Hands-On GUI Programming with C++ and Qt5

Build stunning cross-platform applications and widgets with the most powerful GUI framework

Lee Zhi Eng

BIRMINGHAM - MUMBAI

Hands-On GUI Programming with C++ and Qt5

Commissioning Editor: Richa Tripathi
Acquisition Editor: Alok Dhuri
Content Development Editor: Lawrence Veigas
Technical Editor: Mehul Singh
Copy Editor: Safis Editing
Project Coordinator: Prajakta Naik
Proofreader: Safis Editing
Indexer: Pratik Shirodkar
Graphics: Jisha Chirayil
Production Coordinator: Nilesh Mohite

First published: April 2018

Production reference: 1260418

Published by Packt Publishing Ltd.
Livery Place
35 Livery Street
Birmingham
B3 2PB, UK.

ISBN 978-1-78839-782-7

www.packtpub.com

`mapt.io`

Mapt is an online digital library that gives you full access to over 5,000 books and videos, as well as industry leading tools to help you plan your personal development and advance your career. For more information, please visit our website.

Why subscribe?

- Spend less time learning and more time coding with practical eBooks and Videos from over 4,000 industry professionals

- Improve your learning with Skill Plans built especially for you

- Get a free eBook or video every month

- Mapt is fully searchable

- Copy and paste, print, and bookmark content

PacktPub.com

Did you know that Packt offers eBook versions of every book published, with PDF and ePub files available? You can upgrade to the eBook version at `www.PacktPub.com` and as a print book customer, you are entitled to a discount on the eBook copy. Get in touch with us at `service@packtpub.com` for more details.

At `www.PacktPub.com`, you can also read a collection of free technical articles, sign up for a range of free newsletters, and receive exclusive discounts and offers on Packt books and eBooks.

Contributors

About the author

Lee Zhi Eng is a self-taught programmer who has worked as an artist and programmer at several game studios before becoming a part-time lecturer for 2 years at a university, teaching game development subjects related to Unity and Unreal Engine.

He has not only taken part in various projects related to games, interactive apps, and virtual reality, but has also participated in multiple projects that are more oriented toward software and system development. When he is not writing code, he enjoys traveling, photography, and exploring new technologies.

About the reviewer

Nibedit Dey is a technopreneur with multidisciplinary technology background. He holds a bachelor's degree in biomedical engineering and a master's degree in digital design and embedded systems. Before starting his entrepreneurial journey, he worked for L&T and Tektronix for several years in different R&D roles. He has been using Qt to build complex software products for the past 8 years. Currently, he is a healthcare innovation fellow at IIT, Hyderabad, and is involved in the development of a new medical device.

Packt is searching for authors like you

If you're interested in becoming an author for Packt, please visit `authors.packtpub.com` and apply today. We have worked with thousands of developers and tech professionals, just like you, to help them share their insight with the global tech community. You can make a general application, apply for a specific hot topic that we are recruiting an author for, or submit your own idea.

Table of Contents

Preface   1

Chapter 1: Introduction to Qt   7
  What is Qt?   8
    Why use Qt?   9
    Discovering tools in Qt   9
      Qt Designer   10
      Qt Quick Designer   11
  Downloading and installing Qt   12
    Setting up the working environment   15
  Running our first Hello World Qt program   19
  Summary   25

Chapter 2: Qt Widgets and Style Sheets   27
  Introduction to Qt Designer   28
  Basic Qt widgets   35
  Qt Style Sheets   45
  Summary   52

Chapter 3: Database Connection   53
  Introducing the MySQL database system   54
  Setting up the MySQL database   56
  SQL commands   66
    SELECT   67
    INSERT   68
    UPDATE   68
    DELETE   69
    JOIN   69
  Database connection in Qt   75
  Creating our functional login page   83
  Summary   89

Chapter 4: Graphs and Charts   91
  Types of charts and graphs in Qt   92
    Line and spline charts   92
    Bar charts   93
    Pie charts   94
    Polar charts   95
    Area and scatter charts   96
    Box-and-whiskers charts   98

Candlestick charts	98
Implementing charts and graphs	99
Creating the dashboard page	106
Summary	116
Chapter 5: Item Views and Dialogs	117
Working with item view widgets	117
Creating our Qt Widgets application	120
Making our List Widget functional	124
Adding functionality to the Tree Widget	127
Finally, our Table Widget	127
Working with dialog boxes	128
Creating File Selection Dialogs	134
Image scaling and cropping	136
Summary	143
Chapter 6: Integrating Web Content	145
Creating your own web browser	145
Adding the web view widget	147
Creating a UI for a web browser	150
Managing browser history	161
Sessions, cookies, and cache	162
Managing sessions and cookies	162
Managing cache	163
Integrating JavaScript and C++	164
Calling JavaScript functions from C++	164
Calling C++ functions from JavaScript	168
Summary	172
Chapter 7: Map Viewer	173
Map display	173
Setting up the Qt location module	174
Creating a map display	174
Marker and shape display	178
Displaying position markers on a map	179
Displaying shapes on a map	188
Obtaining a user's location	191
Geo Routing Request	193
Summary	196
Chapter 8: Graphics View	197
Graphics View framework	197
Setting up a new project	198
Movable graphics items	201
Creating an organization chart	204
Summary	220

Chapter 9: The Camera Module 221
The Qt multimedia module 221
Setting up a new project 221
Connecting to the camera 226
Capturing a camera image to file 231
Recording a camera video to file 232
Summary 234

Chapter 10: Instant Messaging 235
The Qt networking module 235
Connection protocols 235
Setting up a new project 237
Creating an instant messaging server 238
Creating TCP Server 238
Listening to clients 240
Creating an instant messaging client 243
Designing the user interface 244
Implementing chat features 247
Summary 252

Chapter 11: Implementing a Graphics Editor 253
Drawing vector shapes 253
Vector versus bitmap 253
Drawing vector shapes using QPainter 255
Drawing text 257
Saving vector images to an SVG File 258
Creating a paint program 263
Setting up a user interface 263
Summary 272

Chapter 12: Cloud Storage 273
Setting up the FTP server 273
Introducing FTP 273
Downloading FileZilla 274
Setting up FileZilla 276
Displaying the file list on the list view 281
Setting up a project 282
Setting up user interface 282
Displaying the file list 283
Writing the code 284
Uploading files to the FTP server 288
Downloading files from the FTP server 294
Summary 297

Chapter 13: Multimedia Viewers 299

Revisiting the multimedia module	299
Dissecting the module	299
The image viewer	301
Designing a user interface for the image viewer	301
Writing C++ code for image viewers	303
The music player	306
Designing a user interface for music players	306
Writing C++ code for music players	308
The video player	313
Designing a user interface for video players	313
Writing C++ code for video players	314
Summary	316
Chapter 14: Qt Quick and QML	317
Introduction to Qt Quick and QML	317
Introducing Qt Quick	317
Introducing QML	319
Qt Quick widgets and controls	325
Qt Quick Designer	328
Qt Quick layouts	329
Basic QML scripting	330
Setting up the project	330
Summary	341
Chapter 15: Cross-Platform Development	343
Understanding compilers	343
What is a compiler?	343
Build automation with Make	344
Build settings	345
Qt Project (.pro) File	346
Comment	347
Modules, configurations, and definitions	347
Platform-specific settings	348
Deploying to PC platforms	349
Windows	349
Linux	351
macOS	359
Deploying to mobile platforms	361
iOS	361
Android	363
Summary	365
Chapter 16: Testing and Debugging	367
Debugging techniques	367
Identifying the problem	368

Print variables using QDebug 368
Setting breakpoints 369
Debuggers supported by Qt 374
Debugging for PC 374
Debugging for Android devices 375
Debugging for macOS and iOS 375
Unit testing 377
Unit testing in Qt 377
Summary 379
Other Books You May Enjoy 381
Index 385

Preface

Qt 5, the latest version of Qt, enables you to develop applications with complex user interfaces for multiple targets. It provides you with faster and smarter ways to create modern UIs and applications for multiple platforms. This book will teach you how to design and build graphical user interfaces that are functional, appealing, and user-friendly.

By the end of this book, you will have successfully learned about high-end GUI applications and will be capable of building many more powerful, cross-platform applications.

Who this book is for

This book will appeal to developers and programmers who would like to build GUI-based applications. Basic knowledge of C++ is necessary, and the basics of Qt would be helpful.

What this book covers

Chapter 1, *Introduction to Qt*, will give you a tour of Qt. In this book, you'll download the SDK, install Qt, and, most importantly, install Qt Creator, which is used as both the user interface designer and the IDE for writing and compiling C++ scripts.

Chapter 2, *Qt Widgets and Style Sheets*, will introduce you to the different types of widgets generally used in Qt to develop desktop applications. You will learn the first step to create your own application, which uses all kinds of widgets and customizations, using the powerful style sheet mechanism provided by Qt, which is very similar to CSS for web.

Chapter 3, *Database Connection*, will introduce you to the MariaDB database and teach you how to connect to it using Qt. You will first learn what is MariaDB database and how to call simple SQL commands to fetch and insert data into a MariaDB database. We will then create a simple but fully functional login page.

Chapter 4, *Graphs and Charts*, explores the Chart feature to allow users to easily render different types of graphs and charts, such as pie chart, bar chart, and line graph. We will make use of the knowledge learned from this chapter to create a dashboard page for an application, which displays all kinds of statistical summary of their company and business.

Chapter 5, *Item Views and Dialogs*, will teach you how to display a list of information by using three different item view widgets—a list widget, tree widget, and table widget. You will also learn how to prompt a message box to display error messages, warnings, and confirmation. You will then create an application that can load, scale, and crop images.

Chapter 6, *Integrating Web Content*, will empower you to use the Qt WebEngine module and make a simple web browser, which displays a web page. We will then go through what is sessions, cookies, and cache and subsequently how to manage them with Qt WebEngine. Finally, you will learn how to make your C++ code communicate with JavaScript content through the WebChannel mechanism.

Chapter 7, *Map Viewer*, will focus on creating a map display. This map will be used to display the location of places and people. You will learn how to implement the QtLocation module, understand the coordinate system, display location markers on the map, and so on.

Chapter 8, *Graphics View*, will provide a platform to manage and interact with a large number of custom-made graphical items and a view widget to visualize the items with support for zooming and rotation. You will learn how to make an organization's chart page that displays the structure of an organization and the relationships and relative ranks of its parts and positions/jobs.

Chapter 9, *The Camera Module*, will explore how to display camera images using Qt. Qt provides us with a multimedia module that enables us to easily take advantage of a platform's multimedia capabilities, such as connecting to the camera of the computer.

Chapter 10, *Instant Messaging*, will discuss the networking module and help us to make our own simple instant messaging program.

Chapter 11, *Implementing a Graphics Editor*, is divided into two sections, based on the two types of graphics in the rendering world–bitmap graphics and vector graphics. Both are quite different but essential to learning in order to understand 2D graphics rendering. You will learn how to draw graphics using Qt in this chapter.

Chapter 12, *Cloud Storage*, will teach you how to upload different types of files to the FTP server and display them in a list. The user will be able to download the file and open them with different types of viewers depending on its file format.

Chapter 13, *Multimedia Viewers*, will deal with creating a media player instead of using the default software on your computer. In this chapter, you will learn how to create an image viewer, a music player, and a video player.

Chapter 14, *Qt Quick and QML,* will introduce you to the basics of QML scripting, which is one of the most recent trends in the Qt world.

Chapter 15, *Cross-Platform Development,* will show you how to export applications to different platforms without re-writing the code from scratch. You will learn some of the essential settings and tips to look out for when porting applications to different platforms. Besides PC platforms, you will also learn how to export applications to mobile platforms.

Chapter 16, *Testing and Debugging,* will teach you the essentials of how to use various techniques to test and debug your Qt application.

To get the most out of this book

In order to successfully execute all the codes and instructions in this book, you would need the following:

- A basic PC/Laptop
- A working internet connection
- Qt 5.10
- MariaDB 10.2 (or MySQL Connector)
- Filezilla Server 0.9

We will deal with the installation processes and details as we go through each chapter.

Download the example code files

You can download the example code files for this book from your account at www.packtpub.com. If you purchased this book elsewhere, you can visit www.packtpub.com/support and register to have the files emailed directly to you.

You can download the code files by following these steps:

1. Log in or register at www.packtpub.com.
2. Select the **SUPPORT** tab.
3. Click on **Code Downloads & Errata**.
4. Enter the name of the book in the **Search** box and follow the onscreen instructions.

Once the file is downloaded, please make sure that you unzip or extract the folder using the latest version of:

- WinRAR/7-Zip for Windows
- Zipeg/iZip/UnRarX for Mac
- 7-Zip/PeaZip for Linux

The code bundle for the book is also hosted on GitHub at `https://github.com/PacktPublishing/Hands-On-GUI-Programming-with-CPP-and-Qt5` In case there's an update to the code, it will be updated on the existing GitHub repository.

We also have other code bundles from our rich catalog of books and videos available at `https://github.com/PacktPublishing/`. Check them out!

Download the color images

We also provide a PDF file that has color images of the screenshots/diagrams used in this book. You can download it here: `https://www.packtpub.com/sites/default/files/downloads/HandsOnGUIProgrammingwithCPPandQt5_ColorImages.pdf`.

Conventions used

There are a number of text conventions used throughout this book.

`CodeInText`: Indicates code words in text, database table names, folder names, filenames, file extensions, pathnames, dummy URLs, user input, and Twitter handles. Here is an example: "We call the `test()` function at the `MainWindow` constructor."

A block of code is set as follows:

```
void MainWindow::test()
{
    int amount = 100;
    amount -= 10;
    qDebug() << "You have obtained" << amount << "apples!";
}
```

When we wish to draw your attention to a particular part of a code block, the relevant lines or items are set in bold:

```
MainWindow::MainWindow(QWidget *parent) :
    QMainWindow(parent),
    ui(new Ui::MainWindow)
{
    ui->setupUi(this);
    test();
}
```

Any command-line input or output is written as follows:

```
********* Start testing of MainWindow *********
Config: Using QtTest library 5.9.1, Qt 5.9.1 (i386-little_endian-ilp32
shared (dynamic) debug build; by GCC 5.3.0)
PASS    : MainWindow::initTestCase()
PASS    : MainWindow::_q_showIfNotHidden()
PASS    : MainWindow::testString()
PASS    : MainWindow::testGui()
PASS    : MainWindow::cleanupTestCase()
Totals: 5 passed, 0 failed, 0 skipped, 0 blacklisted, 880ms
********* Finished testing of MainWindow *********
```

Bold: Indicates a new term, an important word, or words that you see onscreen. For example, words in menus or dialog boxes appear in the text like this. Here is an example: "The third option is **Toggle Bookmark**, which lets you set a bookmark for your own reference."

Warnings or important notes appear like this.

Tips and tricks appear like this.

Get in touch

Feedback from our readers is always welcome.

General feedback: Email `feedback@packtpub.com` and mention the book title in the subject of your message. If you have questions about any aspect of this book, please email us at `questions@packtpub.com`.

Errata: Although we have taken every care to ensure the accuracy of our content, mistakes do happen. If you have found a mistake in this book, we would be grateful if you would report this to us. Please visit `www.packtpub.com/submit-errata`, selecting your book, clicking on the Errata Submission Form link, and entering the details.

Piracy: If you come across any illegal copies of our works in any form on the Internet, we would be grateful if you would provide us with the location address or website name. Please contact us at `copyright@packtpub.com` with a link to the material.

If you are interested in becoming an author: If there is a topic that you have expertise in and you are interested in either writing or contributing to a book, please visit `authors.packtpub.com`.

Reviews

Please leave a review. Once you have read and used this book, why not leave a review on the site that you purchased it from? Potential readers can then see and use your unbiased opinion to make purchase decisions, we at Packt can understand what you think about our products, and our authors can see your feedback on their book. Thank you!

For more information about Packt, please visit `packtpub.com`.

Introduction to Qt 1

Qt (pronounced *cute*) has been used by software engineers and developers for more than two decades to create cross-platform applications since its first release. After several changes of ownership and numerous major code overhauls, Qt has become even more feature rich and supports even more platforms than it used to. Qt not only excels in desktop application development, but is also excellent for both mobile and embedded systems development.

In this chapter, we will cover the following topics :

- What is Qt?
- Why use Qt?
- Using tools in Qt
- Downloading and installing Qt
- Setting up a working environment
- Running our first `Hello World` Qt program

Throughout this chapter, we will learn more about the history of Qt. Then, we'll proceed to build our first example program using the latest version of Qt, which is Qt version 5. For the convenience of our readers, we will simply refer to it as Qt throughout the book.

What is Qt?

Currently, the latest version of Qt (as this book is being written) is version 5.10. This version incorporated a lot of new features as well as thousands of bug fixes, which makes Qt a really powerful and stable development kit for software developers and system engineers alike. Qt has a huge package of SDK (software development kit) that contains a wide range of tools and libraries for helping developers get their job done without worrying too much about technical issues related to a specific platform. Qt handles all the messy integration and compatibility issues for you behind the curtain so you don't have to deal with them. This will not only improve efficiency but also reduces development costs, especially when you're trying to develop cross-platform applications that cater to a wider range of users.

There are two types of license for Qt:

- The first type is the Open Source License, which is free of charge, but only if your project/product fits their terms and conditions. For example, if you made any changes to the Qt's source code, it is an obligation for you to submit back those changes to Qt developers. Failure to do so could result in serious legal issues, and therefore, you might want to pick the second option instead.
- The second type of license is the Commercial License, which gives you full rights to proprietary Qt source code modifications and keeps your application private. But of course, these privileges come with a set of fees.

If you're just starting to learn Qt, don't get pushed back by these terms, as you're certainly not going to modify the source code of Qt libraries or recompile it from source anyway, at least not now.

 For more information regarding Qt's licensing, please visit `https://www.qt.io/licensing-comparison`.

Why use Qt?

It's not hard to see why Qt stands a chance of winning against all other existing SDKs out there in the market; first of all, cross-platform compatibility. You can hardly find any other development kits that support so many platforms without writing different sets of code for each platform. By eliminating these extra steps, programmers can just focus on developing their applications without the need to worry about the implementation of each and every platform-specific feature. Furthermore, your code will look clean without all the `#ifdef` macros and having to load different dependencies for different platforms.

Qt generally uses C++, which is a compiled language that generates small and efficient code. It is also well documented and follows a very consistent set of naming conventions, which reduces the learning curve for the developer.

Do be aware that Qt does include a small amount of features that only work on specific platforms. However, these are minimal and often for special use cases, such as Qt Sensors, which only work on mobile platforms; Qt Web Engine, which only works on desktops; Qt NFC, only for Android and Linux; and so on. Those are some very specific functionalities that only exist on certain platforms that support them. Other than that, common features are usually supported on all platforms.

Discovering tools in Qt

Qt comes with a set of tools that make programmers' lives easier. One of the tools is **Qt Creator** (seen in the following screenshot), which is an **IDE** (**integrated development environment**) that consists of a code editor and a **GUI** (**graphical user interface**) designer that works hand-in-hand with other Qt tools, such as the compiler, debugger, and so on. The most attractive tool among all is, of course, the GUI designer, which comes with two different types of editors: one for widget-based applications, called Qt Designer, and another for Qt Quick Application, called Qt Quick Designer. Both tools can be accessed directly in Qt Creator when you open up a relevant file format. Qt Creator also includes a built-in documentation viewer called Qt Assistant. It is really handy since you can look for the explanation about a certain Qt class or function by simply hovering the mouse cursor over the class name in your source code, and pressing the *F1* key. Qt Assistant will then be opened and show you the documentation related to the Qt class or function:

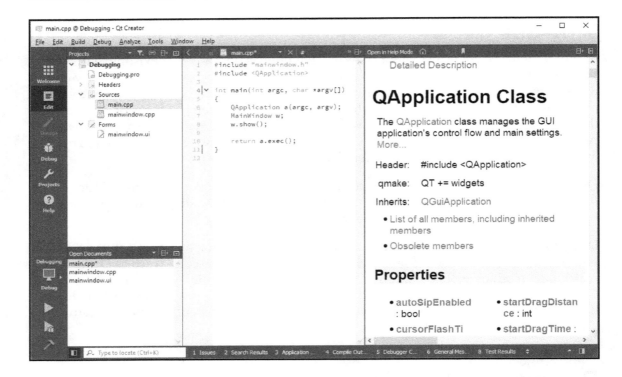

Qt Designer

Qt Designer is normally used by developers to design GUIs for desktop applications, while Qt Quick Designer is usually used for mobile and embedded platforms. With that being said, both formats run just fine on both desktop and mobile formats, the only difference is the look and feel, and the types of languages used.

The GUI file saved by Qt Designer carries the `.ui` extension, which is saved in XML format. The file stores the attributes of each and every widget placed by the GUI designer, such as position, size, margin, tooltip, layout direction, and so on. It also saves the signal-and-slot event names within itself for easily connecting with the code in the later stages. This format does not support coding and only works for Qt C++ projects, namely widget-based application projects.

Qt Quick Designer

On the other hand, Qt Quick Designer saves GUI files in both `.ui.qml` and `.qml` formats. Qt Quick is a very different type of GUI system in terms of technological concept and development approach, which we will cover in `Chapter 14`, *Qt Quick and QML*. Instead of XML format, Qt Quick Designer saves its data in a declarative language similar to JavaScript called **QML**. QML not only allows the designer to customize their GUI in a CSS-like (Cascading Style Sheets) fashion, it also allows the programmer to write functional JavaScript within the QML file. As we mentioned earlier, `.ui.qml` is the file format used for visual decoration only while `.qml` contains application logic.

If you're doing a simple program using Qt Quick, you don't have to touch any C++ coding at all. That's especially welcoming for web developers because they can immediately pick up Qt Quick and develop their own application without a steep learning curve; everything is just so familiar to them. For much more complex software, you can even link C++ functions from QML, and vice versa. Again, if you're interested in learning more about Qt Quick and QML, please head over to `Chapter 14`, *QtQuick and QML*.

Since Qt Creator is also written in Qt libraries itself, it is also totally cross-platform. Hence, you can use the same set of tools across different development environments and develop a unified workflow for your team, resulting in better efficiency and cost-effectiveness.

Other than that, Qt comes with many different modules and plugins, which cover a wide range of functionality you need for your projects. There is often no need for you to look for other external libraries or dependencies and try and implement them yourself. The abstraction layer of Qt makes the backend implementation invisible to the users and results in a unified coding style and syntax. If you try to put together a bunch of external dependencies yourself, what you'll find is each library has its own distinctive coding style. It's quite a mess when mixing up all the different coding styles in the same project, unless you make your own abstraction layer, which is a very time-consuming task. Since Qt already includes most, if not all the modules that you need to create feature-rich applications, there is no need for you to implement your own.

 For more information regarding the modules that come with Qt, please visit: `http://doc.qt.io/qt-5/qtmodules.html`.

That being said, there are also many third libraries out there that extend Qt for features that Qt itself does not support, such as libraries that focus on game development or any other features that are designed for the specific user group.

Downloading and installing Qt

Without wasting any time, let's begin with our installation! To get the free installer for Open Source Qt, first go to their website at https://www.qt.io. There, look for the button that says **Download Qt** (the website might look different if they have updated it). Do note that you might be downloading the free trial version for the Commercial Qt, which you cannot use after 30 days. Make sure that you are downloading the open source version of Qt instead. Also, you may want to pick the right installer for your platform, since there are many different installers of Qt for different operating systemsWindows, macOS, and Linux.

You might wonder why the installer is so small in size—it is only around 19 MB. This is because the unified online installer doesn't actually contain any of the Qt packages, but is rather a downloader client which helps you to download all the relevant files and install them to your computer once the download has completed. Once you have downloaded the online installer, double-click on it and you will be presented with an interface like this (the following example is running on a Windows system):

Click the **Next** button, and a **DRM (Digital Rights Management)** page will appear and ask you to log in with your Qt account. If you don't have one, you can also create your account on the same page:

Once you have logged in, you will see a message that says **No valid commercial license available in your Qt Account for this host platform**. Don't worry about that, just click the **Next** button to proceed.

Next, you will be asked to specify the installation path. The default path is usually just fine, but you can change it to any other path as you please. Also, you can either leave the **Associate this common file types with Qt Creator** option checked, or uncheck it manually if otherwise.

After that, you will be presented with a series of checkboxes with which you can select the version(s) of Qt you need to install to your computer. Typically, for new users, the default options are sufficient. If you don't need some of the options, such as support for Qt on Android, you can unselect them here to reduce the size of the download. You can always go back and add or remove Qt components later if needed, using the Maintenance Tool:

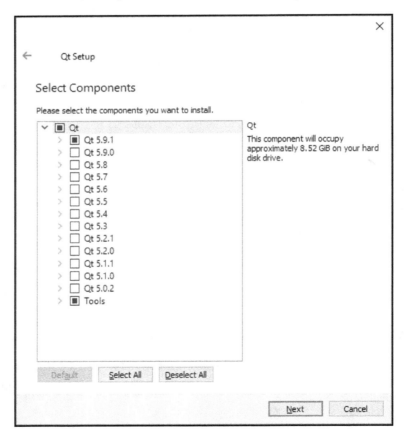

Next, you will be presented with the license agreement. Check the first option, which says **I have read and agree to the terms contained in the license agreements**, and click the **Next** button. Make sure you do read the terms and conditions stated in the license agreement!

Finally, the installer will ask you to enter a name to create a start menu shortcut for Qt. Once you're done, just click **Next** and then click **Install**. The download process will take a couple of minutes to a couple of hours, depending on your internet speed. Once all the files have been downloaded, the installer will automatically proceed to install the files to the installation path that you have just set in one of the previous steps.

Setting up the working environment

Since you have installed the latest version of Qt, let's fire up Qt Creator and start messing around by creating our first project! You should be able to find Qt Creator's shortcut icon either on your desktop or somewhere within your start menu.

Let's look at the steps to set up our environment:

1. When you first start Qt Creator, you should see the following interface:

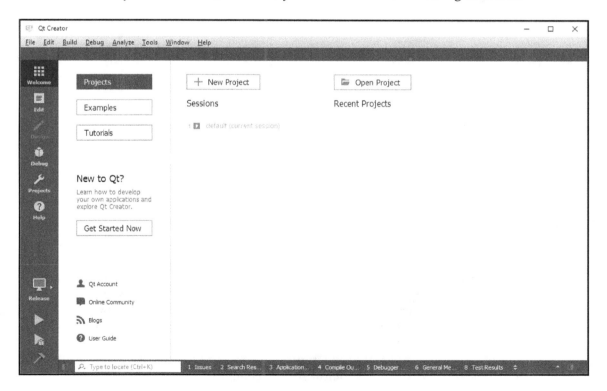

2. Before you start creating your first project, there are several settings that you might want to tweak. Go to the top menu and select **Tools | Options**. A window that looks something like this will pop up on the screen:

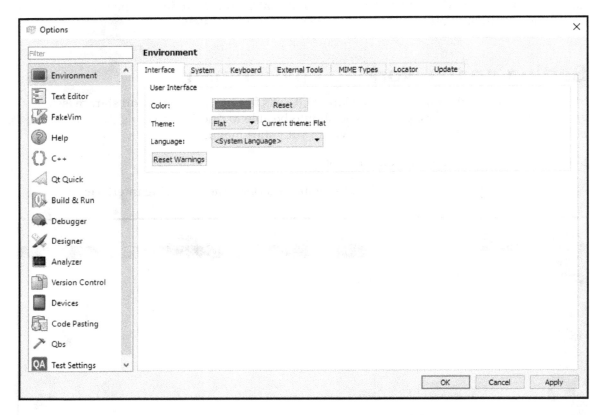

3. There are quite a number of different categories available on the left of the window. Each category represents a set of options you can set to customize how Qt Creator will look and operate. You may not want to touch the settings at all, but it's good to learn about them first. One of the first settings you might want to change is the **Language** option, which is available in the **Environment** category. Qt Creator provides us with an option to switch between different languages. Although it doesn't support all languages, most of the popular ones are available, such as English, French, German, Japanese, Chinese, Russian, and so on. Once you have selected your desired language, click **Apply** and restart Qt Creator. You must restart Qt Creator in order to see the changes.

4. The next setting you probably need is the setting for indentation. By default, Qt uses **space indentation**, in which four spaces will be added to your script whenever you press the *Tab* key on your keyboard. Some people, like me, prefer **tab indentation** instead. You can change the indentation setting at **C++ category**.

> Do note that if you are contributing to Qt project's source code, it's required that you use space indentation instead of tabs, which is the coding standard and style of the Qt project.

5. Under the C++ category, you can find a **Copy** button located beside the **Edit** button, somewhere in the top right position. Click it and a new window will pop up.

6. Insert a code style name of your own, as you can't edit the default built-in coding style. After you have created your own settings, click the **Edit** button. You can now see the actual **Tabs And Indentation** settings under the **General** tab:

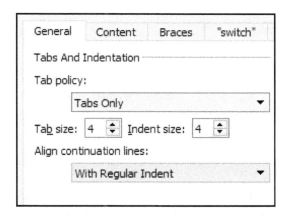

7. Do note that even though there is a **Tabs And Indentation** setting located at the **Text Editor** category, I believe it's an old setting that no longer has any effect in Qt Creator. There is also a note written on the UI that says **Code indentation is configured in C++ and Qt Quick settings**. A possible reason for this is that since Qt Creator now supports both C++ project and QML projects, Qt developers probably felt there was a need to separate the settings into two, so therefore the old setting is no longer valid. I'm pretty sure this section on Text Editor will be deprecated in the near future.

8. Next, under the **Build and Run** category, you'll see a tab labeled **Kits**.

9. This is where you can set the compile settings for each platform. As you can see from the next screenshot, my Qt does not support desktop build under MSVC (Microsoft Visual Studio Compiler) because I never installed Visual Studio on my computer. Instead, my Qt only supports desktop build under the MinGW (Minimal GNU for Windows) compiler. From this window, you can check and see if your Qt supports the platform and compiler you wanted for your project and make changes to it if necessary. But for now, we'll just leave it as it is. To learn more about what is a *kit* is and how to configure the build settings, please head over to Chapter 15, *Cross-Platform Development*:

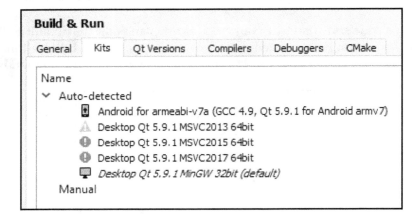

10. Finally, we can link our project to our version control server at the **Version Control** category.

11. Version control allows you or your team to submit code changes to a centralized system so that each and every team member can obtain the same code without passing files around manually. When you're working in a big team, it's very difficult to manually keep track of the code changes, and even more so to merge the code done by different programmers. Version control systems are designed to solve these issues. Qt supports different types of version control systems, such as Git, SVN, Mercurial, Perforce, and so on. Although this is a very useful feature, especially if you're working in a team, we don't need to configure it for now:

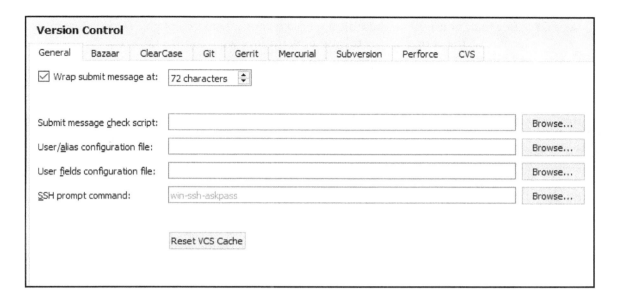

Running our first Hello World Qt program

A Hello World program is a very simple program that does nothing more than display an output that says Hello, World! (or any other thing, not necessarily this) to show that the SDK is working properly. We don't need to write very long code to produce a Hello World program, we can do it using only the very minimum and the most basic code. In fact, we don't have to write any code in Qt, as it will generate the code when you first create your project!

Let's begin our project by following these steps:

1. To create a new project in Qt, click the **New Project** button located at the welcome screen on your Qt Creator. Alternatively, you can also go to the top menu and select **File** | **New File or Project**.

2. After that, you will be presented with a window which lets you select a template for your project or file. For this demonstration, we will pick **Qt Widgets Application**:

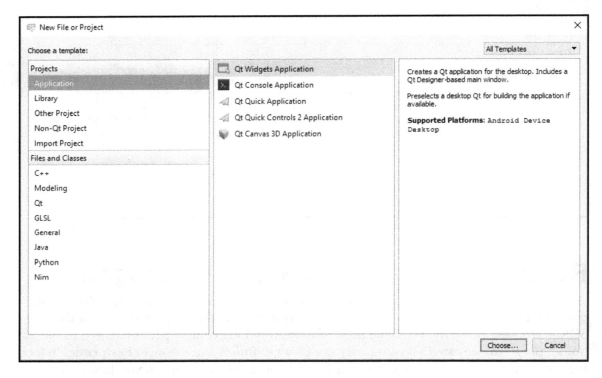

3. After that, set your project name and project directory. You can also check the checkbox that says **Use as default project location** so that you can automatically get the same path when you create a new project in Qt next time.

4. Next, Qt Creator will ask you to select one or more kits for your project. For this demonstration, we'll pick **Desktop Qt** with the MinGW compiler. Don't worry, as you are allowed to add or remove kits from your project later on during development:

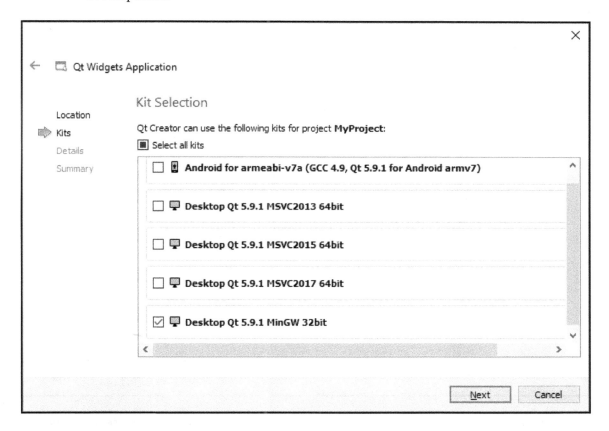

5. After that, you will be presented with a page that says **Class Information**. This is basically where you set the class name for your base window, but we're not going to change anything, so just click the **Next** button to proceed:

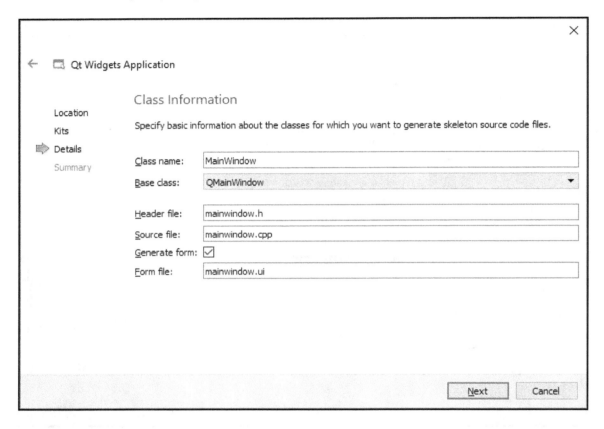

6. Finally, it will ask you to link your project to your version control server. If you have not added any to Qt before, you can click the **Configure** button, which will bring you to the settings dialog that I showed you in the previous section of this chapter.

7. For this demonstration, however, we'll keep the settings as **<None>** and press the **Finish** button. Qt Creator will then proceed to generate the necessary files for your project. After a second or two, Qt Creator will automatically switch to **Edit** mode and you should be able to see the files it created for you under the **Project** panel. You can open up any of the files by double-clicking on them in Qt Creator and they will be shown in the editor located on the right-hand side:

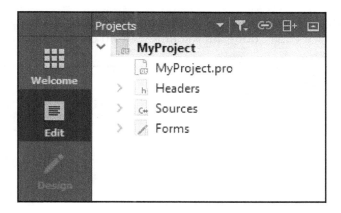

8. Before we start compiling the project, let's open up the `mainwindow.ui` file under the `Forms` directory in your project panel. Don't worry too much about the user interface as we will cover it in the following chapter. What we need to do is to click and drag the **Label** icon under the **Display Widgets** category to the center of the window on the right, as shown in the following screenshot:

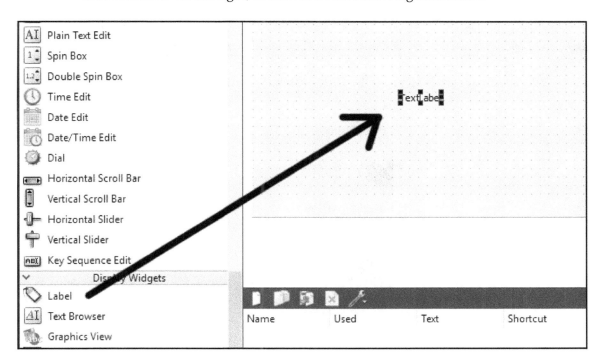

9. After that, double-click on the `Text Label` widget and change the text to `Hello World!`. Once you're done, hit the *Enter* button on your keyboard:

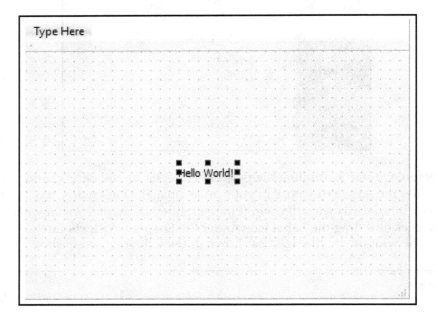

10. The final step is to press the **Run** button located at the bottom left corner that looks like this:

11. We would normally build the program first and then run the program, but Qt Creator is smart enough to figure out that it needs to build it. However, it is still a good habit to build and run your application separately. After a few seconds of compiling, ... voila! You have created your first `Hello World` program using Qt!:

Summary

The existence of tools such as Qt Creator has made designing applications' user interfaces an easy and fun job for the developers. We no longer need to write a bunch of code just to create a single button, or change a bunch just to adjust the position of a text label, since Qt Designer will generate that code for us when we design our GUI. Qt has applied the **WYSIWYG (what you see is what you get)** philosophy into the working pipeline and it provides us with all the convenience and efficiency we need to get our jobs done.

In the next chapter, we will learn the ins and outs of Qt Creator and start designing our first GUI with Qt!

Qt Widgets and Style Sheets

2

One of the advantages of using Qt for software development is that it's very easy to design a program's **graphical user interface (GUI)** using the tools provided by Qt. Throughout this book, we will try and create a single project that involves many different components and modules of Qt. We will go through each section of the project in each chapter, so that you will eventually be able to grasp the entire Qt Framework and at the same time complete demo projects, which is a really valuable item to add to your portfolio. You can find all the source code at `https://github.com/PacktPublishing/Hands-On-GUI-Programming-with-C-QT5.`

In this chapter, we will cover the following topics:

- Introduction to Qt Designer
- Basic Qt widgets
- Qt Style Sheets

In this chapter, we will take a deep look into what Qt can offer us when it comes to designing sleek-looking GUIs with ease. At the beginning of this chapter, you will be introduced to the types of widgets provided by Qt and their functionalities. After that, we will walk through a series of steps and design our first form application using Qt.

Introduction to Qt Designer

There are two types of GUI applications in Qt, namely Qt Quick Application and Qt Widgets Application. In this book, we will cover mostly the latter, as it is the standard way of designing a GUI for desktop applications, and Qt Quick is more widely used for mobile and embedded systems:

1. The first thing we need to do is to open up Qt Creator and create a new project. You can do so by either going to **File | New File or Project**, or by clicking the **New Project** button located at the welcome screen:

2. After that, a new window will pop up and ask you to pick the type of project you want to create. Choose **Qt Widgets Application** under the **Application** category and click **Choose...**, Then, create a name for your project (I have chosen Chapter2 for mine) and select the project directory by clicking the **Browse...** button:

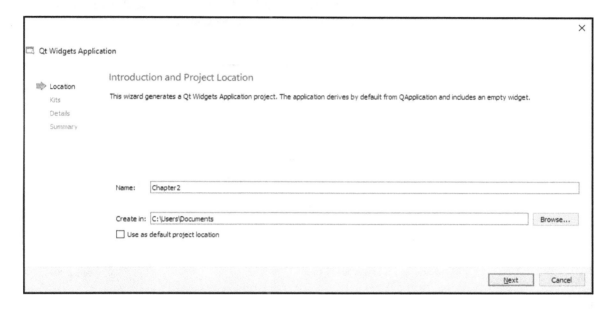

3. Next, you will be asked to select a kit for your project. If you are running this on a Windows system and you have Microsoft Visual Studio installed, you can pick the relevant kit with the MSVC compiler; otherwise, choose the one running MinGW compiler. Qt normally comes with MinGW compiler pre-installed so you don't need to download it separately. If you're running this on a Linux system, then you will see the GCC kit, or the Clang kit if you're running this on macOS. To learn more about *Kits and Builds Settings*, please check out `Chapter 15`, *Cross-Platform Development*:

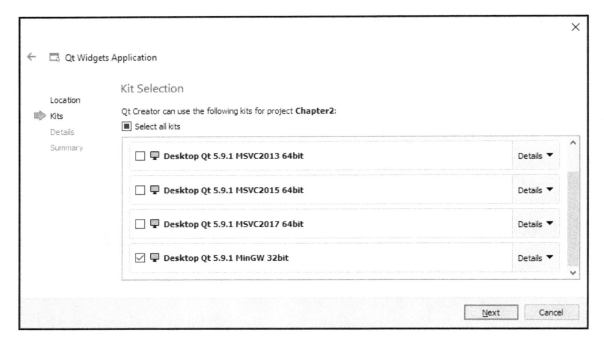

4. After that, the new project wizard will ask you to name your main window class. We'll just go with the default settings and click the **Next** button to proceed:

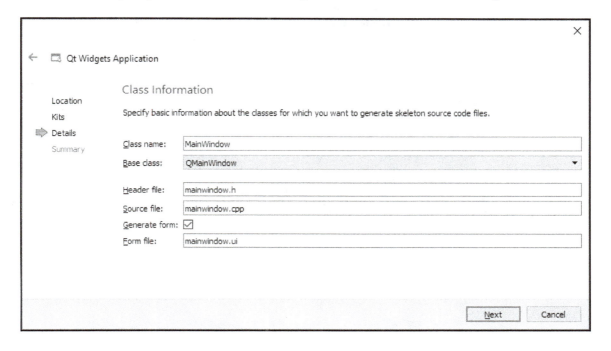

5. Finally, you will be asked to link your version control tool to your project. By linking a version control tool to your project, you will be able to keep every revision of your code on a remote server and keep track of all the changes being made to the project. This is especially useful if you're working in a team. In this tutorial, however, we will not be using any version control, so let's just proceed by clicking the **Finish** button:

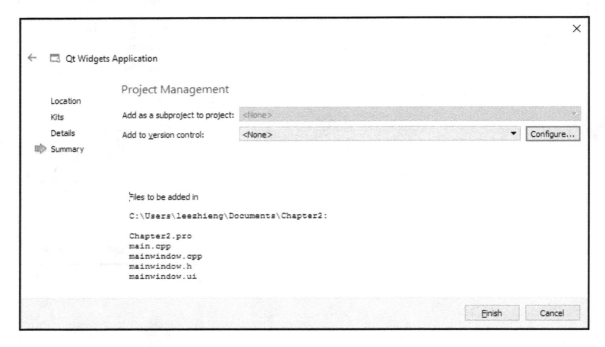

6. Once you're done with that, Qt Creator will open up your new project and you will be able to see your project directory displayed at the top left corner, like so:

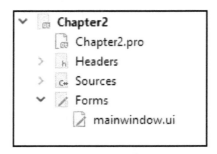

7. Now, open up `mainwindow.ui` by double-clicking on it on the project directory panel. Qt Creator will then switch to another mode, called Qt Designer, which is essentially a tool used to design widget-based GUIs for your program. Once Qt Designer is activated, you will see a list of widgets available on the left panel and a place for you to design your GUI on the right. Let's take a bit of time to get ourselves familiar with Qt Designer's interface before we start learning how to design our own UI:

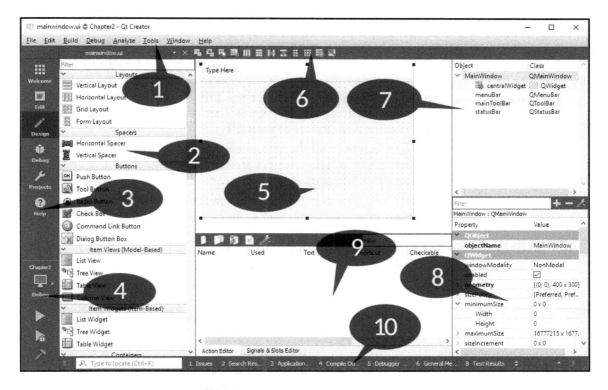

The following numbers represent the UI shown in the preceding screenshot:

1. **Menu bar**: The menu bar is where you find all the basic functions of Qt Creator, such as to create new projects, save files, change compiler settings, and so on.
2. **Widget box**: The widget box is sort of like a toolbox, where all the different widgets provided by Qt Designer are being displayed and are ready to be used. You can drag-and-drop any of the widgets from the widget box directly onto the canvas in the form editor and they will appear in your program.

3. **Mode selector**: The mode selector is where you can quickly and easily switch between source code editing or UI design by clicking the **Edit** or **Design** buttons. You can also easily navigate to the debugger and profiler tools by clicking on their respective buttons located on the mode selector panel.

4. **Build shortcuts**: There are three different shortcut buttons being displayed here—**Build**, **Run**, and **Debug**. You can easily build and test run your application by pressing the buttons here instead of doing so on the menu bar.

5. **Form editor**: This is where you apply your creative idea and design your application's UI. You can drag and drop any of the widgets from the **Widget Box** onto the canvas in the **Form Editor** for it to appear in your program.

6. **Form toolbar**: The form toolbar is where you can quickly select a different form to edit. You can change to a different form by clicking on the drop-down box located above the widget box and selecting the UI file you want to open with Qt Designer. There are also buttons that allow you to switch between different modes for the form editor and layout of your UI.

7. **Object inspector**: This is where all the widgets in your current .ui file are being listed in a hierarchical fashion. The widgets are being arranged in the tree list in accordance to its parent-child relationship with other widgets. The widgets' hierarchy can be easily re-arranged by moving it in the form editor.

8. **Property editor**: When you select a widget from the object inspector window (or from the form editor window), the properties of that particular widget will be displayed on the property editor. You can change any of the properties here and the result will instantly show up on the form editor.

9. **Action editor and signals and slots editor**: Both the action editor and signals and slots editor are located in this window. You can create actions that are linked to your menu bar and toolbar buttons by using the action editor. The signal and slots editor is where you

10. **Output panes**: The output panes are where you look for issues or debugging information when testing your application. It consists of several windows that display different information, such as **Issues**, **Search Results**, **Application Output**, and so on.

In a nutshell, Qt provides an all-in-one editor called Qt Creator. Qt Creator works hand-in-hand with several different tools that come with Qt, such as the script editor, compiler, debugger, profiler, and UI editor. The UI editor, which you can see in the preceding screenshot, is called Qt Designer. Qt Designer is the perfect tool for designers to design their program's UI without writing any code. This is because Qt Designer adopted the **WYSIWYG (what you see is what you get)** approach by providing an accurate visual representation of the final result, which means whatever you design with Qt Designer will turn out exactly the same when the program is compiled and run. Do note that each tool that comes with Qt can, in fact, be run individually, but if you're a beginner or just doing a simple project, it's recommended to just use the Qt Creator, which connects all those tools together in one interface.

Basic Qt widgets

Now, we will take a look at the default set of widgets available in Qt Designer. You can actually create custom widgets by yourself, but that's an advanced topic which is out of the scope of this book. Let's take a look at the first two categories listed on the widget box—**Layouts** and **Spacers**:

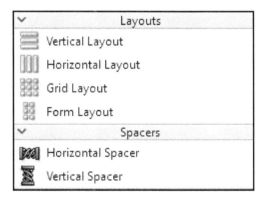

Layouts and **Spacers** are not really something that you can directly observe, but they can affect the positions and orientations of your widgets:

1. **Vertical Layout**: A vertical layout widget lays out widgets in a vertical column, from top to bottom.
2. **Horizontal Layout**: A horizontal layout widget lays out widgets in a horizontal row, from left to right (or right to left for right-to-left languages).

3. **Grid Layout**: A grid layout widget lays out widgets in a two-dimensional grid. Each widget can occupy more than one cell.

4. **Form Layout**: A form layout widget lays out widgets in a two-column field style. Just as the name implies, this type of layout is best suited for forms of input widgets.

Layouts provided by Qt are very important for creating quality applications and are really powerful. Qt programs don't typically lay elements out using the fixed position because layouts allow dialogs and windows to be dynamically resized in a sensible manner while handling a varying length of text when it's localized in different languages. If you don't make use of layouts in your Qt programs, its UI may very look very different on different computers or devices, which in most cases will create an unpleasant user experience.

Next, let's take a look at the spacer widget. A spacer is a non-visible widget that pushes widgets along a specific direction until it reaches the limit of the layout container. **Spacers** must be used within a layout, otherwise they will not carry any effect.

There are two types of spacer, namely the **Horizontal Spacer** and **Vertical Spacer**:

1. **Horizontal Spacer**: A horizontal spacer widget is a widget that occupies the space within a layout and pushes other widgets within the layout along a horizontal space.

2. **Vertical Spacer**: A vertical spacer is similar to a horizontal spacer, except it pushes the widgets along the vertical space.

It's kind of hard to imagine how the **Layouts** and **Spacers** work without actually working with them. Don't worry about that, as we will be trying it out in a moment. One of the most powerful features of Qt Designer is that you can experiment with and test your layouts without have to change and compile your code after each change.

Besides **Layouts** and **Spacers**, there are a few more categories, namely **Buttons**, **Item Views**, **Containers**, **Input Widgets**, and **Display Widgets**. I won't go and explain every single one of them as their names are pretty much self-explanatory. You can also drag and drop the widget on the **Form Editor** to see what it does. Let's do it:

1. Click and drag the **Push Button** widget from the **Widget Box** to the **Form Editor**, as shown in the following screenshot:

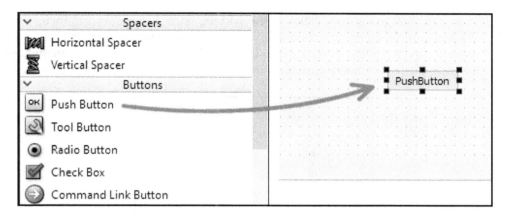

2. Then, select the newly added **Push Button** widget, and you will see that all the information related to this particular widget is now appearing on the **Properties Editor** panel:

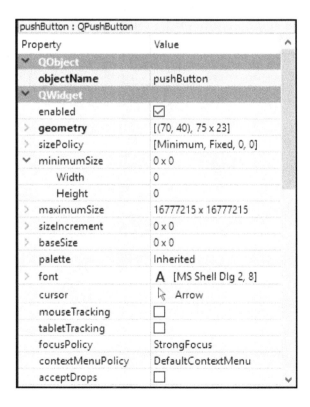

3. You can change the properties of the widget, such as appearance, focus policy, tooltip, and so on programmatically in C++ code. Some properties can also be edited directly in the **Form Editor**. Let's double-click on the **Push Button** and change the text of the button, and then resize the button by dragging its edge:

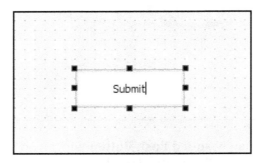

4. Once you're done with that, let's drag and drop a **Horizontal Layout** to the **Form Editor**. Then, drag the **Push Button** to the newly added layout. You will now see that the button automatically fits into the layout:

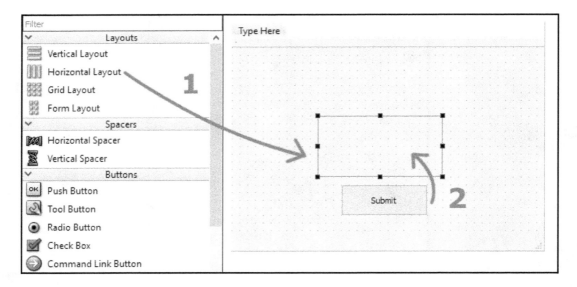

5. By default, the main window does not carry any layout effect, and therefore the widgets will stay where they were originally placed, even when the window is being resized, which does not look very good. To add a layout effect to the main window, right-click on the window in the **Form Editor**, select **Lay out**, and finally select **Lay Out Vertically**. You will now see the **Horizontal Layout** widget we added previously is now automatically expanding to fit the entire window. This is the correct behavior of a layout in Qt:

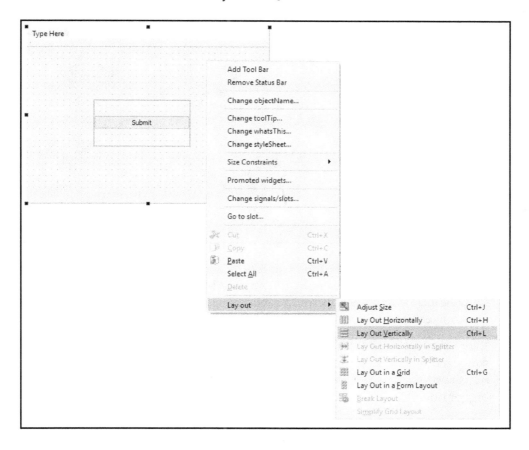

6. Next, we can play around with the spacer and see what effect it has. We will drag and drop a **Vertical Spacer** to the top of the layout containing the **Push Button**, and then we'll place two **Horizontal Spacers** on both sides of the button, within its layout:

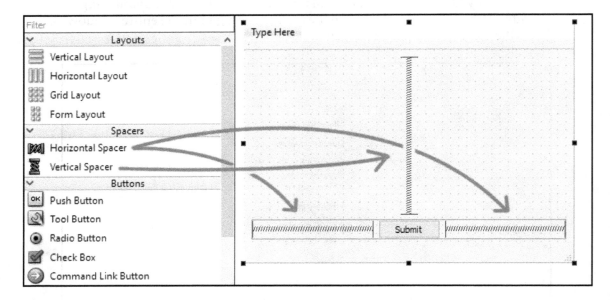

The spacers will push all of the widgets located on both of their ends and occupy the space itself. In this example, the **Submit** button will always stay at the bottom of the window and keep its middle position, regardless of the size of the window. This makes the GUI look good, even on different screen sizes.

Ever since we added the spacers to the window, our **Push Button** has been squeezed to its minimum size. Let's enlarge the button by setting its `minimumSize` property to 120 x 40, and you'll see that the button appears a lot bigger now:

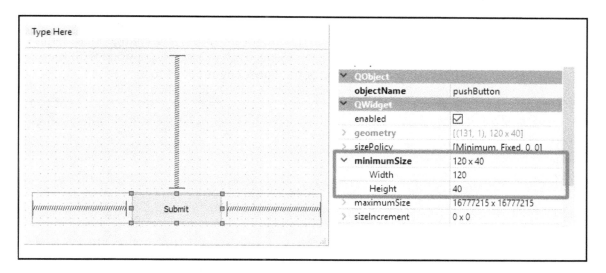

7. After that, let's add a **Form Layout** above the layout of the **Push Button** and a **Vertical Spacer** below it. You will now see that the **Form Layout** is really thin because it has been squeezed by the **Vertical Spacers** we placed earlier onto the main window, which can be troublesome when you want to drag and drop a widget into the **Form Layout**. To solve this problem, temporarily set the layoutTopMargin property to 20 or higher:

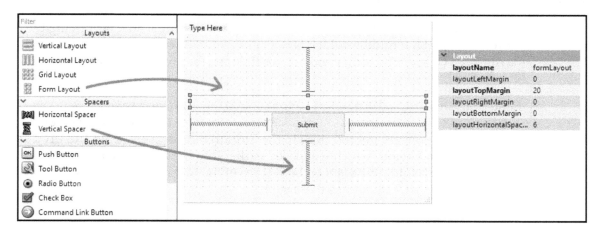

8. Then, drag and drop two **Labels** to the left side of the **Form Layout** and two **Line Edits** to its right side. Double click on both of the labels and change their display texts to `Username:` and `Password:`, respectively. Once you're done with that, set the `layoutTopMargin` property of the **Form Layout** back to `0`:

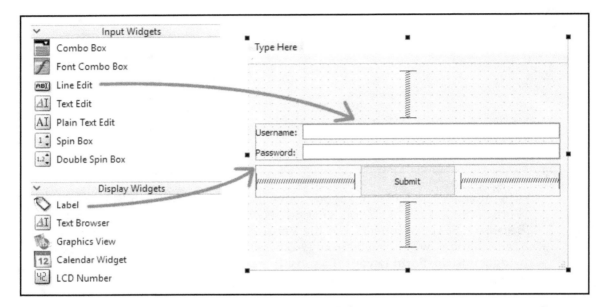

Currently, the GUI looks pretty great, but the **Form Layout** is now occupying the entire spacing in the middle, which is not very pleasant when the main window is maximized. To keep the form compact, we'll do the following steps, which are a little tricky:

9. First, drag and drop a **Horizontal Layout** above the form, and set its `layoutTopMargin` and `layoutBottomMargin` to `20` so that the widgets that we place in it, later on, are not too close to the **Submit** button. Next, drag and drop the entire **Form Layout**, which we placed earlier into the **Horizontal Layout**. Then, place **Horizontal Spacers** on both sides of the form to keep it centered. The following screenshot illustrates these steps:

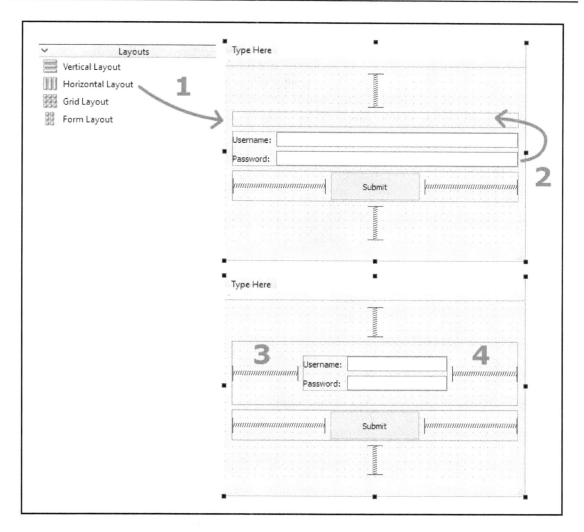

10. After that, we can make further adjustments to the GUI to make it look tidy before we proceed to the next section, where we will be customizing the widgets' style. Let's start off by setting the `minimumSize` property of the two **Line Edit** widgets to 150 x 25. Then, set the `layoutLeftMargin`, `layoutRightMargin`, `layoutTopMargin`, and `layoutBottomMargin` properties of the **Form Layout** to 25. The reason why we want to do this is that we will be adding an outline to the **Form Layout** in the following section.

11. Since the **Push Button** is now way too distanced from the **Form Layout**, let's set the `layoutBottomMargin` property of the **Horizontal Layout**, which sets the **Form Layout** to 0. This will make the **Push Button** move slightly above and closer to the **Form Layout**. After that, we'll adjust the size of the **Push Button** to make it align with the **Form Layout**. Let's set the `minimumSize` property of the **Push Button** to 260 x 35, and we're done!:

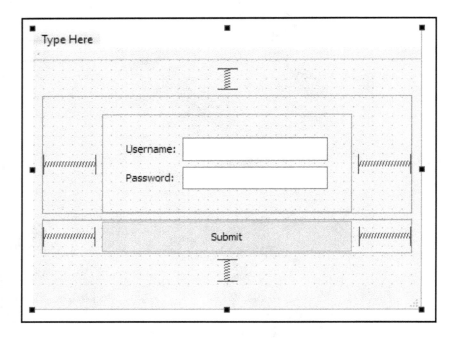

You can also preview your GUI without building your program by going to **Tools | Form Editor | Preview**. Qt Designer is a very handy tool when it comes to designing sleek GUIs for Qt programs without a steep learning curve. In the following section, we will learn how to customize the appearance of the widgets using Qt Style Sheets.

Qt Style Sheets

Qt's Widgets Application uses a styling system called Qt Style Sheets, which is similar to the web technology's styling system—**CSS (Cascading Style Sheet)**. All you need to do is write the style description of the widget and Qt will render it accordingly. The syntax of Qt Style Sheets is pretty much the same as CSS.

Qt Style Sheets has been inspired by CSS and thus they are both very similar to each other:

- Qt Style Sheets:

    ```
    QLineEdit { color: blue; background-color: black; }
    ```

- CSS:

    ```
    h1 { color: blue; background-color: black; }
    ```

In the preceding example, both Qt Style Sheet and CSS contain a declaration block and a selector. Each declaration consists of a property and value, which are separated by a colon.

You can change a widget's style sheet by using two methods—using C++ code directly or by using the properties editor. If you're using C++ code, you can call the `QObject::setStyleSheet()` function, like so:

```
myButton->setStyleSheet("background-color: green");
```

The preceding code changes the background color of our push button widget to green. You can also achieve the same result by writing the same declaration into the `styleSheet` property of the widget in Qt Designer:

```
QPushButton#myButton { background-color: green }
```

To learn more about the syntax and properties of Qt Style Sheets, please refer to the following link: `http://doc.qt.io/qt-5/stylesheet-reference.html`

Let's continue with our project and apply a custom Qt Style Sheet to our GUI!

1. First, right-click on the **Submit** button and select **Change styleSheet...** A window will pop up for you to edit the widget's Style Sheet:

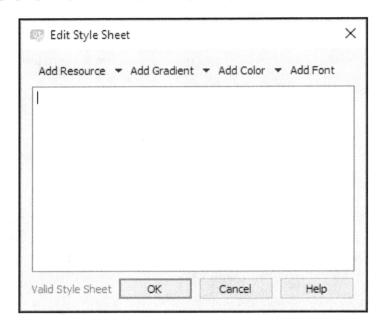

2. Then, add the following to the Style Sheet Editor window:

```
border: 1px solid rgb(24, 103, 155);
border-radius: 5px;
background-color: rgb(124, 203, 255);
color: white;
```

3. Once you're done, click the **OK** button and you should be able to see that the **Submit** button changes its appearance to this:

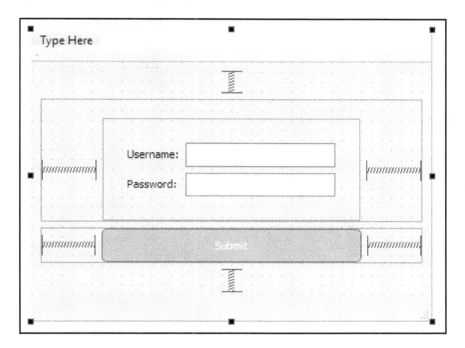

The Style Sheet we used earlier is pretty much self-explanatory. It enables the borderline of the **Push Button** and sets the border color to dark blue using RGB values. Then, it also applies a rounded corner effect to the button and changes its background color to light blue. Finally, the **Submit** text has also been changed to white.

4. Next, we want to apply a custom Style Sheet to the **Form Layout**. However, you will notice that there is no **Change styleSheet...** option when right clicking on it. This is because layouts do not carry that property with it. In order to apply styling to the **Form Layout**, we must first convert it into a **QWidget** or **QFrame** object. To do so, right-click on the **Form Layout** and select **Morph into | QFrame**:

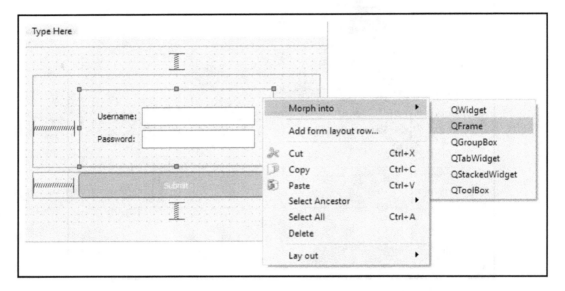

5. Once you're done with that, you will notice it is now carrying the styleSheet property and thus we are now able to customize its appearance. Let's right-click on it and select **Change styleSheet...** to open up the Style Sheet Editor window. Then, insert the following script:

```
#formFrame {
border: 1px solid rgb(24, 103, 155);
border-radius: 5px;
background-color: white; }
```

The word `formFrame` is referring to the widget's `objectName` property and it must match the exact name of the widget, otherwise the style will not be applied to it. The reason why we define the widget name for this example (which we didn't do in the previous one) is because the style will also be applied to all its children if we don't specify the widget name. You can try and remove `#formFrame {}` from the preceding script and see what happens—now, even the **Labels** and **Line Edits** have borderlines, and that is not what we intended to do. The GUI now looks like this:

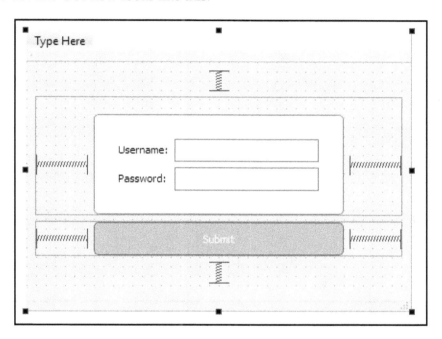

6. Lastly, we want to have a nice-looking background, and we can do this by attaching a background image. To do so, we first need to import the image into Qt's resource system. Go to **File** | **New File or Project...**Then, select Qt under the **Files and Classes** category. After that, pick the **Qt Resource File** and click the **Choose...** button. The Qt resource system is a platform-independent mechanism for storing binary files in the application's executable. You can basically store all of those important files here, such as icon images or language files, directly into your executable by using the Qt resource file. These important files will be directly embedded into your program during the compilation process.

7. Then, key in the file name and set its location before pressing the **Next** button, and follow this by clicking the **Finish** button. Now, you will see a new resource file being created, which I named `resource.qrc`:

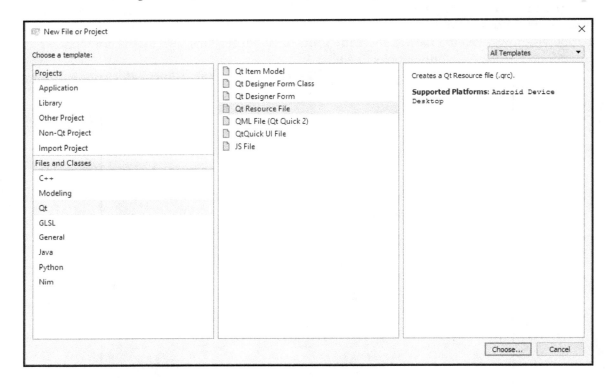

8. Open up `resource.qrc` with Qt Creator and select **Add | Add Prefix**. After that, key in your preferred prefix, for example, `/images`. Once you're done with that, select **Add again** and this time, pick **Add Files**. Add the image file provided by the sample project called `login_bg.png`. Then, save `resource.qrc` and right-click on the image and select **Copy Resource Path to Clipboard**. After that, close `resource.qrc` and open up `mainwindow.ui` again:

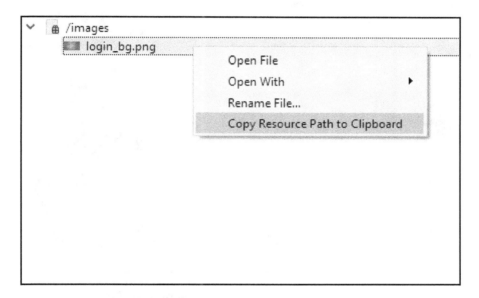

9. The next thing we need to do is to right-click on the `centralWidget` object from the **Object Inspector** and select **Change styleSheet...**, and then insert the following script:

```
#centralWidget {
border-image: url(:/images/login_bg.png); }
```

10. The text within `url()` can be inserted by pressing *Ctrl + V* (or paste) because it was copied to the clipboard when we selected **Copy Resource Path to Clipboard** in the previous step. The final outcome looks like this:

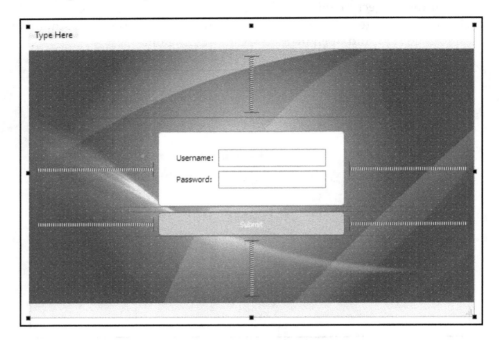

Please make sure that you also build and run the application, and then check whether the final outcome looks the same, as intended. There are a lot more things to tweak in order to make it look truly professional, but so far it's looking pretty great!

Summary

Qt Designer really revolutionized the way we design program GUIs. Not only does it include all the common widgets but it also has handy stuff like the layout and spacer, which makes our program run perfectly fine on different types of monitors and screen sizes. Also, notice that we have successfully created a working application with a beautiful user interface without writing a single line of C++ code!

What we've learned in this chapter merely scratches the surface of Qt, as there are many more features that we are yet to cover! Join us in the next chapter to learn how we can make our program truly functional!

Database Connection 3

In the previous chapter, we learned how to create a login page from scratch. However, it is not functional yet, as the login page is not connected to a database. In this chapter, you will learn how to connect your Qt application to a MySQL (or MariaDB) database that validates login credentials.

In this chapter, we will cover the following topics:

- Introducing the MySQL database system
- Setting up the MySQL database
- SQL commands
- Database connection in Qt
- Functional login page

We will walk through this chapter in a step-by-step approach to discover the powerful features that come with Qt and allow your application to connect directly to a database without any additional third-party dependencies. Database querying is a huge topic by itself, but we will be able to learn the most basic commands from scratch through examples and practical methods.

Qt supports multiple different types of database systems:

- MySQL (or MariaDB)
- SQLite (version 2 and 3)
- IBM DB2
- Oracle
- ODBC
- PostgreSQL
- Sybase Adaptive Server

Two of the most popular ones are MySQL and SQLite. The SQLite database is usually used offline and it doesn't require any setup as it uses an on-disk file format for storing data. Therefore, in this chapter, we will learn how to set up a MySQL database system instead, and at the same time learn how to connect our Qt application to a MySQL database. The C++ code used to connect to the MySQL database can be reused for connecting to other database systems without many alterations.

Introducing the MySQL database system

MySQL is an open source database management system based on the relational model, which is the most common method used by modern database systems to store information for various purposes.

Unlike some other legacy models—such as an object database system or a hierarchical database system—the relational model has been proven to be more user friendly and performs well beyond the other models. That's the reason why most of the modern database systems we see today are mostly using this method.

MySQL was originally developed by a Swedish company called **MySQL AB**, and its name is the combination of *My*, the name of the daughter of the company's co-founder, and *SQL*, the abbreviation for **Structured Query Language**.

Similar to Qt, MySQL has also been owned by multiple different people throughout its history. The most notable acquisition happened in 2008, where **Sun Microsystems** bought MySQL AB for $1 billion. One year later in 2009, **Oracle Corporation** acquired Sun Microsystems, and so MySQL is owned by Oracle up to this day. Even though MySQL changed hands several times, it still remains as an open source software that allows users to change the code to suit their own purposes.

Due to its open source nature, there are also other database systems out there that were derived/forked from the MySQL project, such as **MariaDB**, **Percona Server**, and so on. However, these alternatives are not fully compatible with MySQL as they have modified it to suit their own needs, and therefore some of the commands may be varied among these systems.

According to a 2017 survey carried out by **Stack Overflow**, **MySQL** is the most widely used database system among web developers, as we can see in the following screenshot:

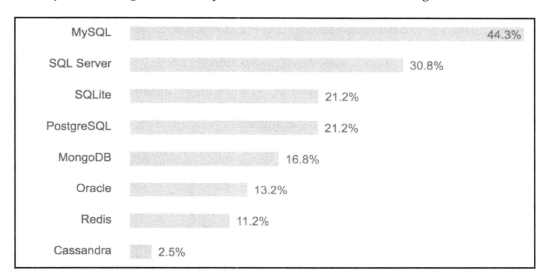

The survey result indicates that what you learn in this chapter can be applied to not just Qt projects but also web, mobile app, and other types of applications.

Furthermore, MySQL and its variants are being used by big corporations and project groups such as Facebook, YouTube, Twitter, NASA, Wordpress, Drupal, Airbnb, Spotify, and so on and so forth. This means that you can easily get answers when encountering any technical issues during development.

 For more information regarding MySQL, please visit:
`https://www.mysql.com`

Setting up the MySQL database

There are many different ways to set up your MySQL database. It really depends on the type of platforms you are running, whether it is **Windows**, **Linux**, **Mac**, or any other type of operating system; it will also depend on the purpose of your database—whether it's for development and testing, or for a large-scale production server.

For large scale services (such as social media), the best way is to compile MySQL from the source, because such as project requires a ton of optimization, configuration, and sometimes customization in order to handle the large amount of users and traffic.

However, you can just download the pre-compiled binaries if you're going for normal use, as the default configuration is pretty sufficient for that. You can install a standalone MySQL installer from their official website or the download installation packages that come with several other pieces of software besides MySQL.

In this chapter, we will be using a software package called **XAMPP**, which is a web server stack package developed by a group called **Apache Friends**. This package comes with **Apache**, **MariaDB**, **PHP**, and other optional services that you can add on during the installation process. Previously, MySQL was part of the package, but it has since been replaced with **MariaDB** starting from version 5.5.30 and 5.6.14. MariaDB works almost the same as MySQL, except those commands involving advanced features, which we will not be using in this book.

The reason why we use XAMPP is that it has a control panel that can easily start and stop the services without using Command Prompt, and provides easy access to the configuration files without you having to dig into the installation directory by yourself. It is very quick and efficient for application development that involves frequent testings. However, it is not recommended that you use XAMPP on a production server as some of the security features have been disabled by default.

Alternatively, you may also install MySQL through other similar software packages such as **AppServ**, **AMPPS**, **LAMP** (Linux only), **WAMP** (Windows only), **ZendServer**, and so on.

Now, let's learn how to install XAMPP:

1. First, go to their website at `https://www.apachefriends.org` and click on one of the download buttons located at the bottom of your screen, which displays the icon of your current operating system:

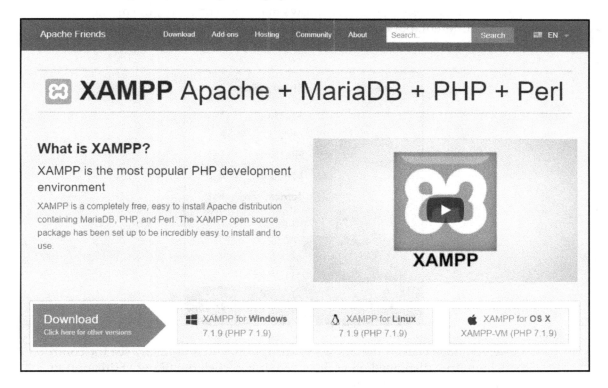

2. Once you click on the **Download** button, the download process should start automatically within a few seconds, and it should proceed to install the program once it's done. Make sure that **Apache** and **MySQL/MariaDB** are included before the installation process starts.

3. After you have installed XAMPP, launch the control panel from the start menu or from the desktop shortcut. After that, you may notice that nothing has happened. This is because the XAMPP control panel is hidden within the taskbar by default. You may display the control panel window by right-clicking on it and selecting the **Show / Hide** option in the pop-up menu. The following screenshot shows you what this looks like on a Windows machine. For Linux, the menu may look slightly different, but overall it is very similar. For macOS, you must launch XAMPP from the launchpad or from the dock:

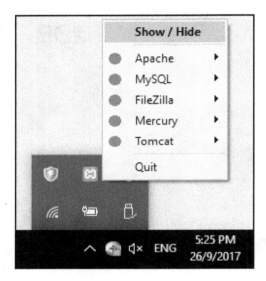

4. Once you have clicked the **Show / Hide** option, you will finally see the control panel window displayed on your screen. If you click the **Show / Hide** option again, the window will be hidden away:

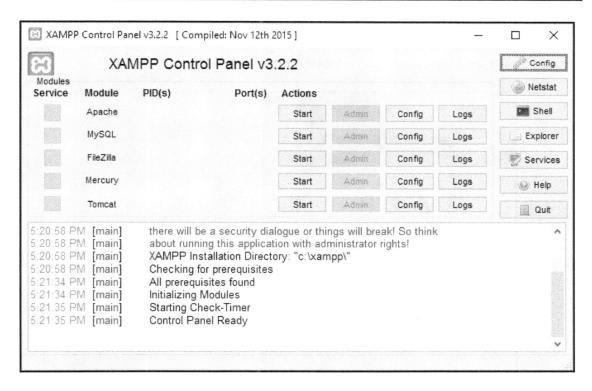

5. Their control panel is pretty much self-explanatory at first glance. On the left, you can see the names of the services that are available in XAMPP, and on the right, you will see the buttons that indicate **Start**, **Config**, **Logs**, and so on. For some reason, XAMPP is showing MySQL as the module name but it is in fact running MariaDB. Don't worry; both work pretty much the same since MariaDB is a fork of MySQL.

6. In this chapter, we'll only need **Apache** and **MySQL** (MariaDB), so let's click the **Start** buttons of these services. After a second or two, you'll see that the **Start** buttons are now labeled as **Stop**, which means the services have been launched!:

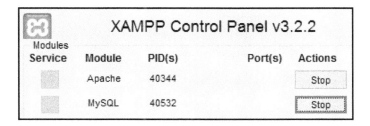

7. To verify this, let's open up the browser and type `localhost` as the website address. If you see something like the following image, it means that the Apache web server has been successfully launched!:

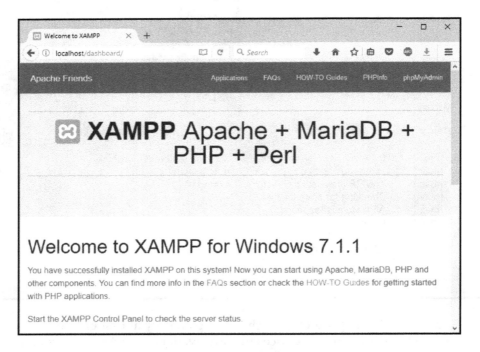

8. **Apache** is very important here as we'll be using it to configure the database using a web-based administrative tool called **phpMyAdmin**. phpMyAdmin is an administrative tool for MySQL written in PHP scripting language, hence its name. Even though it was originally designed for MySQL, it works pretty well for MariaDB as well.

9. To access the **phpMyAdmin** control panel, type `localhost/phpmyadmin` on your browser. After that, you should see something like this:

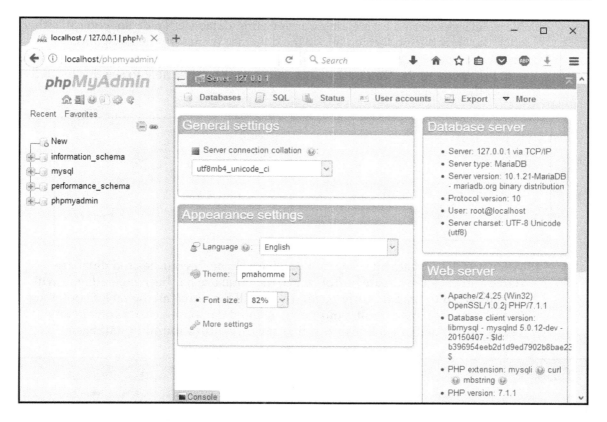

10. On the left-hand side of the page, you will see the navigation panel, which allows you access to the different databases available in your MariaDB database. On the right-hand side of the page are various tools that let you view table, edit table, run SQL command, export data to spreadsheet, set privileges, and so on.

11. By default, you can only modify the **General settings** of the database on the setting panel located on the right. You must select a database from the **navigation panel** on the left before you are able to modify the settings of a particular database.

12. A database is like a cabinet that you can store log books within. Each log book is called a table and each table contains data, which is sorted like a spreadsheet. When you want to obtain a data from MariaDB, you must specify which cabinet (database) and log book (table) you would like to access before getting the data from it. Hopefully, this will make you better understand the concept behind MariaDB and other similar database systems.

13. Now, let's get started by creating our very first database! To do so, you can either click the **New** button located above the database names on the navigation panel or click the **Databases** button located at the top of the menu. Both buttons will bring you to the **Databases** page, and you should be able to see this located below the menu buttons:

14. After that, let's create our very first database! Type in your desired database name and click the **Create** button. Once the database has been created, you will be redirected to the **Structure** page, which will list down all the tables contained in this database. By default, your newly created database doesn't contain any tables, so you will see a line of text that says **No tables found in database**:

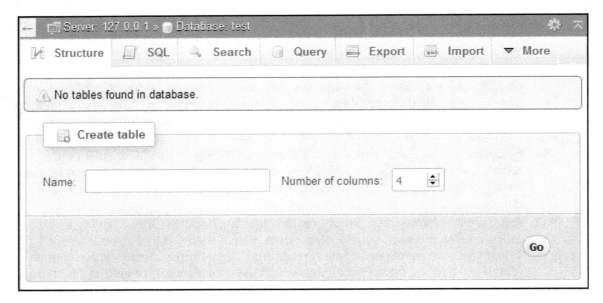

15. Guess what we'll be doing next? Correct, we will create our first table! First, let's insert the name of the table you want to create. Since we'll be doing a login page later in this chapter, let's name our table `user`. We'll leave the default number of columns as it is and click **Go**.

16. After that, you will be redirected to another page, which contains many columns of input fields for you to fill in. Each column represents a data structure which will be added to your table after it's been created.

17. The first thing you need to add to the table structure is an ID that will automatically increase upon each new data insertion. Then, add a timestamp column to indicate the date and time of the data insertion, which is good for debugging. Last but not least, we will add a username column and password column for login validation. If you're unsure on how to do this, please refer to the following image. Make sure you follow the settings that are being circled in the image:

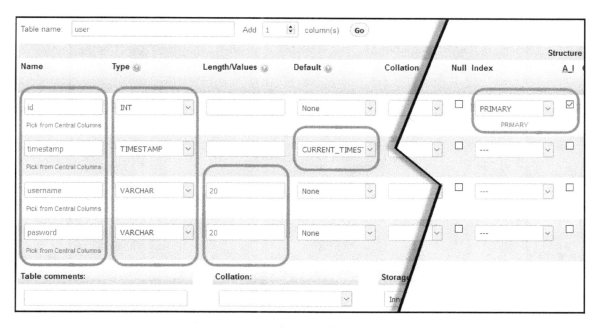

18. The type of the structure is very important and must be set according to its intended purpose. For example, the **id** column must be set as **INT** (integer number) as it must be a full number, while **username** and **password** must be set as either **VARCHAR** or other similar data types (CHAR, TEXT, and so on) in order for it to save the data correctly.

19. The **timestamp**, on the other hand, must be set to **TIMESTAMP** type, and must set the default value to **CURRENT_TIMESTAMP,** which notifies MariaDB to automatically generate the current timestamp upon data insertion.

20. Please note that the index setting for the ID column must be set to **PRIMARY,** and make sure that the **A_I** (auto increment) checkbox is ticked. When you check the **A_I** checkbox, an Add Index window will appear. You can keep the default settings as they are and then you can click the **Go** button to complete the steps and start creating the table:

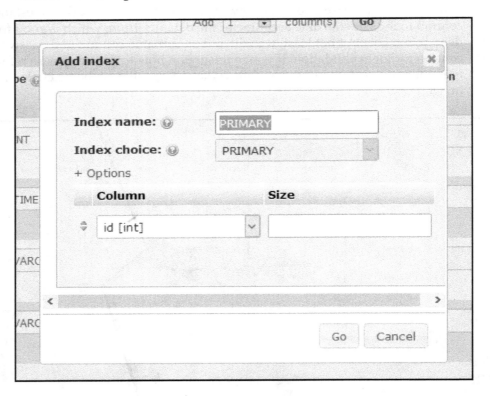

21. After you have created the new table, you should be able to see something similar like the following image. You can still edit the structure settings anytime by clicking the **Change** button; you can also remove any of the columns by clicking on the **Drop** button located at the right-hand side of the column. Please note that deleting a column will also remove all the existing data belonging to that column, and this action cannot be undone:

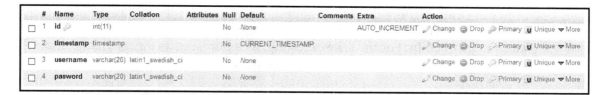

#	Name	Type	Collation	Attributes	Null	Default	Comments	Extra	Action
☐ 1	id	int(11)			No	None		AUTO_INCREMENT	Change ⊜ Drop Primary Unique ▼More
☐ 2	timestamp	timestamp			No	CURRENT_TIMESTAMP			Change ⊜ Drop Primary Unique ▼More
☐ 3	username	varchar(20)	latin1_swedish_ci		No	None			Change ⊜ Drop Primary Unique ▼More
☐ 4	pasword	varchar(20)	latin1_swedish_ci		No	None			Change ⊜ Drop Primary Unique ▼More

22. Even though we'll usually add data to the database through our programs or web pages, we can also add data directly on **phpMyAdmin** for testing purposes. To add data using **phpMyAdmin**, first, you must create a database and table, which we have done in the previous steps. Then, click the **Insert** button located at the top of the menu:

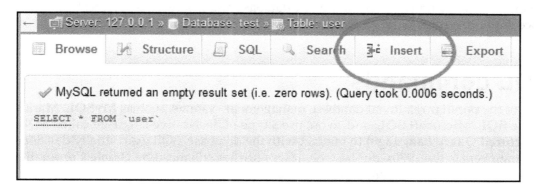

23. After that, you'll see that a form has appeared, which resembles the data structure that we created previously:

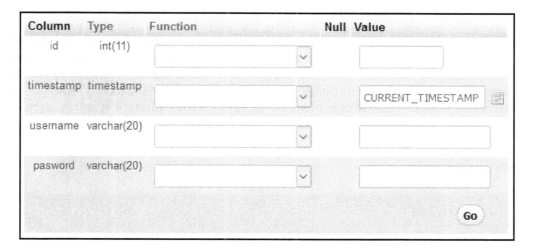

24. You can simply ignore the ID and timestamp values as they will be automatically generated when you save the data. In this case, only **username** and **password** need to be filled in. For the sake of testing, let's put `test` as the username and `123456` as the password. Then, click the **Go** button to save the data.

 Please note that you should not save your password in a human-readable format on your actual production server. You must encrypt the password with a **cryptographic hash** function such as SHA-512, RIPEEMD-512, BLAKE2b, and so on before passing it to the database. This will ensure that the password is not readable by hackers in case your database is being compromised. We will cover this topic at the end of this chapter.

Now that we have finished setting up our database and inserted our first test data, let's proceed to learn some of the SQL commands!

SQL commands

Most of the popular relational database management systems, such as **MySQL**, **MariaDB**, **Oracle SQL**, **Microsoft SQL**, and so on, use a type of declarative language called **SQL** (**Structured Query Language**) to interact with the database. SQL was initially developed by IBM engineers in the 1970s, but later on, it was further enhanced by **Oracle Corporation** and other emerging tech companies of that era.

Today, SQL has become a standard of the **American National Standards Institute** (**ANSI**) and of the **International Organization for Standardization** (**ISO**). SQL language has since been adopted by many different database systems and has become one of the most popular database languages in the modern era.

In this section, we will learn what some of the basic SQL commands you can use to interact with your MariaDB database are, specifically for obtaining, saving, modifying, and deleting your data from/to the database. These basic commands can be used in other types of SQL-based database systems as well as under the ANSI and ISO standards. Only, some of the more advanced/customized features could be different across different systems, so make sure that you read the system manual before using these advanced features.

Alright, let's get started!

SELECT

Most of the SQL statements are one-word short and self-explanatory. This statement, for example, is used to select one or more columns from a specific table and to obtain the data from the said columns. Let's check out some of the sample commands that use the SELECT statement.

The following command retrieves all the data of all the columns from the user table:

```
SELECT * FROM user;
```

The following command retrieves only the username column from the user table:

```
SELECT username FROM user;
```

The following command retrieves the username and password columns from the user table with the condition that the id equals 1:

```
SELECT username, password FROM user WHERE id = 1;
```

You can try out these commands by yourself using phpMyAdmin. To do that, click the **SQL** button located at the top of the menu in **phpMyAdmin**. After that, you can type the command in the text field below and click **Go** to execute the query:

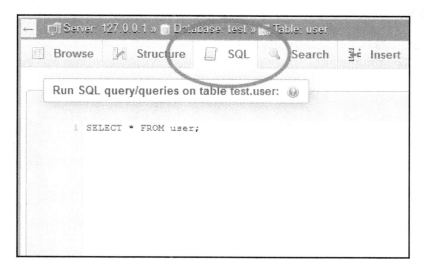

To learn more about the SELECT statement, please refer to the following link:
https://dev.mysql.com/doc/refman/5.7/en/select.html

INSERT

Next, the INSERT statement is used to save new data into a database table. For example:

```
INSERT INTO user (username, password) VALUES ("test2", "123456");
```

The preceding SQL command inserts username and password data into the user table. There are some other statements that can be used together with INSERT, such as LOW_PRIORITY, DELAYED, HIGH_PRIORITY, and so on.

Please refer to the following link to learn more about these options:
https://dev.mysql.com/doc/refman/5.7/en/insert.html

UPDATE

The UPDATE statement modifies existing data in the database. You must specify a condition for the UPDATE command as otherwise, it will modify every single piece of data in a table, which is not our intended behavior. Try the following command, which will change the username and password of the first user:

```
UPDATE user SET username = "test1", password = "1234321" WHERE id = 1;
```

The command will fail, however, if the user with ID 1 does not exist. The command will also return the status 0 rows affected if the username and password data you provided matches exactly with the one stored in the database (nothing to change). For more information regarding the UPDATE statement, please refer to the following link:

https://dev.mysql.com/doc/refman/5.7/en/update.html

DELETE

The `DELETE` statement deletes data from a specific table of a database. For example, the following command deletes a data from the `user` table that carries the ID `1`:

```
DELETE FROM user WHERE id = 1;
```

Even though you can use this statement to delete unwanted data, it is not recommended to delete any data from your database because the action cannot be undone. It is better to add another column to your table called status and use that to indicate whether data should be shown or not. For example, if your user deletes data on the front end application, set the **status** of that data to (let's say) `1` instead of `0`. Then, when you want to display data on the front end, display only the data that carries a **status** of `0`:

This way, any data that has been accidentally deleted can be recovered with ease. You can also use a BOOLEAN type for this if you only plan to use true or false. I usually use **TINYINT** just in case I need a third or fourth status in the future. For more information regarding the `DELETE` statement, you can refer to the following link:

```
https://dev.mysql.com/doc/refman/5.7/en/delete.html
```

JOIN

The advantage of using a relational database management system is that the data can be easily joined together from different tables and can be returned to the user in a single bulk. This greatly improves the productivity of the developers as it allows fluidity and flexibility when it comes to designing a complex database structure.

There are many types of **JOIN** statements in MariaDB/MySQL—**INNER JOIN, FULL OUTER JOIN, LEFT JOIN**, and **RIGHT JOIN**. All of these different **JOIN** statements behave differently when executed, which you can see in the following image:

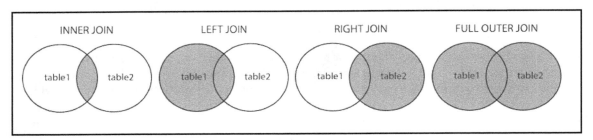

Most of the time, we'll be using the **INNER JOIN** statement, as it only returns the data that has matching values in both tables, and thus only returns a small amount of the data that is needed. The **JOIN** command is much more complicated than the others as you need to design the tables to be join-able in the first place. Before we start testing the **JOIN** command, let's create another table to make this possible. We will call this new table **department**:

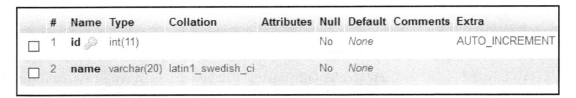

After that, add two departments, like so:

Then, go to the **user** table, and at the structure page, scroll all the way to the bottom and look for the form shown, then click the **Go** button:

Add a new column called **deptID** (which stands for department ID) and set its data type to `int` (integer number):

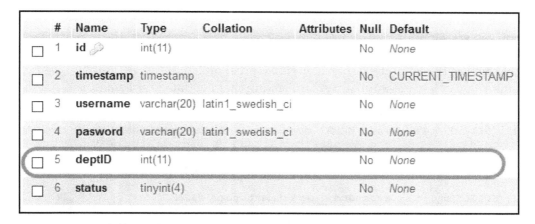

After that, set up a few test users and put each of their **deptID** as either `1` or `2`:

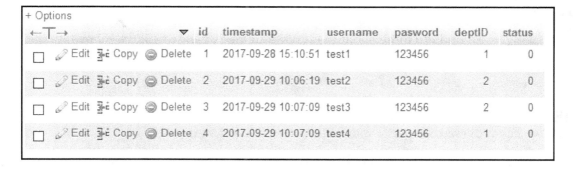

Please notice that I have also added the status column here for checking whether the user has been deleted or not. Once you have done with that, let's try to run a sample command!:

```
SELECT my_user.username, department.name FROM (SELECT * FROM user WHERE
deptID = 1) AS my_user INNER JOIN department ON department.id =
my_user.deptID AND my_user.status = 0
```

That looks quite complicated at first glance, but it really isn't if you separate it into a few parts. We'll start from the command within the () bracket first, in which we asked MariaDB/MySQL to select all columns within the user table that carry deptID = 1:

```
SELECT * FROM user WHERE deptID = 1
```

After that, contain it within a () bracket and name this entire command as my_user. After that, you can start joining your user table (now called my_user) with the department table by using the INNER JOIN statement. Here, we also added some conditions for it to look up the data, such as the ID of the department table must match the deptID of my_user, and the status value of my_user must be 0, indicating that the data is still valid and not tagged as removed:

```
(SELECT * FROM user WHERE deptID = 1) AS my_user INNER JOIN department
ON department.id = my_user.deptID AND my_user.status = 0
```

Lastly, add the following code in front to complete the SQL command:

```
SELECT my_user.username, department.name FROM
```

Let's try the preceding command and see if the result is what you expected.

You can join infinite numbers of tables using this method as long as the tables are linked to each another through matching columns.

 To find out more about the **JOIN** statement, please visit the following link: https://dev.mysql.com/doc/refman/5.7/en/join.html

There are many other SQL statements that we have not covered in this chapter, but the ones that we have covered are pretty much all you need to get started.

One last thing before we move on to the next section—we must create a user account for the application to access to our MariaDB/MySQL database. First of all, go to your **phpMyAdmin** home page and click **User accounts** on the top menu:

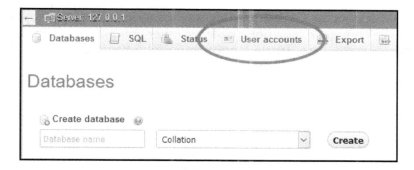

Then, go to the bottom and look for this link called **Add user account**:

Once you're in the **Add user account** page, type in the **User name** and **Password** information in the **Login Information** form. Make sure that the **Host name** is set to **Local**:

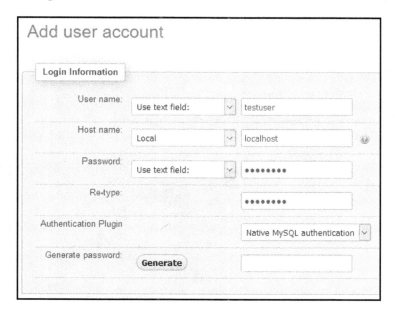

Then, scroll down and set the **Global privileges** of the user. Enabling the options within the **Data** section is well enough, but do not enable the other options as it might give hackers the privilege to alter your database structure once your server has been compromised:

Once you have created the user account, follow the following steps to allow the newly-created user access to the database called **test** (or any other table name of your choice):

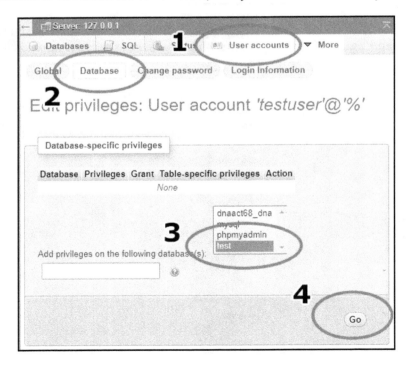

After you have clicked the **Go** button, you have now given the user account the privilege to access the database! In the next section, we'll be learning how to connect our Qt application to the database.

Database connection in Qt

Now that we have learned how to set up a functional MySQL/MariaDB database system, let's move a step further and discover the database connection module in Qt!

Before we continue working on our login page from the previous chapter, let's start off with a new Qt project first so that it's easier to demonstrate the functionality solely related to database connection and so that we don't get distracted by the other stuff. This time, we'll go for the Terminal-style application called **Qt Console Application**, as we don't really need any GUI for this demonstration:

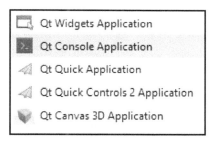

After you have created the new project, you should only see two files in the project, that is, **[project_name].pro** and **main.cpp**:

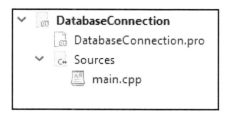

The first thing you need to do is to open up your project file (.pro), which in my case is **DatabaseConnection.pro**, and add the sql keyword at the back of the first line, like so:

```
QT += core sql
```

As simple as that, we have successfully imported the `sql` module into our Qt project! Then, open up `main.cpp` and you should see a very simple script that contains only eight lines of code. This is basically all you need to create an empty console application:

```
#include <QCoreApplication>
int main(int argc, char *argv[])
{
    QCoreApplication a(argc, argv);
    return a.exec();
}
```

In order for us to connect to our database, we must first import the relevant headers to `main.cpp`, like so:

```
#include <QCoreApplication>
#include <QtSql>
#include <QSqlDatabase>
#include <QSqlQuery>
#include <QDebug>
int main(int argc, char *argv[])
{
    QCoreApplication a(argc, argv);
    return a.exec();
}
```

Without these header files, we won't be able to use the functions provided by Qt's `sql` module, which we have imported previously. Additionally, we also added the `QDebug` header so that we can easily print out any text on the console display (similar to the `std::cout` function provided by C++'s standard library).

Next, we'll add some code to the `main.cpp` file. Add the following highlighted code before `return a.exec()`:

```
int main(int argc, char *argv[])
{
    QCoreApplication a(argc, argv);
    QSqlDatabase db = QSqlDatabase::addDatabase("QMYSQL");
    db.setHostName("127.0.0.1");
    db.setPort(3306);
    db.setDatabaseName("test");
    db.setUserName("testuser");
    db.setPassword("testpass");
    if (db.open())
    {
        qDebug() << "Connected!";
    }
```

```
else
{
        qDebug() << "Failed to connect.";
        return 0;
}
return a.exec();
}
```

Do note that the database name, username, and password could be different from what you have set in your database, so please make sure they are correct before compiling the project.

Once you are done with that, let's click the **Run** button and see what happens!:

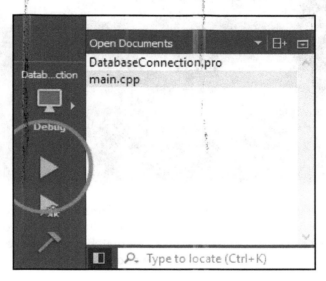

If you see the following error, don't worry:

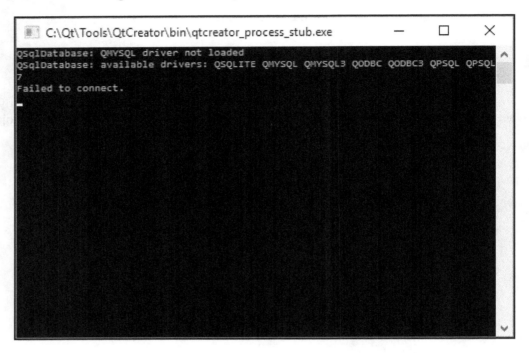

That is simply because you must install the **MariaDB Connector** (or **MySQL Connector** if you're running MySQL) to your computer and copy the DLL file over to your Qt installation path. Please make sure that the DLL file matches your server's database library. You can open up your **phpMyAdmin** home page and see which library it is currently using.

For some reason, even though I'm running XAMPP with MariaDB, the library name here shows **libmysql** instead of **libmariadb**, so I had to install MySQL Connector instead:

Database server

- Server: 127.0.0.1 via TCP/IP
- Server type: MariaDB
- Server version: 10.1.21-MariaDB - mariadb.org binary distribution
- Protocol version: 10
- User: root@localhost
- Server charset: UTF-8 Unicode (utf8)

Web server

- Apache/2.4.25 (Win32) OpenSSL/1.0.2j PHP/7.1.1
- Database client version: libmysql - mysqlnd 5.0.12-dev - 20150407 - $Id: b396954eeb2d1d9ed7902b8bae237b287f21ad9e $
- PHP extension: mysqli ◎ curl ◎ mbstring ◎
- PHP version: 7.1.1

If you're using MariaDB, please download the MariaDB Connector at the following link:
`https://downloads.mariadb.org/connector-c`
If you're using MySQL instead (or are having the same issue as I did), please visit the other link and download MySQL Connector:
`https://dev.mysql.com/downloads/connector/cpp/`

After you have downloaded the **MariaDB Connector**, install it on your computer:

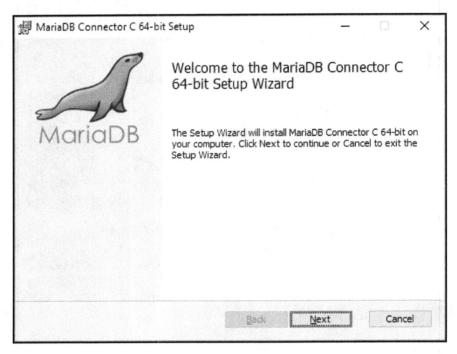

The preceding screenshot shows the installation process for a Windows machine. If you're running Linux, you must download the right package for your Linux distribution. If you're running Debian, Ubuntu, or one of its variants, download the Debian and Ubuntu packages. If you're running Red Hat, Fedora, CentOS, or one of its variants, download the Red Hat, Fedora, and CentOS packages. The installation for these packages are automated, so you're good to go. However, if you're running neither of those, you'll have to download one of the gzipped tar files listed on the download page that fits your system requirement.

For more information about installing MariaDB binary tarballs on Linux, please refer to the following link:
`https://mariadb.com/kb/en/library/installing-mariadb-binary-tarballs/`

As for macOS, you need to use a package manager called **Homebrew** to install MariaDB server.

For more information, check out the following link:
https://mariadb.com/kb/en/library/installing-mariadb-on-macos-us
ing-homebrew/

Once you have installed it, go to its installation directory and look for the DLL file
(libmariadb.dll for MariaDB or libmysql.dll for MySQL). For Linux and macOS, it's
libmariadb.so or libmysql.so instead of DLL.

Then, copy the file over to your application's build directory (the same folder as your
application's executable file). After that, try and run your application again:

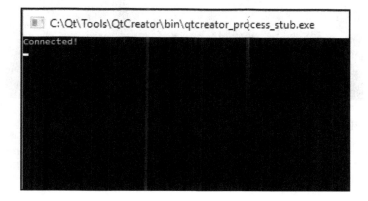

If you still getting Failed to connect but without the QMYSQL driver not
loaded message, please check your XAMPP control panel and make sure that your
database service is running; also make sure that the database name, username, and
password that you put in the code is all the correct information.

Next, we can start playing around with SQL commands! Add the following code before
return a.exec():

```
QString command = "SELECT name FROM department";
QSqlQuery query(db);
if (query.exec(command))
{
    while(query.next())
    {
        QString name = query.value("name").toString();
        qDebug() << name;
    }
}
```

The preceding code sends the command text to the database and synchronously waits for the result to return from the server. After that, use a `while` loop to go through every single result and convert it to a string format. Then, display the result on the console window. If everything went right, you should see something like this:

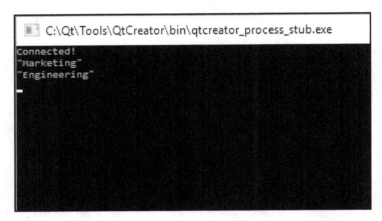

Let's try out something more complex:

```
QString command = "SELECT my_user.username, department.name AS deptname
FROM (SELECT * FROM user WHERE status = 0) AS my_user INNER JOIN
department ON department.id = my_user.deptID";
QSqlQuery query(db);
if (query.exec(command))
{
    while(query.next())
    {
        QString username = query.value("username").toString();
        QString department = query.value("deptname").toString();
        qDebug() << username << department;
    }
}
```

This time, we used **INNER JOIN** to combine two tables to select the `username` and `department` name. To avoid confusion regarding the variable called `name`, rename it to `deptname` using the `AS` statement. After that, display both the `username` and `department` name on the console window:

We're done... for now. Let's move on to the next section, where we will learn how to make our login page functional!

Creating our functional login page

Since we have learned how to connect our Qt application to the MariaDB/MySQL database system, it's time to continue working on the login page! In the previous chapter, we learned how to set up the GUI of our login page. However, it didn't have any functionality at all as a login page since it doesn't connect to the database and verify login credentials. Therefore, we will learn how to achieve that by empowering Qt's `sql` module.

Just to recap—this is what the login screen looks like:

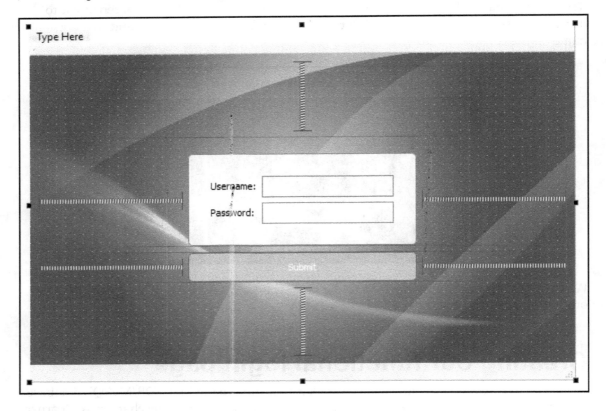

The very first thing we need to do now is to name the widgets that are important in this login page, which are the **Username** input, **Password** input, and the **Submit** button. You can set these properties by selecting the widget and looking for the property in the property editor:

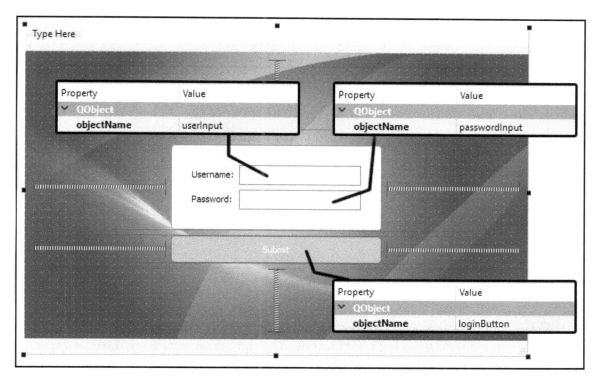

Then, set the **echoMode** of the password input as **Password**. This setting will hide the password visually by replacing it with dots:

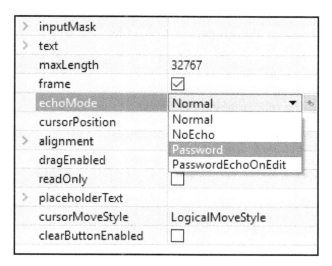

After that, right-click on the **Submit** button and select **Go to slot...** A window will pop up and ask you which signal to use. Select **clicked()** and click **OK**:

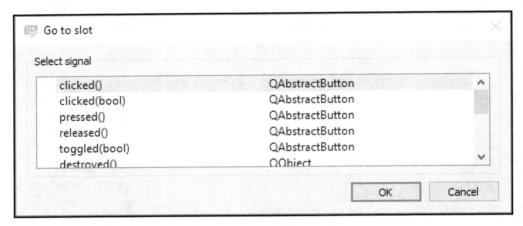

A new function called `on_loginButton_clicked()` will be automatically added to the `MainWindow` class. This function will be triggered by Qt when the **Submit** button is pressed by the user, and thus you just need to write the code here to submit the `username` and `password` to the database for login verification. The signal and slots mechanism is a special feature provided by Qt which is used for communication between objects. When one widget is emitting a signal, another widget will be notified and will proceed to run a specific function that is designed to react to the particular signal.

Let's check out the code.

First, add in the `sql` keyword at your project (.pro) file:

```
QT += core gui
sql
```

Then, proceed and add the relevant headers to `mainwindow.cpp`:

```
#ifndef MAINWINDOW_H
#define MAINWINDOW_H

#include <QMainWindow>

#include <QtSql>
#include <QSqlDatabase>
#include <QSqlQuery>
#include <QDebug>
#include <QMessageBox>
```

Then, go back to `mainwindow.cpp` and add the following code to the
`on_loginButton_clicked()` function:

```cpp
void MainWindow::on_loginButton_clicked()
{
    QString username = ui->userInput->text();
    QString password = ui->passwordInput->text();
    qDebug() << username << password;
}
```

Now, click the **Run** button and wait for the application to start. Then, key in any random
`username` and `password`, followed by clicking on the **submit** button. You should now see
your `username` and `password` being displayed on the application output window in Qt
Creator.

Next, we'll copy the SQL integration code we have written previously into
`mainwindow.cpp`:

```cpp
MainWindow::MainWindow(QWidget *parent) :
    QMainWindow(parent),
    ui(new Ui::MainWindow)
{
    ui->setupUi(this);

    db = QSqlDatabase::addDatabase("QMYSQL");
    db.setHostName("127.0.0.1");
    db.setPort(3306);
    db.setDatabaseName("test");
    db.setUserName("testuser");
    db.setPassword("testpass");

    if (db.open())
    {
        qDebug() << "Connected!";
    }
    else
    {
        qDebug() << "Failed to connect.";
    }
}
```

Do note that I've used some random text for the database name, username, and password. Please make sure you enter the correct details here and that they match with what you've set in the database system.

One minor thing we have changed for the preceding code is that we only need to call db = QSqlDatabase::addDatabase("QMYSQL") in mainwindow.cpp without the class name as the declaration QSqlDatabase db has now been relocated to mainwindow.h:

```
private:
    Ui::MainWindow *ui;
    QSqlDatabase db;
```

Lastly, we add in the code that combines the username and password information with the SQL command, and send the whole thing to the database for execution. If there is a result that matches the login information, then it means that the login has been successful, otherwise, it means the login has failed:

```
void MainWindow::on_loginButton_clicked()
{
    QString username = ui->userInput->text();
    QString password = ui->passwordInput->text();

    qDebug() << username << password;

    QString command = "SELECT * FROM user WHERE username = '" + username
    + "' AND password = '" + password + "' AND status = 0";
    QSqlQuery query(db);
    if (query.exec(command))
    {
        if (query.size() > 0)
        {
            QMessageBox::information(this, "Login success.", "You
            have successfully logged in!");
        }
        else
        {
            QMessageBox::information(this, "Login failed.", "Login
            failed. Please try again...");
        }
    }
}
```

Click the **Run** button again and see what happens when you click the **Submit** button:

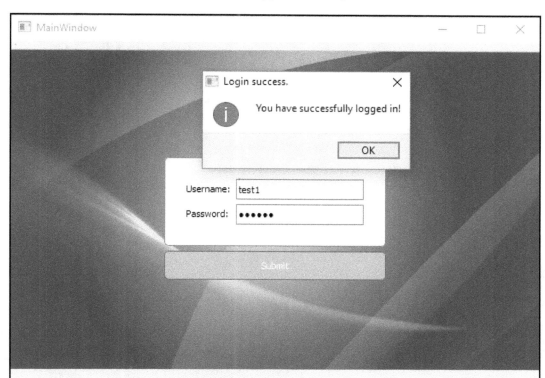

Hip hip hooray! The login page is now fully functional!

Summary

In this chapter, we learned how to set up a database system and make our Qt application connect to it. In the next chapter, we will learn how to draw graphs and charts using the powerful Qt Framework.

4
Graphs and Charts

In the previous chapter, we learned how to retrieve data from a database using Qt's `sql` module. There are many ways to present this data to the users, such as displaying it in the form of tables or diagrams. In this chapter, we will learn how to do the latter—presenting data with different types of graphs and charts using Qt's charts module.

In this chapter, we will cover the following topics:

- Types of charts and graphs in Qt
- Charts and graphs implementation
- Creating the dashboard page

Since Qt 5.7, several modules that were only available for commercial users before have become free for all the open source package users, which includes the **Qt Charts** module. Therefore, it is considered a very new module for most Qt users who don't own the commercial license.

Do note that, unlike most of the Qt modules that are available under an LGPLv3 license, the Qt Chart module is offered under an GPLv3 license. Unlike LGPLv3, a GPLv3 license requires you to release the source code of your application, while your application must also be licensed under GPLv3. This means that you are not allowed to static-link Qt Chart with your application. It also prevents the module from being used in proprietary software.

 To learn more about the GNU licenses, please head over to the following link: https://www.gnu.org/licenses/gpl-faq.html.

Let's get started!

Types of charts and graphs in Qt

Qt supports most commonly used diagrams, and even allows the developer to customize the look and feel of them so that they can be used for many different purposes. The Qt Charts module provides the following chart types:

- Line and spline charts
- Bar charts
- Pie charts
- Polar charts
- Area and scatter charts
- Box-and-whiskers charts
- Candlestick charts

Line and spline charts

The first type of chart is the **line and spline chart**. These charts are typically presented as a series of points/markers that are connected by lines. In a line chart, the points are connected by straight lines to show the changes of the variables over a period of time. On the other hand, spline charts are very similar to line charts except the points are connected by a spline/curve line instead of straight lines:

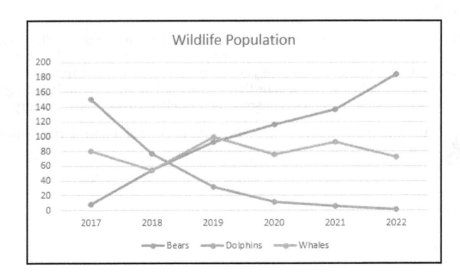

Bar charts

Bar charts are one of the most commonly used diagrams beside line charts and pie charts. A bar chart is quite similar to a line chart, except it doesn't connect the data along an axis. Instead, a bar chart displays its data using individual rectangular shapes, where its height is determined by the value of the data. This means that the higher the value, the taller the rectangular shape will become:

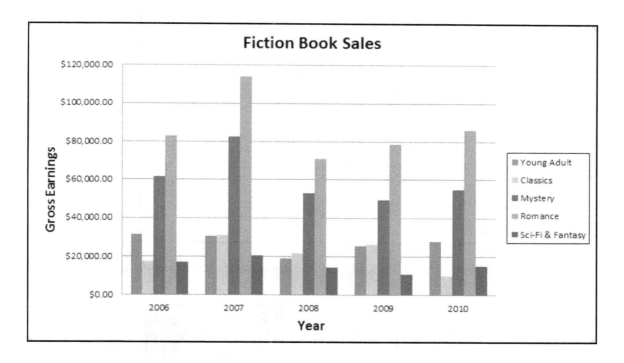

Pie charts

A **pie chart**, as its name implies, is a type of chart that looks like a pie. A pie chart presents its data in the form of pie slices. The size of each slice of pie will be determined by the overall percentage of its value compared to the rest of the data. Therefore, pie charts are normally used to display fraction, ratio, percentage, or a share of a set of data:

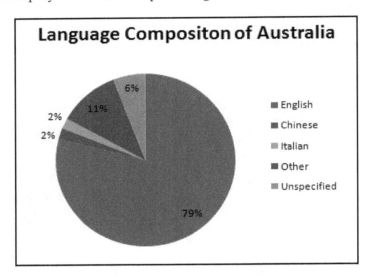

Sometimes, a pie chart can also be displayed in a donut shape (also known as donut chart):

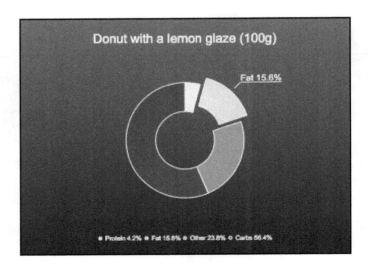

Polar charts

Polar charts present data in a circular graph, where the placement of the data is based on both the angle and the distance from the center of the graph, which means the higher the value of the data, the further away the point is from the center of the chart. You can display multiple types of graphs within the polar chart, such as line, spline, area, and scatter to visualize the data:

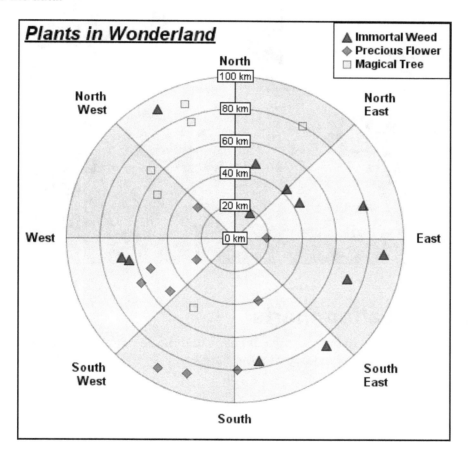

If you are a gamer, you should have noticed this type of graph being used in some video games to display the in-game character's attributes:

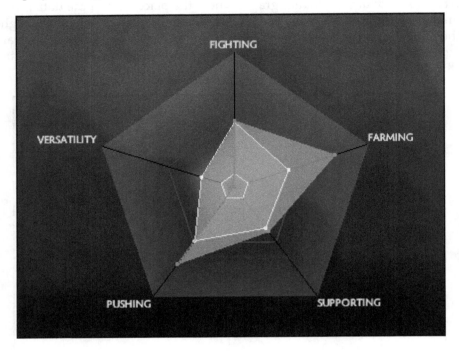

Area and scatter charts

An **area chart** displays its data as an area or shape to indicate volume. It's usually used to compare the differences between two or more datasets.

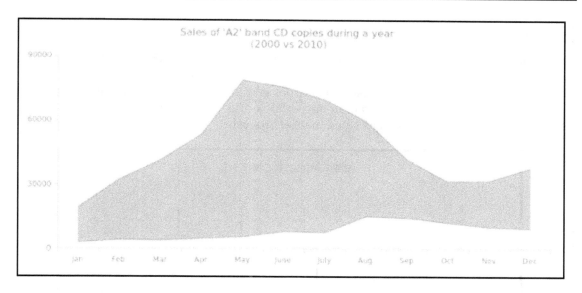

Scatter charts, on the other hand, are used to display a collection of data points, and for showing the non-linear relationship between two or more datasets.

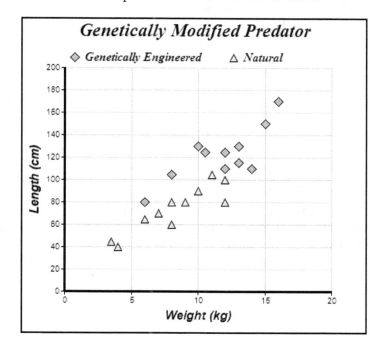

Box-and-whiskers charts

Box-and-whiskers charts present data as quartiles extended with whiskers that show the variability of the values. The boxes may have lines extending vertically called *whiskers*. These lines indicate variability outside the upper and lower quartiles, and any point outside those lines or whiskers is considered an outlier. Box-and-whisker charts are most commonly used in statistical analysis, such as stock market analysis:

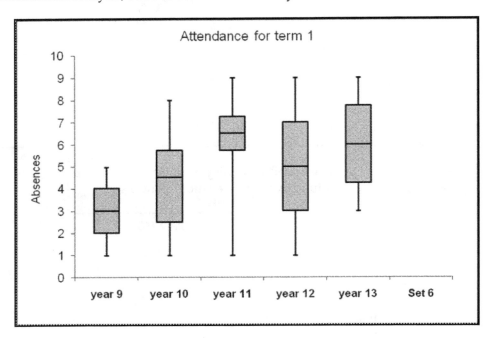

Candlestick charts

Candlestick charts are visually quite similar to the box-and-whiskers charts, except they are used to represent the difference between the opening and closing value, while showing the direction of the value (whether increasing or decreasing) through different colors. If the value of a particular piece of data stays the same, the rectangular shape will not be shown at all:

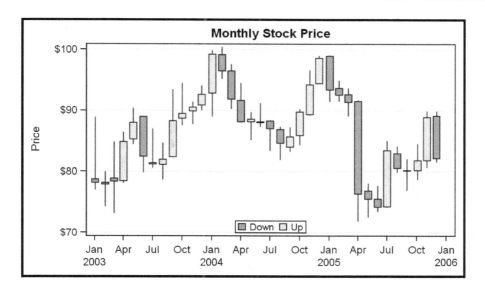

 For more information regarding the different types of charts supported by Qt, please head over to the following link: https://doc.qt.io/qt-5/qtcharts-overview.html.

Qt supports most of the diagram types you need for your project. It is also extremely easy to implement these diagrams in Qt. Let's see how we can do it!

Implementing charts and graphs

Qt makes drawing different types of diagrams easy by putting the complex drawing algorithms behind different abstraction layers, and providing us with a set of classes and functions that can be used to easily create these diagrams without knowing how the drawing algorithm works behind the scenes. These classes and functions are all included in the chart module that comes together with Qt.

Let's create a new **Qt Widgets Application** project and try to create our first chart in Qt.

After you have created the new project, open up the project file (.pro) and add the charts module to your project, like so:

```
QT += core gui charts
```

Then, open up `mainwindow.h` and add the following to include the header files that are required for using the `charts` module:

```
#include <QtCharts>
#include <QChartView>
#include <QBarSet>
#include <QBarSeries>
```

The `QtCharts` and `QtChartView` headers are both essential for Qt's `charts` module. You must include both of them for any type of chart to work at all. The other two headers, namely `QBarSet` and `QBarSeries`, are used here because we're going to create a bar chart. The headers that get included in your project will be different depending on the type of chart you want to create.

Next, open `mainwindow.ui` and drag either **Vertical Layout** or **Horizontal Layout** to the central widget. Then, select the central widget and click either **Layout Horizontally** or **Layout Vertically**. The layout direction is not particularly important, as we will only create a single chart here:

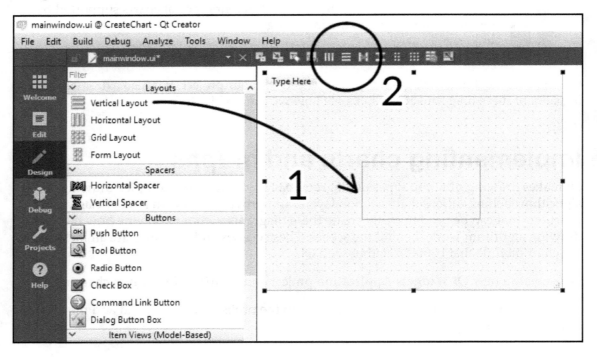

After that, right-click on the layout widget you just dragged to the central widget, and select **Morph into | QFrame**. This will change the layout widget into a QFrame widget while still maintaining its layout properties. If you create a QFrame from Widget Box, it won't have the layout properties that we need. This step is important so that we can set it as the parent of our chart later:

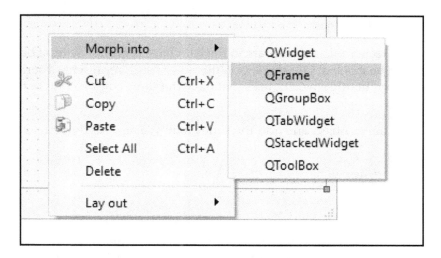

Now open up `mainwindow.cpp` and add the following code:

```
MainWindow::MainWindow(QWidget *parent) :
    QMainWindow(parent),
    ui(new Ui::MainWindow)
{
    ui->setupUi(this);

    QBarSet *set0 = new QBarSet("Jane");
    QBarSet *set1 = new QBarSet("John");
    QBarSet *set2 = new QBarSet("Axel");
    QBarSet *set3 = new QBarSet("Mary");
    QBarSet *set4 = new QBarSet("Samantha");

    *set0 << 10 << 20 << 30 << 40 << 50 << 60;
    *set1 << 50 << 70 << 40 << 45 << 80 << 70;
    *set2 << 30 << 50 << 80 << 13 << 80 << 50;
    *set3 << 50 << 60 << 70 << 30 << 40 << 25;
    *set4 << 90 << 70 << 50 << 30 << 16 << 42;

    QBarSeries *series = new QBarSeries();
    series->append(set0);
    series->append(set1);
```

```
    series->append(set2);
    series->append(set3);
    series->append(set4);
}
```

The code above initializes all the categories that will be displayed in the bar chart. Then, we also added six different items of data to each category, which will later be represented in the form of bars/rectangular shapes.

The QBarSet class represents a set of bars in the bar chart. It groups several bars into a bar set, which can then be labeled. QBarSeries, on the other hand, represents a series of bars grouped by category. In other words, bars that have the same color belong to the same series.

Next, initiate the QChart object and add the series to it. We also set the chart's title and enable animation:

```
QChart *chart = new QChart();
chart->addSeries(series);
chart->setTitle("Student Performance");
chart->setAnimationOptions(QChart::SeriesAnimations);
```

After that, we create a bar chart category axis and apply it to the bar chart's *x* axis. We used a QStringList variable, which is similar to an array, but explicitly for storing strings. The QBarCategoryAxis will then take the string list and populate it over the *x* axis:

```
QStringList categories;
categories << "Jan" << "Feb" << "Mar" << "Apr" << "May" << "Jun";
QBarCategoryAxis *axis = new QBarCategoryAxis();
axis->append(categories);
chart->createDefaultAxes();
chart->setAxisX(axis, series);
```

Then, we create a chart view for Qt to render the bar chart and set it as a child of the frame widget in the main window; otherwise, it won't be rendered on the main window:

```
QChartView *chartView = new QChartView(chart);
chartView->setParent(ui->verticalFrame);
```

Click the **Run** button in Qt Creator, and you should see something like this:

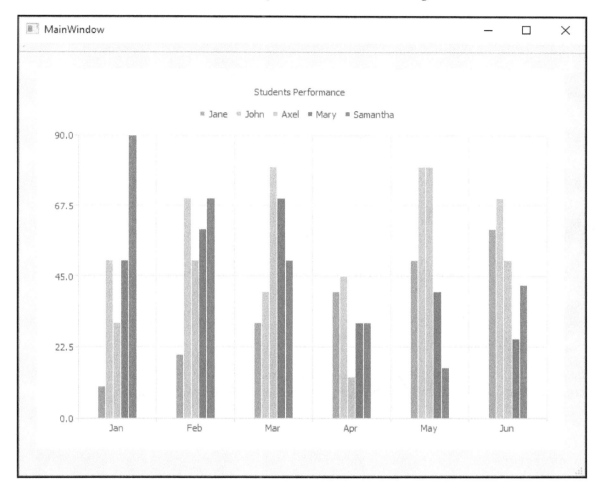

Next, let's do a pie chart; it's really easy. First, instead of QBarSet and QBarSeries, we include QPieSeries and QPieSlice:

```
#include <QPieSeries>
#include <QPieSlice>
```

Then, create a QPieSeries object and set up the name and value of each data. After that, set one of the slices to a different visual style and make it pop out from the rest. Then, create a QChart object and link it with the QPieSeriesobject that we have created:

```
QPieSeries *series = new QPieSeries();
series->append("Jane", 10);
series->append("Joe", 20);
series->append("Andy", 30);
series->append("Barbara", 40);
series->append("Jason", 50);

QPieSlice *slice = series->slices().at(1);
slice->setExploded(); // Explode this chart
slice->setLabelVisible(); // Make label visible
slice->setPen(QPen(Qt::darkGreen, 2)); // Set line color
slice->setBrush(Qt::green); // Set slice color

QChart *chart = new QChart();
chart->addSeries(series);
chart->setTitle("Students Performance");
```

Last, but not least, create the QChartView object and link it with the QChart object we just created. Then, set it as a child of the frame widget, and we're good to go!

```
QChartView *chartView = new QChartView(chart);
chartView->setParent(ui->verticalFrame);
```

Press the **Run** button now, and you should be able to see something like this:

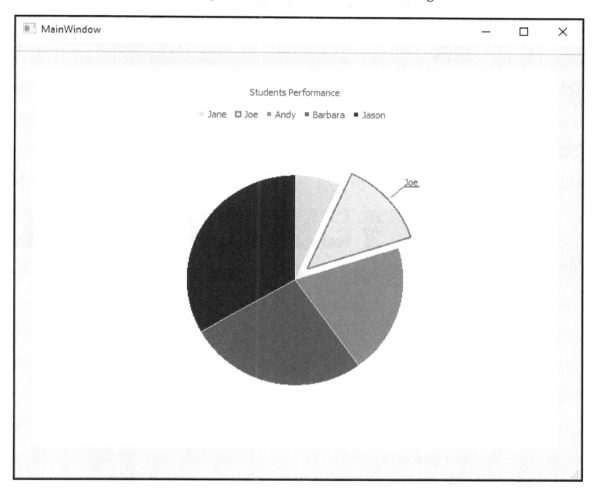

 For more examples of how to create different charts in Qt, please check out their sample code at the following link: `https://doc.qt.io/qt-5/qtcharts-examples.html`.

Now that we've seen that it is easy to create graphs and charts with Qt, let's expand the project we started in the previous chapters and create a dashboard for it!

Creating the dashboard page

In the previous chapter, we created a functional login page that allows the user to sign in using their username and password. What we need to do next is to create the dashboard page, which the user will automatically get directed to upon successful login.

The dashboard page usually serves as a quick overview for the user about the status of their company, business, project, assets, and/or other statistics. The following image shows an example of what a dashboard page could look like:

As you can see, there are quite a number of charts and graphs that are being used on the dashboard page because it is the best way for displaying a huge number of data without making the users feel overwhelmed. Moreover, graphs and charts can let the users understand the overall situation easily without digging too much into the details.

Let's open up our previous project and open the `mainwindow.ui` file. The user interface should look something like this:

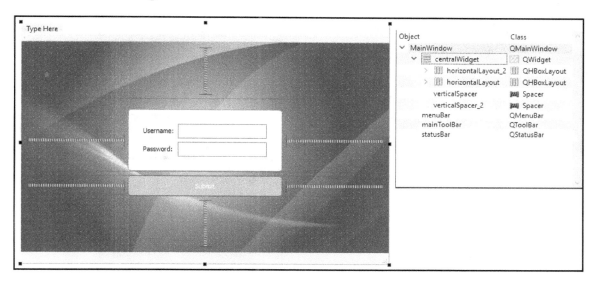

As you can see, we already have the login page now, but we need to add in another page for the dashboard as well. For multiple pages to co-exist in the same program and to be able to switch between different pages at any time, Qt provides us with something called **QStackedWidget**.

A stacked widget is just like a book that you can add more and more pages to, but it shows only one page at a time. Each page is a completely different GUI, so it won't interfere with other pages in the stacked widget.

Since the previous login page was not made with a stacked widget in mind, we have to make some adjustments to it. First, drag and drop a stacked widget from the **Widget Box** to the central widget of your application, and then, we need to move everything previously under the central widget into the first page of the stacked widget, which we renamed **loginPage**:

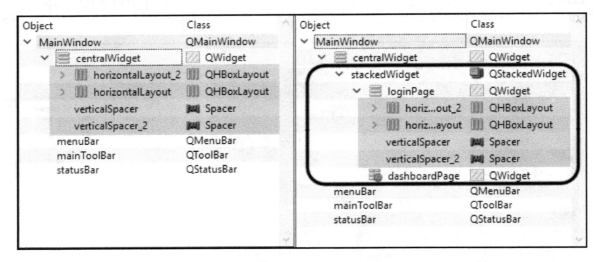

Next, set all the layout settings of the central widget to 0, so that it contains no margin at all, like so:

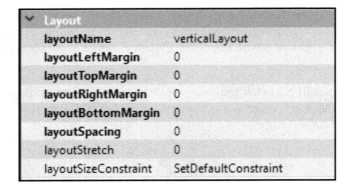

After that, we must cut away the code in the style sheet property of the central widget, and paste it to the login page's style sheet property. In other words, the background image, button style, and other visual settings are now only applied to the login page.

Once you're done, you should be getting two completely different GUIs (the dashboard page is empty for now) when switching between pages on the stacked widget:

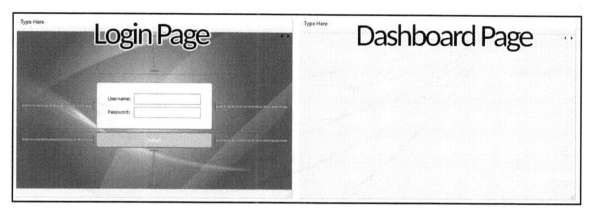

Next, drag and drop a grid layout to the dashboard page, and apply **Layout Vertically** to the dashboard page:

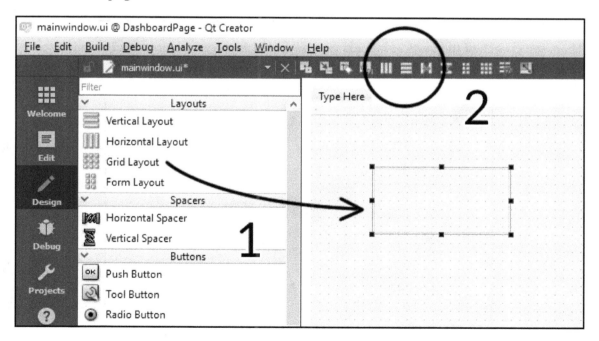

After that, drag and drop six **Vertical Layout** into the **Grid Layout**, like so:

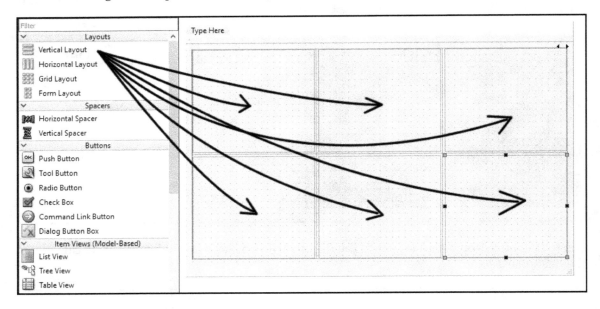

Then, select each of the vertical layouts we just added to the grid layout, and turn it into **QFrame**:

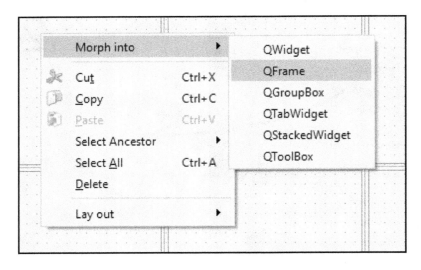

Just as we did in the charts implementation examples, we must turn the layout into a QFrame (or QWidget) so that we can attach the chart on it as a child object. If you directly drag a QFrame from the widget box and don't use morphing, the QFrame objects do not have the layout properties, and hence the charts may not be resizing themselves to fit the QFrame's geometry. Also, name those QFrame objects as chart1 to chart6 as we're going to need them in the following steps. Once you're done with that, let's proceed to the code.

First, open your project (.pro) file and add the charts module, just as we did in the earlier example in this chapter. Then, open up mainwindow.h and include all the headers required. This time around, we also include the QLineSeries header for creating the line chart:

```
#include <QtCharts>
#include <QChartView>

#include <QBarSet>
#include <QBarSeries>

#include <QPieSeries>
#include <QPieSlice>

#include <QLineSeries>
```

After that, declare the pointers for the charts, like so:

```
QChartView *chartViewBar;
QChartView *chartViewPie;
QChartView *chartViewLine;
```

Then, we'll add the code for creating a bar chart. This is the same bar chart we created earlier in the chart implementation example, except it's now attached to the QFrame object called chart1, and is set to enable *anti-aliasing* when rendering. The anti-aliasing feature removes the jagged edges of all charts and thus makes the rendering appear smoother:

```
MainWindow::MainWindow(QWidget *parent) :
    QMainWindow(parent),
    ui(new Ui::MainWindow)
{
    ui->setupUi(this);

    ////////BAR CHART////////////
    QBarSet *set0 = new QBarSet("Jane");
    QBarSet *set1 = new QBarSet("John");
    QBarSet *set2 = new QBarSet("Axel");
    QBarSet *set3 = new QBarSet("Mary");
    QBarSet *set4 = new QBarSet("Samantha");
```

```
*set0 << 10 << 20 << 30 << 40 << 50 << 60;
*set1 << 50 << 70 << 40 << 45 << 80 << 70;
*set2 << 30 << 50 << 80 << 13 << 80 << 50;
*set3 << 50 << 60 << 70 << 30 << 40 << 25;
*set4 << 90 << 70 << 50 << 30 << 16 << 42;

QBarSeries *seriesBar = new QBarSeries();
seriesBar->append(set0);
seriesBar->append(set1);
seriesBar->append(set2);
seriesBar->append(set3);
seriesBar->append(set4);

QChart *chartBar = new QChart();
chartBar->addSeries(seriesBar);
chartBar->setTitle("Students Performance");
chartBar->setAnimationOptions(QChart::SeriesAnimations);

QStringList categories;
categories << "Jan" << "Feb" << "Mar" << "Apr" << "May" << "Jun";
QBarCategoryAxis *axis = new QBarCategoryAxis();
axis->append(categories);
chartBar->createDefaultAxes();
chartBar->setAxisX(axis, seriesBar);

chartViewBar = new QChartView(chartBar);
chartViewBar->setRenderHint(QPainter::Antialiasing);
chartViewBar->setParent(ui->chart1);
}
```

Next, we also add the code for the pie chart. Again, this is the same pie chart from the previous example:

```
QPieSeries *seriesPie = new QPieSeries();
seriesPie->append("Jane", 10);
seriesPie->append("Joe", 20);
seriesPie->append("Andy", 30);
seriesPie->append("Barbara", 40);
seriesPie->append("Jason", 50);

QPieSlice *slice = seriesPie->slices().at(1);
slice->setExploded();
slice->setLabelVisible();
slice->setPen(QPen(Qt::darkGreen, 2));
slice->setBrush(Qt::green);

QChart *chartPie = new QChart();
chartPie->addSeries(seriesPie);
```

```
chartPie->setTitle("Students Performance");

chartViewPie = new QChartView(chartPie);
chartViewPie->setRenderHint(QPainter::Antialiasing);
chartViewPie->setParent(ui->chart2);
```

Finally, we also add a line graph to the dashboard, which is something new. The code is very simple and very similar to the pie chart:

```
QLineSeries *seriesLine = new QLineSeries();
seriesLine->append(0, 6);
seriesLine->append(2, 4);
seriesLine->append(3, 8);
seriesLine->append(7, 4);
seriesLine->append(10, 5);
seriesLine->append(11, 10);
seriesLine->append(13, 3);
seriesLine->append(17, 6);
seriesLine->append(18, 3);
seriesLine->append(20, 2);

QChart *chartLine = new QChart();
chartLine->addSeries(seriesLine);
chartLine->createDefaultAxes();
chartLine->setTitle("Students Performance");

chartViewLine = new QChartView(chartLine);
chartViewLine->setRenderHint(QPainter::Antialiasing);
chartViewLine->setParent(ui->chart3);
```

Once you're done with that, we must add a resize-event slot to the main window class, and make the charts follow the size of their respective parent when the main window is being resized. This can be done by first going to the mainwindow.h and adding in the event-handler declaration:

```
protected:
    void resizeEvent(QResizeEvent* event);
```

Then, open up `mainwindow.cpp` and add the following code:

```
void MainWindow::resizeEvent(QResizeEvent* event)
{
    QMainWindow::resizeEvent(event);

    chartViewBar->resize(chartViewBar->parentWidget()->size());
    chartViewPie->resize(chartViewPie->parentWidget()->size());
    chartViewLine->resize(chartViewLine->parentWidget()->size());
}
```

Do note that the `QMainWindow::resizeEvent(event)` must be called first so that the default behavior will be triggered before you call your custom methods below it. `resizeEvent()` is one of the many event handlers provided by Qt for reacting to its events, such as mouse events, window events, paint events, and so on. Unlike the signal-and-slots mechanism, you need to replace the virtual function of the event handler to make it do what you want it to do when the event is being called.

If we build and run the project now, we should be getting something like this:

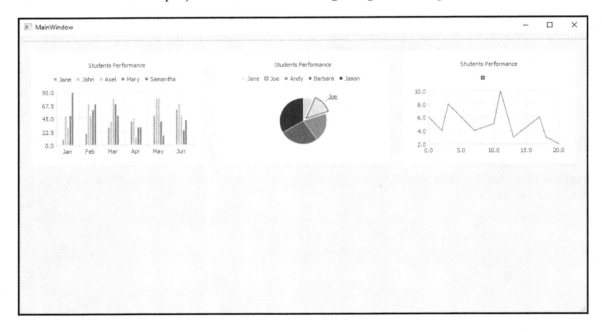

Looks pretty neat, doesn't it! However, for the sake of simplicity and so as not to confuse the readers, the charts are all hard-coded and are not using any data from the database. If you intend to use data from the database, don't make any SQL query during program startup, as this will make your program freeze if the data you're loading is very large, or your server is very slow.

The best way to do it is to load the data only when you're switching from the login page to the dashboard page (or upon switching to any other pages) so that the loading time is less obvious to the user. To do this, right-click on the stacked widget and select **Go to slot.** Then, select **currentChanged(int)** and click **OK**.

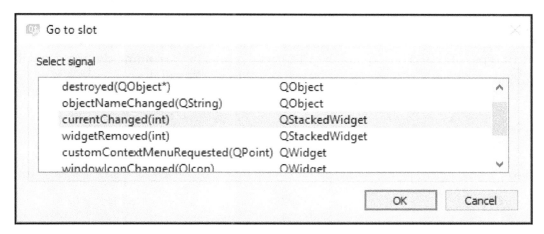

After that, a new slot function will be created automatically by Qt. This function will be called automatically when the stacked widget is switching between pages. You can check which page it is currently switching over to by checking the arg1 variable. The arg1 value will be 0 if the target page is the first page within stacked widget, or 1 if the target is the second page, and so on.

You can submit the SQL query only when the stacked widget is showing the dashboard page, which is the second page (arg1equals to 1):

```
void MainWindow::on_stackedWidget_currentChanged(int arg1)
{
    if (arg1 == 1)
    {
        // Do it here
    }
}
```

Phew! That's a lot to digest for this chapter! Hopefully, this chapter will help you understand how to create a beautiful and informative page for your project.

Summary

The chart module in Qt is the combination of feature and visual aesthetic. Not only is it easy to implement without the need to write a very long code just to display the chart, but it is also customizable to suit your visual requirements. We really need to be thankful to Qt developers for opening up this module and allowing non-commercial users to use it for free!

In this chapter, we have learned how to create a really nice-looking dashboard, and display different types of charts on it using the Qt Chart module. In the coming chapter, we will learn how to use view widget, dialog boxes, and file-selection dialogs.

Item Views and Dialogs

5

In the previous chapter, we learned how to display data using different types of chart. Charts are one of many ways to present information to the users on screen. It is very important for your application to present vital information to the users so that they know exactly what's happening to the application—whether data has been saved successfully, or the application is waiting for the user's input, or warning/error messages that the users should be aware of, and so on—it's all very important to ensure your application's user-friendliness and usability.

In this chapter, we will cover the following topics :

- Working with item view widgets
- Working with dialog boxes
- Working with file selection dialogs
- Image scaling and cropping

Qt provides us with many types of widget and dialog that we can easily use to display important information to the users. Let's check out what these widgets are!

Working with item view widgets

Other than displaying data using different types of chart, we can also display this data using different types of item view. An item view widget presents data by rendering it visually, usually along the vertical axis.

A two-dimensional item view, often known as a **table view**, displays data in both vertical and horizontal directions. That allows it to display huge volumes of data within a compact space, and enables the users to search for an item very quickly and easily.

There are two ways to display data in an item view. The most common method is to use the **model-view architecture**, which uses three different components, model, view, and delegate, to retrieve data from a data source and display it in the item view. These components all make use of the **signal-slot architecture** provided by Qt to communicate with each other:

- Signals from the model inform the view about changes to the data held by the data source
- Signals from the view provide information about the user's interaction with the items being displayed
- Signals from the delegate are used during editing to tell the model and view about the state of the editor

The other method is the manual way, in which the programmer must tell Qt which data goes into which column and row. This method is much simpler than the model-view, but much slower when compared to its performance. However, for small amounts of data, the performance issue can be negligible, making this a good approach.

If you open up Qt Designer, you will see the two different categories for Item View Widgets, namely **Item Views (Model-Based)** and **Item Widgets (Item-Based)**:

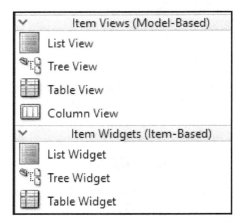

Even though they might look the same, in actual fact the widgets within the two categories work very differently. In this chapter, we will learn how to use the latter category, as it is more straightforward and easy to understand, and able to serve as prerequisite knowledge for the former category.

Under the **Item Widgets (Item-Based)** category are three different widgets called **List Widget**, **Tree Widget**, and **Table Widget**. Each of these item widgets displays data in a different way. Pick the one that suits your needs:

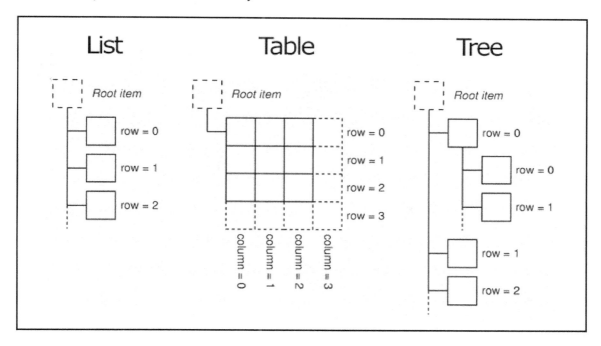

As you can see from the preceding diagram, the **List Widget** displays its items in a one-dimensional list, while the **Table Widget** displays its item in a two-dimensional table. Even though the **Tree Widget** works almost similar to the **List Widget**, its items are displayed in a hierarchical structure, in which each item can have multiple children items under it, recursively. One good example of this is the filesystem in our operating system, which displays the directory structure using the tree widget.

To illustrate the differences, let's create a new Qt Widgets application project and try it out ourselves.

Creating our Qt Widgets application

Once you have created the project, open up `mainwindow.ui` and drag the three different item widgets to your main window. After that, select the main window and click the **Layout Vertically** button located at the top:

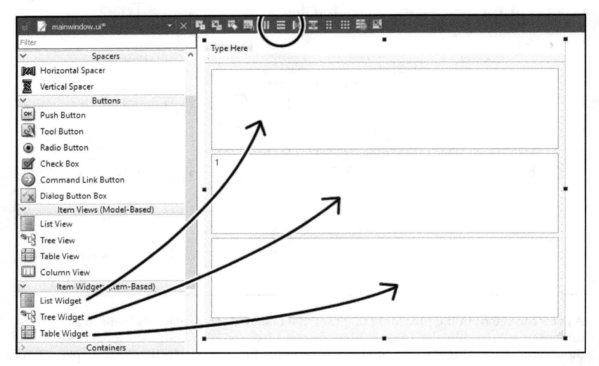

Then, double-click on the **List Widget** and a new window will pop out. Here, you can add a few dummy items to the **List Widget** by clicking the + icon, or remove them by selecting an item from the list and clicking the - icon. Click the **OK** button to apply the final result to the widget:

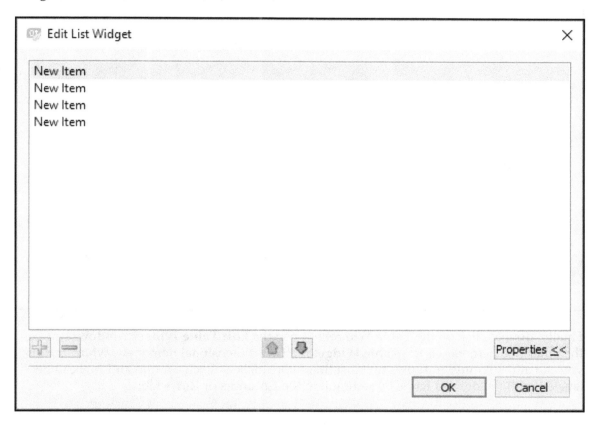

You can do the same to the **Tree Widget**. It's almost the same as the **List Widget**, except that you can add sub-items to an item, recursively. You can also add columns to the Tree Widget and name the columns:

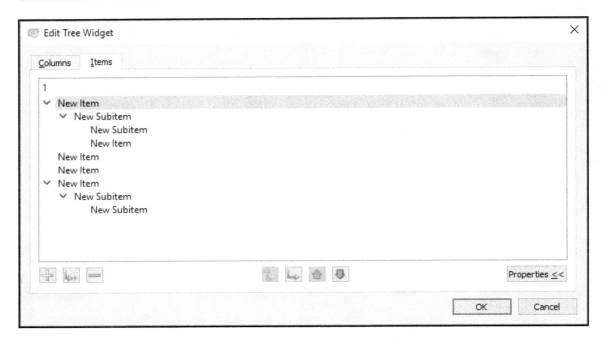

Finally, double-click on the **Table Widget** to open the **Edit Table Widget** window. Unlike the other two item views, the **Table Widget** is a two-dimensional item view, which means you can add columns and rows to it just like a spreadsheet. Each column and row can be labeled with the desired name by setting it in the **Columns** or **Rows** tab:

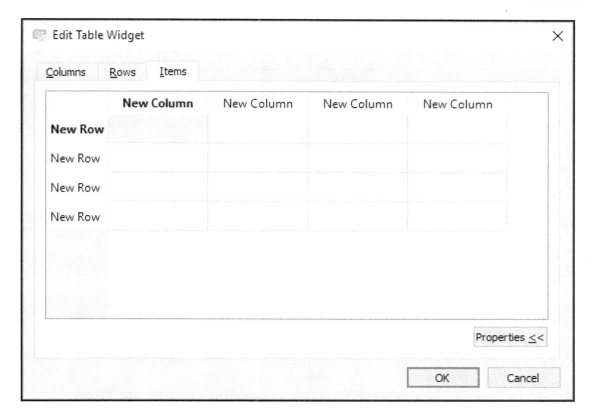

It's really easy to understand how a widget works by using the Qt Designer. Just drag and drop the widget into the window and play around with its settings, then build and run the project to see the result for yourself.

In this case, we have demonstrated the differences between the three item views widgets without writing a single line of code:

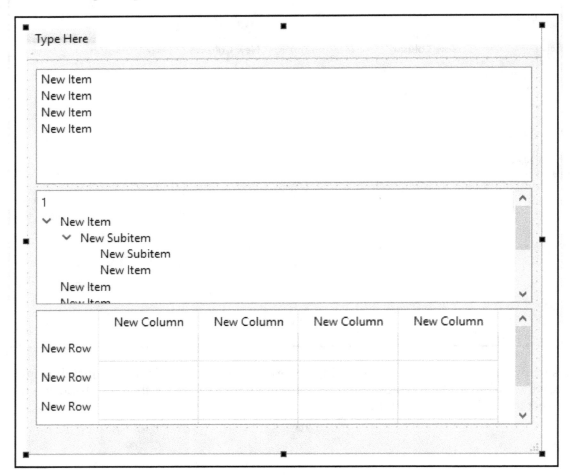

Making our List Widget functional

Writing code, however, is still required in order for the widgets to be fully functional in your application. Let's learn how to add items to our item view widgets using C++ code!

First, open up `mainwindow.cpp` and write the following code to the class constructor, right after `ui->setupui(this)`:

```
ui->listWidget->addItem("My Test Item");
```

As simple as that, you have successfully added an item to the List Widget!

There is another way to add an item to the **List Widget**. But before that, we must add the following headers to `mainwindow.h`:

```
#ifndef MAINWINDOW_H
#define MAINWINDOW_H

#include <QMainWindow>
#include <QDebug>
#include <QListWidgetItem>
```

The `QDebug` header is for us to print out debug message, and the `QListWidgetItem` header is for us to declare **List Widget** `Item` objects. Next, open up `mainwindow.cpp` and add the following code:

```
QListWidgetItem* listItem = new QListWidgetItem;
listItem->setText("My Second Item");
listItem->setData(100, 1000);
ui->listWidget->addItem(listItem);
```

The preceding code does the same as the previous one-line code. Except, this time, I've added an extra data to the item. The `setData()` function takes in two input variables—the first variable is the data-role of item, which indicates how it should be treated by Qt. If you put a value that matches the `Qt::ItemDataRole` enumerator, the data will affect the display, decoration, tooltip, and so on, and that may change its appearance.

In my case, I just simply set a number that doesn't match any of the enumerators in `Qt::ItemDataRole` so that I can store it as a hidden data for later use. To retrieve the data, you can simply call `data()` and insert the number that matches the one you've just set:

```
qDebug() << listItem->data(100);
```

Build and run the project; you should be able to see that the new item is now being added to the List Widget:

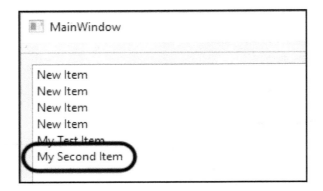

 For more information about `Qt::ItemDataRole` enumerators, please check out the following link: `http://doc.qt.io/qt-5/qt.html#ItemDataRole-enum`

As mentioned earlier, hidden data can be attached to a list item for later use. For example, you could use the list widget to display a list of products ready to be purchased by the user. Each of these items can be attached with its product ID so that when the user selects the item and places it on the cart, your system can automatically identify which product has been added to the cart by identifying the product ID stored as the data role.

In the preceding example, I stored custom data, `1000`, in my list item and set its data role as `100`, which does not match any of the `Qt::ItemDataRole` enumerators. This way, the data won't be shown to the users, and thus it can only be retrieved through C++ code.

Adding functionality to the Tree Widget

Next, let's move on to the **Tree Widget**. It is actually not that different from the **List Widget**. Let's take a look at the following code:

```
QTreeWidgetItem* treeItem = new QTreeWidgetItem;
treeItem->setText(0, "My Test Item");
ui->treeWidget->addTopLevelItem(treeItem);
```

It's pretty much the same as the **List Widget**, except we have to set the column ID in the `setText()` function. This is because the **Tree Widget** is somewhere between a **List Widget** and a **Table Widget**—it can have more than one column but can't have any rows.

The most obvious distinction between a **Tree Widget** and other view widgets is that all its items can contain children items, recursively. Let's look at the following code to see how we can add a child item to an existing item in the **Tree Widget**:

```
QTreeWidgetItem* treeItem2 = new QTreeWidgetItem;
treeItem2->setText(0, "My Test Subitem");
treeItem->addChild(treeItem2);
```

It's really that simple! The final result looks like this:

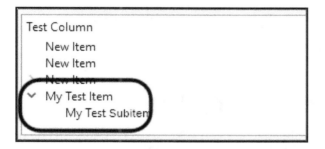

Finally, our Table Widget

Next, let's do the same for the **Table Widget**. Technically, the items already exist and are reserved in the **Table Widget** when the columns and rows are being created. What we need to do is to create a new item and replace it with the (currently empty) item located at a specific column and row, which is why the function name is called `setItem()`, instead of `addItem()` used by the List Widget.

Let's take a look at the code:

```
QTableWidgetItem* tableItem = new QTableWidgetItem;
tableItem->setText("Testing1");
ui->tableWidget->setItem(0, 0, tableItem);

QTableWidgetItem* tableItem2 = new QTableWidgetItem;
tableItem2->setText("Testing2");
ui->tableWidget->setItem(1, 2, tableItem2);
```

As you can see from the code, I have added two sections of data to two different locations, which translates into the following result:

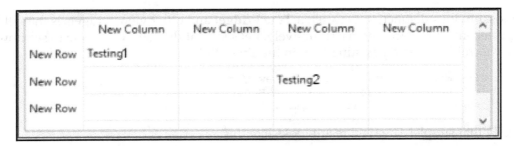

That's it! It's all that simple and easy to display data using item views in Qt. If you are looking for more examples related to item views, please visit the following link: `http://doc.qt.io/qt-5/examples-itemviews.html`

Working with dialog boxes

One very important aspect of creating a user-friendly application is the ability to display vital information regarding the status of the application when a certain event (intended or unintended) occurs. To display such information, we need an external window that can be dismissed by the user once he/she has acknowledged the information.

Qt comes with this functionality, and it's all residing in the `QMessageBox` class. There are several types of message box you can use in Qt; the most basic one uses just a single line of code, like so:

```
QMessageBox::information(this, "Alert", "Just to let you know,
something happened!");
```

There are three parameters you need to provide for this function. The first one is the parent of the message box, which we have set as the main window. The second parameter is for the window title, and the third parameter is for the message we want to deliver to the user. The preceding code will produce the following result:

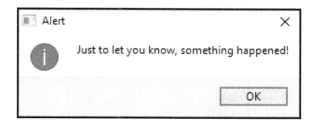

The appearance shown here is running on a Windows system. The appearance may look different on different operating systems (Linux, macOS, and so forth). As you can see, the dialog box even comes with an icon located before the text. There are a few types of icon you can use, such as information, warning, and critical. The following code shows you the code for calling all the different message boxes with icons:

```
QMessageBox::question(this, "Alert", "Just to let you know, something
happened!");
QMessageBox::warning(this, "Alert", "Just to let you know, something
happened!");
QMessageBox::information(this, "Alert", "Just to let you know,
something happened!");
QMessageBox::critical(this, "Alert", "Just to let you know, something
happened!");
```

The preceding code produces the following results:

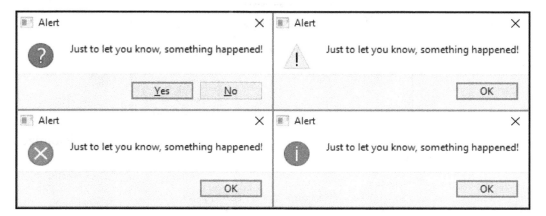

If you don't need any icons, just call the `QMessageBox::about()` function instead. You can also set the buttons you want by picking from a list of standard buttons provided by Qt, for example:

```
QMessageBox::question(this, "Serious Question", "Am I an awesome guy?",
QMessageBox::Ignore, QMessageBox::Yes);
```

The preceding code will produce the following result:

Since these are the built-in functions provided by Qt to create message boxes with ease, it doesn't give developers the freedom to fully customize a message box. However, Qt does allow you to create your message boxes manually using another method, which is much more customizable than the built-in method. It takes a couple more lines of code, but is still pretty simple to write:

```
QMessageBox msgBox;
msgBox.setWindowTitle("Alert");
msgBox.setText("Just to let you know, something happened!");
msgBox.exec();
```

The preceding code will produce the following result:

It looks just the same, you're telling me. What about adding our own icon and customized buttons? No problem with that:

```
QMessageBox msgBox;
msgBox.setWindowTitle("Serious Question");
msgBox.setText("Am I an awesome guy?");
```

```
msgBox.addButton("Seriously Yes!", QMessageBox::YesRole);
msgBox.addButton("Well no thanks", QMessageBox::NoRole);
msgBox.setIcon(QMessageBox::Question);
msgBox.exec();
```

The preceding code produces the following result:

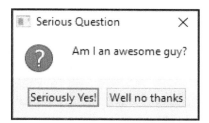

In the preceding code example, I have loaded the question icon that comes with Qt, but you can also load your own icon from the resource file if you intended to do so:

```
QMessageBox msgBox;
msgBox.setWindowTitle("Serious Question");
msgBox.setText("Am I an awesome guy?");
msgBox.addButton("Seriously Yes!", QMessageBox::YesRole);
msgBox.addButton("Well no thanks", QMessageBox::NoRole);
QPixmap myIcon(":/images/icon.png");
msgBox.setIconPixmap(myIcon);
msgBox.exec();
```

Build and run the project now, and you should be able to see this fantastic message box:

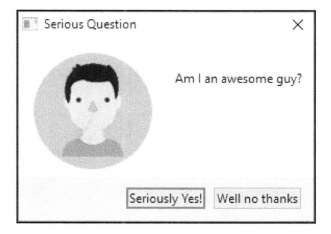

Once you have understood how to create your own message boxes, let's proceed to learn about the event system that comes with the message box.

When a user is presented with a message box with multiple different choices, he/she would expect a different reaction from the application when pressing a different button.

For example, when a message box pops up and asks the user whether they wish to quit the program or not, the button **Yes** should make the program terminate, while the **No** button will do nothing.

Qt's QMessageBox class provides us with a simple solution for checking the button event. When the message box is being created, Qt will wait for the user to pick their choice; then, it will return the button that gets triggered. By checking which button is being clicked, the developer can then proceed to trigger the relevant event. Let's take a look at the example code:

```
if (QMessageBox::question(this, "Question", "Some random question. Yes
or no?") == QMessageBox::Yes)
{
    QMessageBox::warning(this, "Yes", "You have pressed Yes!");
}
else
{
    QMessageBox::warning(this, "No", "You have pressed No!");
}
```

The preceding code will produce the following result:

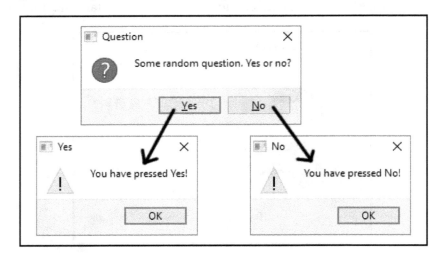

If you prefer the manual way to create your message box, the code for checking the button event is slightly longer:

```
QMessageBox msgBox;
msgBox.setWindowTitle("Serious Question");
msgBox.setText("Am I an awesome guy?");
QPushButton* yesButton = msgBox.addButton("Seriously Yes!",
QMessageBox::YesRole);
QPushButton* noButton = msgBox.addButton("Well no thanks",
QMessageBox::NoRole);
msgBox.setIcon(QMessageBox::Question);
msgBox.exec();
if (msgBox.clickedButton() == (QAbstractButton*) yesButton)
{
    QMessageBox::warning(this, "Yes", "Oh thanks! :)");
}
else if (msgBox.clickedButton() == (QAbstractButton*) noButton)
{
    QMessageBox::warning(this, "No", "Oh why... :(");
}
```

Even though the code is slightly longer, the basic concept is pretty much the same—the clicked button will always be able to be retrieved by the developer for triggering the appropriate action. This time, however, instead of checking the enumerator, Qt directly checks the button pointer instead, since the preceding code does not use the built-in standard buttons from the QMessageBox class.

Build the project, and you should be able to get the following result:

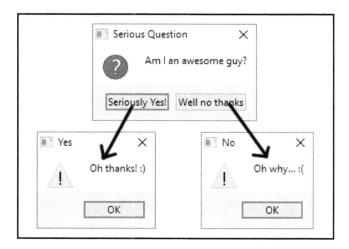

For more information regarding the dialog boxes, please visit the API documents located at the following link:
http://doc.qt.io/qt-5/qdialog.html

Creating File Selection Dialogs

Since we have covered the topic about message boxes, let's also learn about the other type of dialog—the File Selection Dialog. The File Selection Dialog is also very useful, especially if your application frequently deals with files. It is extremely unpleasant to ask users to key in the absolute path of the file they wanted to open, so the File Selection Dialog is very handy in this kind of situation.

Qt provides us with a built-in File Selection Dialog that looks exactly the same as the one we see in our operating system, and therefore, it won't feel unfamiliar to the users. The File Selection Dialog essentially only does one thing—it lets the user pick the file(s) or folder they want and return the path(s) of the selected file(s) or folder; that's all. In fact, it is not in charge of opening the file and reading its content.

Let's look at how we can trigger the File Selection Dialog. First, open up `mainwindow.h` and add in the following header files:

```
#ifndef MAINWINDOW_H
#define MAINWINDOW_H

#include <QMainWindow>
#include <QFileDialog>
#include <QDebug>
```

Next, open up `mainwindow.cpp` and insert the following code:

```
QString fileName = QFileDialog::getOpenFileName(this);
qDebug() << fileName;
```

It's that simple! Build and run the project now, and you should get this:

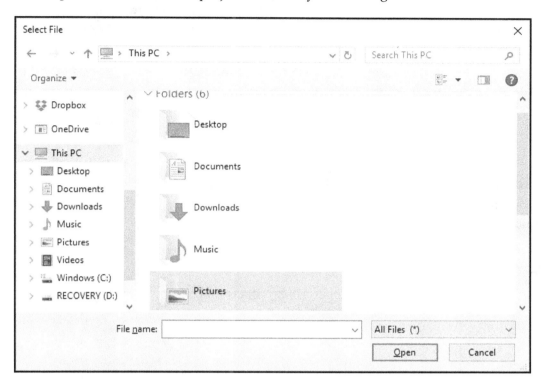

If the user has selected a file and pressed **Open**, the fileName variable will be filled with the absolute path of the selected file. If the user clicked the **Cancel** button, the fileName variable will be an empty string.

The File Selection Dialog also contains several options that can be set during the initialization step. For example:

```
QString fileName = QFileDialog::getOpenFileName(this, "Your title",
QDir::currentPath(), "All files (*.*) ;; Document files (*.doc *.rtf);;
PNG files (*.png)");
qDebug() << fileName;
```

There are three things that we have set in the preceding code they are as follows:

- The window title of the File Selection Dialog
- The default path that the users see when the dialog is being created
- File type filters

The file type filter is very handy when you only allow the users to select a specific type of file (for example, only JPEG image files) and hide the rest. Besides `getOpenFileName()`, you can also use `getSaveFileName()`, which will allow the user to specify a filename that does not already exist.

For more information regarding the File Selection Dialog, please visit the API documents located at the following link:
`http://doc.qt.io/qt-5/qfiledialog.html`

Image scaling and cropping

Since we learned about the File Selection Dialog in the previous section, I'd thought we should learn something fun this time!

First off, let's create a new Qt Widgets Application. Then, open up `mainwindow.ui` and create the following user interface:

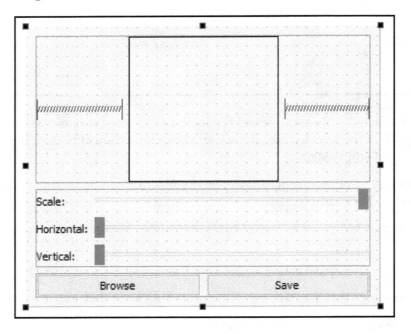

Let's dissect this user interface into three parts:

- Top—Image preview:
    - First, add a **Horizontal Layout** to the window.
    - Then, add a **Label** widget into the **Horizontal Layout** we just added, then set the **text** property to empty. Set both the label's **minimumSize** and **maximumSize** properties to 150x150. Finally, set the **frameShape** property under the **QFrame** category to **Box**.
    - Add two **Horizontal Spacers** to the sides of the label to make it centered.
- Middle—Sliders for adjustments:
    - Add a **Form Layout** to the window, below the **Horizontal Layout** we just added previously in step 1.
    - Add three **Labels** to the **Form Layout**, and set their **text** property to Scale:, Horizontal:, and Vertical: respectively.
    - Add three **Horizontal Sliders** to the **Form Layout**. Set the **minimum** property to 1 and **maximum** to 100. Then, set the **pageStep** property to 1.
    - Set the **value** property of the scale slider to 100.
- Bottom—Browse button and Save button:
    - Add a **Horizontal Layout** to the window, below the **Form Layout** we previously added during step 2.
    - Add two **Push Buttons** to the **Horizontal Layout** and set their **text** property to Browse and Save respectively.
    - Lastly, delete the **Menu Bar**, **Tool Bar**, and **Status Bar** from the central widget.

Now that we have created the user interface, let's dive into the coding! First, open up mainwindow.h and add in the following headers:

```
#ifndef MAINWINDOW_H
#define MAINWINDOW_H

#include <QMainWindow>
#include <QMessageBox>
#include <QFileDialog>
#include <QPainter>
```

After that, add the following variables to `mainwindow.h`:

```
private:
    Ui::MainWindow *ui;
    bool canDraw;
    QPixmap* pix;
    QSize imageSize;
    QSize drawSize;
    QPoint drawPos;
```

Then, go back to `mainwindow.ui` and right-click on the **Browse** button, followed by selecting **Go to slot**. Then, a window will pop up and ask you to select a signal. Pick the `clicked()` signal located at the top of the list, and then press the **OK** button:

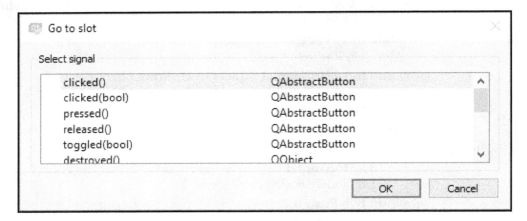

A new `slot` function will be automatically added to your source file. Now, add the following code to open up the File Selection Dialog when the **Browse** button is clicked. The dialog only lists JPEG images and hides the other files:

```
void MainWindow::on_browseButton_clicked()
{
    QString fileName = QFileDialog::getOpenFileName(this, tr("Open
    Image"), QDir::currentPath(), tr("Image Files (*.jpg *.jpeg)"));

    if (!fileName.isEmpty())
    {
        QPixmap* newPix = new QPixmap(fileName);

        if (!newPix->isNull())
        {
            if (newPix->width() < 150 || newPix->height() < 150)
            {
```

```
                    QMessageBox::warning(this, tr("Invalid Size"),
                    tr("Image size too small. Please use an image
                    larger than 150x150."));
                    return;
            }

            pix = newPix;
            imageSize = pix->size();
            drawSize = pix->size();

            canDraw = true;

        }
        else
        {

            canDraw = false;

            QMessageBox::warning(this, tr("Invalid Image"),
            tr("Invalid or corrupted file. Please try again with
            another image file."));
        }
    }
}
```

As you can see, the code checks whether any image has been selected by the user. If it has its checks again and see whether the image resolution is at least 150 x 150. If no problem is found, we will save the image's pixel map to a pointer called `pix`, then save the image size to the `imageSize` variable, and the initial drawing size to the `drawSize` variable. Finally, we set the `canDraw` variable to `true`.

After that, open up `mainwindow.h` again and declare these two functions:

```
public:
    explicit MainWindow(QWidget *parent = 0);
    ~MainWindow();
    virtual void paintEvent(QPaintEvent *event);
    void paintImage(QString fileName, int x, int y);
```

The first function, `paintEvent()`, is a virtual function that automatically gets called whenever Qt needs to refresh the user interface, such as when the main window is being resized. We'll override this function and draw the newly loaded image onto the image preview widget. In this case, we'll call the `paintImage()` function within the `paintEvent()` virtual function:

```
void MainWindow::paintEvent(QPaintEvent *event)
{
```

```
if (canDraw)
{
        paintImage("", ui->productImage->pos().x(), ui->productImage-
        >pos().y());
}
}
```

After that, we'll write the `paintImage()` function in `mainwindow.cpp`:

```
void MainWindow::paintImage(QString fileName, int x, int y)
{
    QPainter painter;
    QImage saveImage(150, 150, QImage::Format_RGB16);

    if (!fileName.isEmpty())
    {
        painter.begin(&saveImage);
    }
    else
    {
        painter.begin(this);
    }

    if (!pix->isNull())
    {
        painter.setClipRect(x, y, 150, 150);
        painter.fillRect(QRect(x, y, 150, 150), Qt::SolidPattern);
        painter.drawPixmap(x - drawPos.x(), y - drawPos.y(),
        drawSize.width(), drawSize.height(), *pix);
    }

    painter.end();

    if (fileName != "")
    {
        saveImage.save(fileName);
        QMessageBox::information(this, "Success", "Image has been
        successfully saved!");
    }
}
```

This function does two things—if we don't set the `fileName` variable, it will proceed to draw the image on top of the image preview widget, otherwise, it will crop the image based on the dimension of the image preview widget and save it to the disk following the `fileName` variable.

We'll call this function again when the save button is being clicked. This time, we'll set the `fileName` variable as the desired directory path and filename, so that the `QPainter` class can save the image correctly:

```
void MainWindow::on_saveButton_clicked()
{
    if (canDraw)
    {
        if (!pix->isNull())
        {
            // Save new pic from painter
            paintImage(QCoreApplication::applicationDirPath() +
            "/image.jpg", 0, 0);
        }
    }
}
```

Lastly, right-click on each of the three sliders and select **Go to slot**. Then, select `valueChanged(int)` and click **OK**.

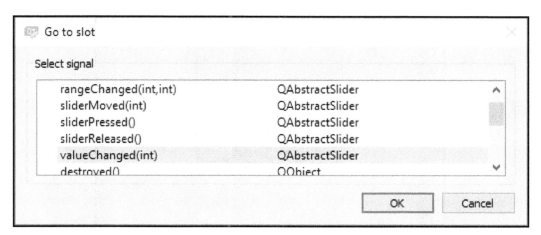

After that, we'll write the code for the `slot` functions resulting from the previous step:

```
void MainWindow::on_scaleSlider_valueChanged(int value)
{
    drawSize = imageSize * value / 100;
    update();
}

void MainWindow::on_leftSlider_valueChanged(int value)
{
```

```
        drawPos.setX(value * drawSize.width() / 100 * 0.5);
        update();
    }

    void MainWindow::on_topSlider_valueChanged(int value)
    {
        drawPos.setY(value * drawSize.height() / 100 * 0.5);
        update();
    }
```

The scale slider is basically for users to resize the image to their desired scale within the image preview widget. The left slider is for the users to move the image horizontally, while the top slider is used by the users to move the image vertically. By combining these three different sliders, users can adjust and crop the image to their liking before proceeding to upload the image to the server, or use it for other purposes.

If you build and run the project now, you should be able to get this result:

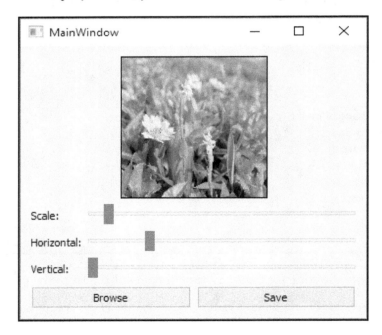

You can click on the **Browse** button to select a JPG image file to load. After that, the image should appear on the preview area. You can then move the sliders around for adjusting the cropping size. Once you're satisfied with the result, click the **Save** button to save your image in the current directory.

Do check out the sample code that comes together with this book if you want to learn more about it in detail. You can find the source code at the following GitHub page: `https://github.com/PacktPublishing/Hands-On-GUI-Programming-with-C-QT5`

Summary

Input and Output (I/O) are the essence of modern computer software. Qt allows us to display our data in many different ways that are both intuitive and engaging to the end users. Other than that, the event system that comes with Qt makes our life as a programmer a lot easier, as it tends to automatically capture the user inputs through the powerful signal-and-slot mechanism and in-response triggering custom-defined behaviors. Without Qt, we would have a hard time trying to figure out how to reinvent the proverbial wheel, and might eventually end up creating a less user-friendly product.

In this chapter, we have learned how to make use of the fantastic features that are provided by Qt—view widgets, dialog boxes, and file selection dialogs used to display important information to the users. Furthermore, we also went through a fun little project that taught us how to scale and crop an image using Qt widgets for user inputs. In the next chapter, we will go for something more advanced (and fun too), which is creating our very own web browser using Qt!

6
Integrating Web Content

In the previous chapter, we learned how to use item views and dialogs in Qt. In this chapter, we will learn how to integrate web content into our Qt application.

Starting from the dotcom era in the late 90s and early 2000s, our world has become more and more connected by the internet. Naturally, the applications running on our computers are also evolving in that direction. Nowadays, most—if not all—of our software is in some way connected to the internet, usually to retrieve useful information and display it to their users. The easiest way to do this is to embed a web browser display (also known as a web view) into the application's user interface. That way, the users can not only view the information, but do so in an aesthetic way.

By using the web view, developers can take advantage of its rendering capability and decorate their contents using the powerful combination of **HTML (Hypertext Markup Language)** and **CSS (Cascading Style Sheets)**. In this chapter, we will explore Qt's web engine module and create our very own web browser.

In this chapter, we will cover the following topics:

- Creating your own web browser
- Sessions, cookies, and cache
- Integrating JavaScript and C++

Without further ado, let's check out how to create our own web browser in Qt!

Creating your own web browser

Once upon a time, Qt used a different module called **WebKit** to render web contents on its user interface. However, the WebKit module has been completely deprecated since version 5.5 and replaced by a new module called **WebEngine**.

The new WebEngine module is based on the **Chromium** framework built by Google, and it will only work on the **Visual C++** compiler on the Windows platform. Therefore, if you're running Windows, please make sure that you have installed **Microsoft Visual Studio** on your computer as well as all the **MSVC** components for Qt that match the version of Visual Studio installed on your computer. Other than that, the Qt WebEngine component is also required for this particular chapter. If you have skipped the components during Qt's installation, all you need to do is to run the same installer again and install it there:

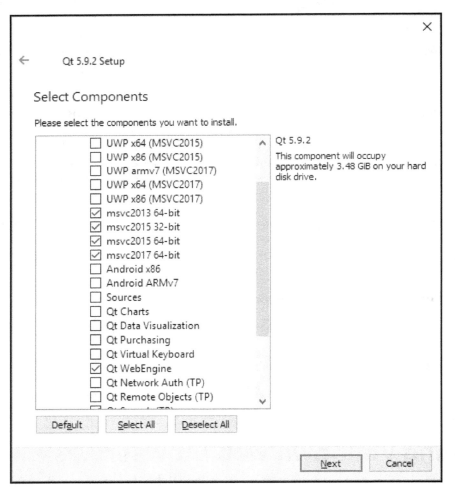

Adding the web view widget

Once you are ready, let's get started! First, open up Qt Creator and create a new Qt Widgets Application project. After that, open up the project (.pro) file and add in the following text to enable the modules:

```
QT += core gui webengine webenginewidgets
```

If you didn't install the MSVC component (on Windows) or the Qt WebEngine component, error messages will appear at this point if you are trying to build the project. Please run the Qt installer again if that's the case.

Next, open up mainwindow.h and add the following header files:

```
#ifndef MAINWINDOW_H
#define MAINWINDOW_H

#include <QMainWindow>
#include <QWebEngineView>
```

After that, open up mainwindow.h and add the following code:

```
private:
    Ui::MainWindow *ui;
    QWebEngineView* webview;
```

Then, add the following code:

```
MainWindow::MainWindow(QWidget *parent) :
    QMainWindow(parent),
    ui(new Ui::MainWindow)
{
    ui->setupUi(this);

    webview = new QWebEngineView(ui->centralWidget);
    webview->load(QUrl("http://www.kloena.com"));
}
```

Build and run the program now and you should see the following result:

It's actually that simple. You have now successfully placed a web view on your application!

The reason why we're writing C++ code to create the web view is that the default **Qt Designer** used by the Qt Creator doesn't have web view in the widget box. The preceding code simply creates the `QWebEngineView` object, sets its parent object (in this case, the central widget), and sets the URL of the web page before showing the web view widget. If you want to use Qt Designer to place a web engine view on your UI, you must run the standalone Qt Designer located in your Qt installation directory. For example, if you're running Windows, it's located in `C:QtQt5.10.25.10.2msvc2017_64bin`. Please note that it's located in the directory with the compiler name that supports the web engine:

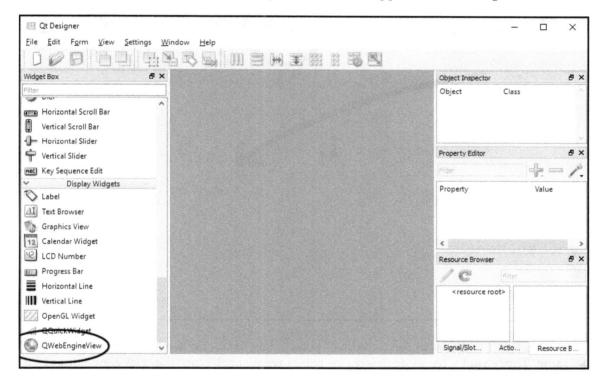

Creating a UI for a web browser

Next, we are going to turn this into a proper web browser. First, we need to add a few layout widgets so that we can put other widgets in place afterwards. Drag a **Vertical Layout** (1) onto the **centralWidget** and select the **centralWidget** from the object list. Then, click the **Lay Out Vertically** button (2) located at the top:

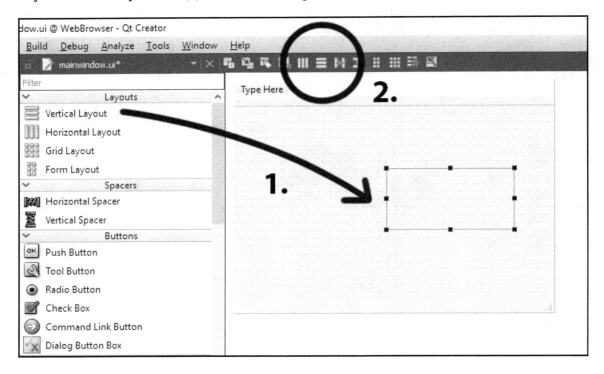

After that, select the newly added vertical layout, right-click and select **Morph into |** **QFrame**. The reason why we're doing this is that we want to place the web view widget under this **QFrame** object instead of the central widget. We must convert the layout widget to a **QFrame** (or any **QWidget**-inherited) object so that it can *adopt* the web view as its child. Finally, rename the **QFrame** object to webviewFrame:

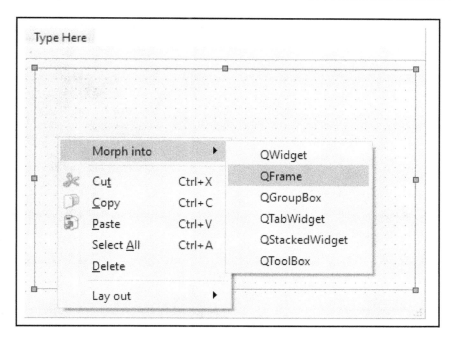

Once you're done with that, let's drag and drop a **Horizontal Layout** widget above the **QFrame** object. Now we can see that the size of both the **Horizontal Layout** widget and the **QFrame** object are the same, and we don't want that. Next, select the **QFrame** object and set its **Vertical Policy** to **Expanding**:

˅ **sizePolicy**	[Preferred, Expanding, 0, 0]
Horizontal Policy	Preferred
Vertical Policy	Expanding ▼
Horizontal Stretch	Fixed
Vertical Stretch	Minimum
	Maximum
˅ minimumSize	Preferred
Width	MinimumExpanding
Height	Expanding
˅ maximumSize	Ignored

Then, you will see the top layout widget is now very thin. Let's temporarily set its height to 20, like so:

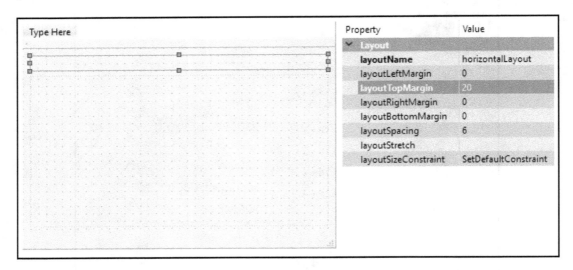

After that, drag and drop three push buttons to the horizontal layout and we can now set its **top margin** back to 0:

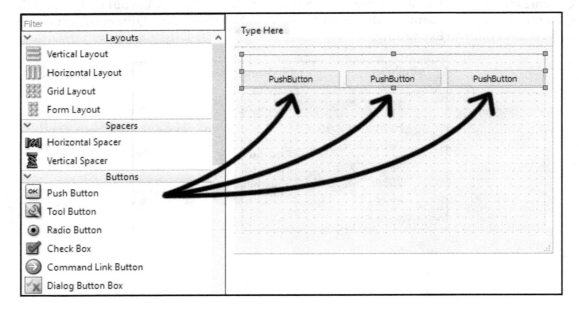

Set the buttons' labels to `Back`, `Forward`, and `Refresh` respectively. You may also use icons instead of text to display on these buttons. If you wish to do that, simply set the text property to empty and select an icon from the icon property. For the sake of simplicity, we'll just display texts on the buttons for this tutorial.

Next, place a line edit widget on the right-hand side of the three buttons, followed by adding another push button with a `Go` label:

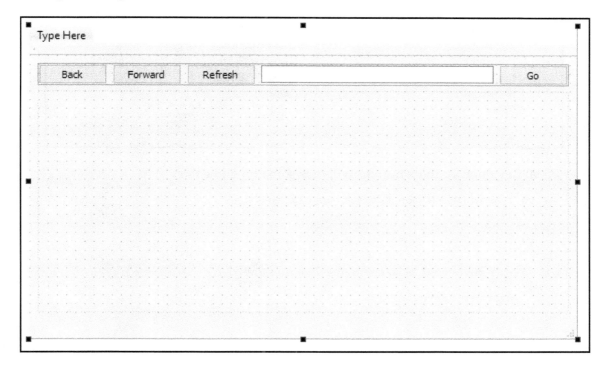

After that, right-click on each of the buttons and select **Go to slot**. A window will pop up, select **clicked()** and press **OK**.

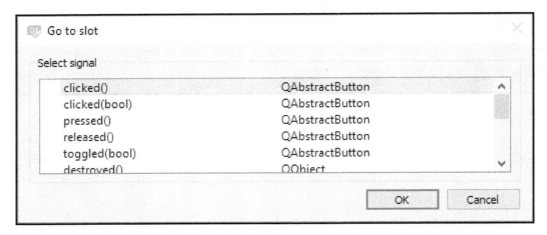

The signal functions for these buttons will look something like this:

```
void MainWindow::on_backButton_clicked()
{
    webview->back();
}

void MainWindow::on_forwardButton_clicked()
{
    webview->forward();
}

void MainWindow::on_refreshButton_clicked()
{
    webview->reload();
}

void MainWindow::on_goButton_clicked()
{
    loadPage();
}
```

Basically, the QWebEngineViewclass already provided us with functions such as back(), forward() and reload(), so we just have to call these functions when the respective button is pressed. The loadPage() function, however, is a custom function that we will write:

```
void MainWindow::loadPage()
{
    QString url = ui->addressInput->text();
    if (!url.startsWith("http://") && !url.startsWith("https://"))
    {
        url = "http://" + url;
    }
    ui->addressInput->setText(url);
    webview->load(QUrl(url));
}
```

Remember to add the declaration for loadPage() in mainwindow.h as well.

Instead of just calling the load() function, I think we should do something more. Normally, users will not include the http:// (or https://) scheme when typing the URL of the web page, but it is required when we are passing the URL to the web view. To solve this problem, we automatically check for the existence of the scheme. If none has been found, we will manually add the http:// scheme to the URL. Also, don't forget to call it at the beginning to replace the load() function:

```
MainWindow::MainWindow(QWidget *parent) :
    QMainWindow(parent),
    ui(new Ui::MainWindow)
{
    ui->setupUi(this);

    webview = new QWebEngineView(ui->webviewFrame);
    loadPage();
}
```

Next, right-click on the text input and select **Go to slot**. Then, select **returnPressed()** and click the **OK** button:

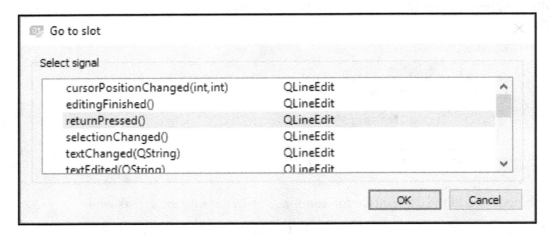

This slot function will be called when the user presses the *Return* key on the keyboard once they have finished typing the web page URL. Logically, the user would expect the page to start loading not have to press the **Go** button every time they are done typing the URL. The code is really simple, we'll just call the `loadPage()` function we just created in the previous step:

```
void MainWindow::on_addressInput_returnPressed()
{
    loadPage();
}
```

Now that we have done a significant amount of code, let's build and run our project and see how it turns out:

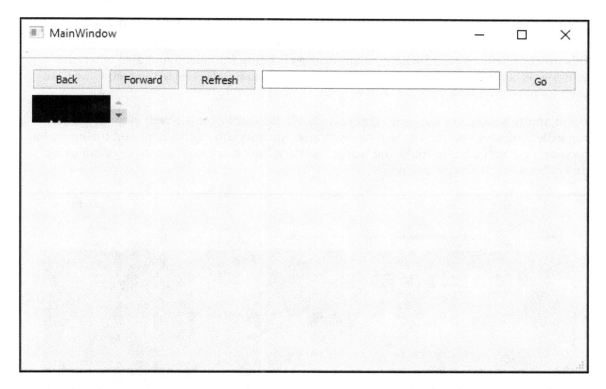

The result shown doesn't really look that great. For some reason, the new web view doesn't seem to scale properly even on an expanding size policy, at least on Qt version 5.10, which is being used when writing this book. It might be fixed in the future version, but let's find a way to solve this issue. What I did was to override an inherited function in the main window called paintEvent(). In mainwindow.h, simply add the function declaration, like this:

```
public:
    explicit MainWindow(QWidget *parent = 0);
    ~MainWindow();
    void paintEvent(QPaintEvent *event);
```

Then, write its definition in mainwindow.cpp like so:

```
void MainWindow::paintEvent(QPaintEvent *event)
{
    QMainWindow::paintEvent(event);
    webview->resize(ui->webviewFrame->size());
}
```

This `paintEvent()` function will be automatically called by Qt whenever the main window needs to re-render its widgets (such as when the window is being resized). Since this function will be called when the application is being initialized and also when the window is being resized, we will use this function to manually resize the web view to fit with its parent widget.

Build and run the program again and you should be able to get the web view to fit nicely, regardless of how you resize the main window. Additionally, I also removed the menu bar, toolbar, and status bar to make the whole interface look more tidy, since we're not using any of those in this application:

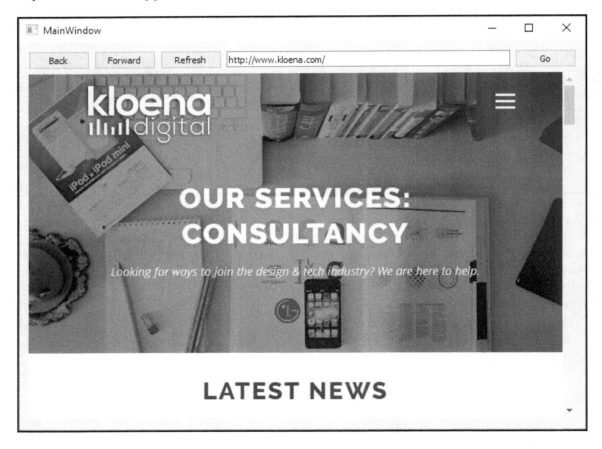

Next, we need a progress bar to show users the current progression of the page load. To do that, first we need to place a progress bar widget below the web view:

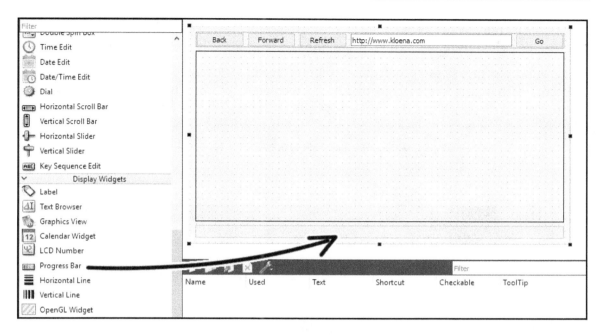

Then, add these two slot functions to `mainwindow.h`:

```
private slots:
    void on_backButton_clicked();
    void on_forwardButton_clicked();
    void on_refreshButton_clicked();
    void on_goButton_clicked();
    void on_addressInput_returnPressed();
    void webviewLoading(int progress);
    void webviewLoaded();
```

Their function definition in `mainwindow.cpp` looks like this:

```
void MainWindow::webviewLoading(int progress)
{
    ui->progressBar->setValue(progress);
}

void MainWindow::webviewLoaded()
{
    ui->addressInput->setText(webview->url().toString());
}
```

The first function, `webviewLoading()` simply takes the progression level (in the form of a percentage value) from the web view and directly supplies it to the progress bar widget.

The second function `webviewLoaded()` will replace the URL text on the address input with the actual URL of the web page loaded by the web view. Without this function, the address input will not display the correct URL after you've pressed the back button or the forward button. Once you're done, let's compile and run the project again. The result looks amazing:

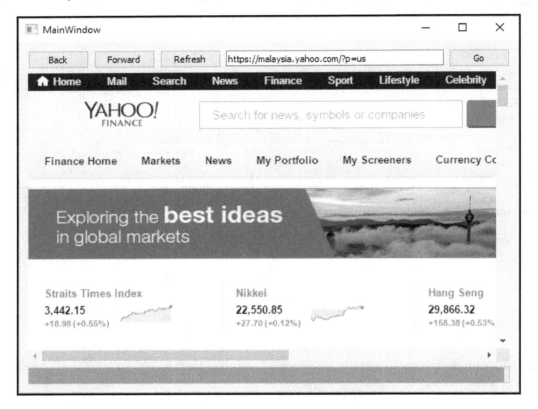

You will ask me, what's the actual use of this if I'm not making a web browser using Qt? There are many other uses for embedding a web view into your application, for instance, showing the latest news and updates of your product to the users through a nicely decorated HTML page, which is a common method used by most of the online games in the gaming market. The stream client, for example, also uses a web view to display the latest games and discounts to their players.

These are often called hybrid applications, which combine web content with native x, so you can leverage both dynamic contents from the web as well as code running natively that has the benefits of high performance and a consistent look and feel.

Other than that, you can also use it to display the printable report in HTML format. You can easily send the report to the printer, or save it as a PDF file by calling `webview->page()->print()` or `webview->page()->printToPdf()`.

> To learn more about printing from the web view, check out the following link: `http://doc.Qt.io/Qt-5/qwebenginepage.html#print`.

You might also want to create the entire user interface of your program using HTML and embed all the HTML, CSS and image files into Qt's resource package and run it locally from the web view. The possibilities are endless, the only limit is your imagination!

> To learn more about Qt **WebEngine**, check out the documentation here: `https://doc.Qt.io/Qt-5/qtwebengine-overview.html`.

Managing browser history

Qt's web engine stores all the links which the user has visited into an array structure for later use. The web view widget uses this to move back and forth between history by calling `back()` and `forward()`.

If you need to manually access this browsing history, add the following header to `mainwindow.h`:

```
#include <QWebEnginePage>
```

After that, use the following code to obtain the browsing history in the form of a `QWebEngineHistory` object:

```
QWebEngineHistory* history = QWebEnginePage::history();
```

You can get the entire list of visited links from `history->items()` or navigate between history using functions such as `back()` or `forward()`. To clear the browsing history, call `history->clear()`. Alternatively, you can also do this:

```
QWebEngineProfile::defaultProfile()->clearAllVisitedLinks();
```

> To learn more about the `QWebEngineHistory` class, visit the following link: `http://doc.Qt.io/Qt-5/qwebenginehistory.html`.

Sessions, cookies, and cache

Just like any other web browser, the `WebEngine` module also supports mechanisms used to store temporary data and persistent data for session and cache. Sessions and cache are very important as they allow websites to remember your last visit and associate you with data, such as a shopping cart. The definitions of a session, a cookie, and a cache are shown as follows:

- **Session**: Normally, sessions are server-side files that contain user information with a unique identifier, which gets sent from the client side to map them to a specific user. In Qt, however, a session simply means a cookie that doesn't have any expiration date, and hence it will be gone when the program is closed.
- **Cookie**: Cookies are client-side files that contain user information or any other information that you want to save. Unlike sessions, cookies have an expiration date which means they will remain valid and can be retrieved before reaching the expiration date, even if the program has been closed and re-opened again.
- **Cache**: Caching is a method used to speed up page loading by saving the page and its resources to a local disk during its first load. If the user loads the same page again on the next visit, the web browser will reuse the cached resources instead of waiting for the download to complete, which can significantly speed up the page loading time.

Managing sessions and cookies

By default, `WebEngine` doesn't save any cookie and treats all user information as temporary sessions, which means when you close the program, your login session on the web page will automatically become invalid.

To enable cookies on Qt's `WebEngine` module, first add the following header to `mainwindow.h`:

```
#include <QWebEngineProfile>
```

Then, simply call the following function to force persistent cookies:

```
QWebEngineProfile::defaultProfile()->setPersistentCookiesPolicy(QWebEng
ineProfile::ForcePersistentCookies);
```

After calling the preceding function, your login session will continue to exist after closing the program. To revert it to non-persistent cookies, we simply call:

```
QWebEngineProfile::defaultProfile()->setPersistentCookiesPolicy(QWebEng
ineProfile::NoPersistentCookies);
```

Other than that, you can also change the directory in which your Qt program stores the cookies. To do that, add the following code to your source file:

```
QWebEngineProfile::defaultProfile()->setPersistentStoragePath("your
folder");
```

If, for some reason, you want to manually delete all the cookies, use the following code:

```
QWebEngineProfile::defaultProfile()->cookieStore()->deleteAllCookies();
```

Managing cache

Next, let's talk about a cache. There are two types of cache which you can use in the web engine module, namely, **Memory Cache** and **Disk Cache**. **Memory Cache** uses the computer's memory to store the cache, which will be gone once you've closed the program. On the other hand, **Disk Cache** saves all the files in the hard disk, and hence they will still remain, even after you've turned off your computer.

By default, the web engine module saves all the cache to the disk, if you need to change them to **Memory Cache**, call the following function:

```
QWebEngineProfile::defaultProfile()->setHttpCacheType(QWebEngineProfile
::MemoryHttpCache);
```

Alternatively, you can also disable caching completely by calling:

```
QWebEngineProfile::defaultProfile()->setHttpCacheType(QWebEngineProfile
::NoCache);
```

As for changing the folder to which your program saves the cache files, call the `setCachePath()` function:

```
QWebEngineProfile::defaultProfile()->setCachePath("your folder");
```

Lastly, to delete all the cache files, call `clearHttpCache()`:

```
QWebEngineProfile::defaultProfile()->clearHttpCache();
```

There are many other functions that you can use to change the settings related to cookies and cache.

 You can read more about it at the following link: `https://doc.Qt.io/Qt-5/qwebengineprofile.html`

Integrating JavaScript and C++

One powerful feature of using Qt's web engine module is that it can call JavaScript functions from C++, as well as calling C++ functions from JavaScript. This makes it more than just a web browser. You can use this to access features that are not supported by the web browser standard, such as file management and hardware integration. Things like that are not possible with W3C standards; hence, it is not possible to do it in native JavaScript. However, you can implement these features using C++ and Qt, then simply call the C++ functions from your JavaScript. Let's take a look at how we can achieve this with Qt.

Calling JavaScript functions from C++

After that, add in the following code to the HTML file we just created:

```
<!DOCTYPE html><html>
    <head>
        <title>Page Title</title>
    </head>
    <body>
        <p>Hello World!</p>
    </body>
</html>
```

These are the basic HTML tags which show you nothing other than a line of words that says `Hello World!`. You can try and load it using your web browser:

After that, let's go back to our Qt project and go to **File** | **New File or Project** and create a **Qt Resource File**:

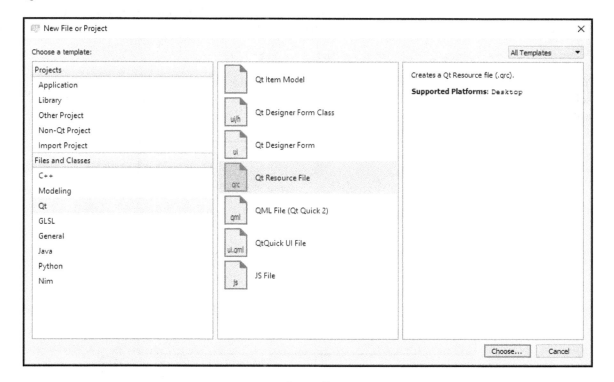

Then, open up the Qt resource file we just created and add in an **/html** prefix followed by adding the HTML file to the resource file, like so:

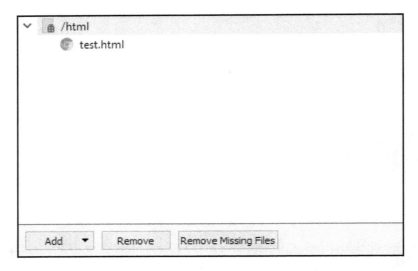

Right-click on **text.html** while the resource file is still opened, then select **Copy Resource Path to Clipboard**. Right after that, change the URL of your web view to:

```
webview->load(QUrl("qrc:///html/test.html"));
```

You can use the link you just copied from the resource file, but make sure you add the URL scheme `qrc://` at the front of the link. Build and run your project now and you should be able to see the result instantly:

Next, we need to set up a function in JavaScript that will be called by C++ in just a moment. We'll just create a simple function that pops up a simple message box and changes the `Hello World!` text to something else when called:

```
<!DOCTYPE html>
<html>
    <head>
            <title>Page Title</title>
            <script>
                function hello()
                {
                    document.getElementById("myText").innerHTML =
                    "Something happened!";
                    alert("Good day sir, how are you?");
                }
            </script>
    </head>
    <body>
            <p id="myText">Hello World!</p>
    </body>
</html>
```

Note that I have added an ID to the `Hello World!` text so that we are able to find it and change its text. Once you're done, let's go to our Qt project again.

Let's proceed to add a push button to our program UI, and when the button is pressed, we want our Qt program to call the `hello()` function we just created in JavaScript. It's actually very easy to do that in Qt; you simply call the `runJavaScript()` function from the `QWebEnginePage` class, like so:

```
void MainWindow::on_pushButton_clicked()
{
    webview->page()->runJavaScript("hello();");
}
```

The result is pretty astounding, as you can see from the following screenshot:

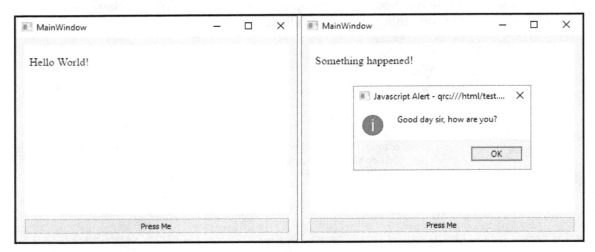

You can do a lot more than just change the text or call a message box. For example, you can start or stop an animation in an HTML canvas, show or hide an HTML element, trigger an Ajax event to retrieve information from a PHP script, and so on and so forth... endless possibilities!

Calling C++ functions from JavaScript

Next, let's take a look at how we can call C++ functions from JavaScript instead. For the sake of demonstration, I'll put a text label above the web view and we will change its text using a JavaScript function:

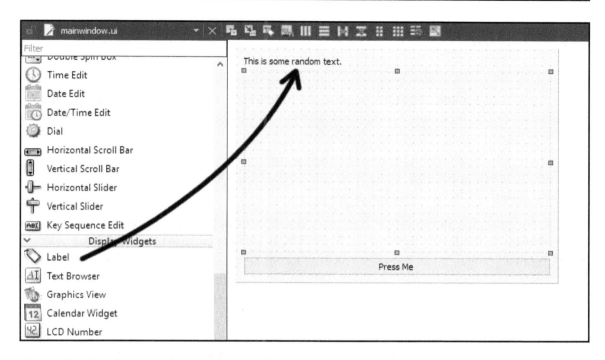

Normally, JavaScript can only work within the HTML environment and hence, is only able to alter HTML elements and not something outside the web view. However, Qt allows us to do just that by using the web channel module. So let's open up our project (.pro) file and add the web channel module to the project:

```
QT += core gui webengine webenginewidgets webchannel
```

After that, open up mainwindow.h and add in the QWebChannel header:

```
#include <QMainWindow>
#include <QWebEngineView>
#include <QWebChannel>
```

At the same time, we also declare a function called `doSomething()`, with a `Q_INVOKABLE` macro in front of it:

```
Q_INVOKABLE void doSomething();
```

The `Q_INVOKABLE` macro tells Qt to expose the function to the JavaScript engine, and thus the function can then be called from JavaScript (and QML, since QML is also based on JavaScript).

Then in `mainwindow.cpp`, we'll have to first create a `QWebChannel` object and register our main window as a JavaScript object. You can register any Qt object as a JavaScript object as long as it is derived from the `QObject` class.

Since we're going to call the `doSomething()` function from JavaScript, we must register the main window to the JavaScript engine. After that, we also need to set the `QWebChannel` object we just created as the web channel of our web view. The code looks like the following:

```
QWebChannel* channel = new QWebChannel(this);
channel->registerObject("mainwindow", this);
webview->page()->setWebChannel(channel);
```

Once you're done with that, let's define the `doSomething()` function. We're just going to do something simple—change the text label on our Qt GUI, and that's all:

```
void MainWindow::doSomething()
{
    ui->label->setText("This text has been changed by javascript!");
}
```

We're done with the C++ code, let's open up our HTML file. There are couple of things we need to do to make this work. First, we need to include the `qwebchannel.js` script that is embedded in your Qt program by default, so you don't have to search for that file in your Qt directory. Add the following code in between the `head` tags:

```
<script type="text/javascript"
src="qrc:///qtwebchannel/qwebchannel.js"></script>
```

Then, we create a `QWebChannel` object in JavaScript when the document is successfully being loaded by web view and link the `mainwindow` variable to the actual main window object from Qt (which we registered earlier in C++). This step must only be done after the web page has been loaded (through `window.onload` callback); otherwise, there might be problems creating the web channel:

```
var mainwindow;
```

```
window.onload = function()
{
    new QWebChannel(Qt.webChannelTransport,function(channel)
    {
        mainwindow = channel.objects.mainwindow;
    });
}
```

After that, we create a JavaScript function that calls the doSomething() function:

```
function myFunction()
{
    mainwindow.doSomething();
}
```

Finally, add a button to the HTML body and make sure myFunction() is called when the button is pressed:

```
<body>
    <p id="myText">Hello World!</p>
    <button onclick="myFunction()">Do Something</button>
</body>
```

Build and run the program now and you should be able to get the following result:

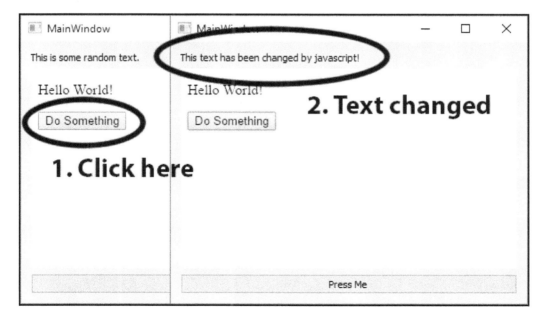

You can do a lot of useful things using this method other than altering the properties of a Qt widget. For example, saving a file to the local hard disk, getting scanned data from a barcode scanner, and so on. There is no longer any barrier between native and web technology. However, do be extra aware of any possible security implications of this technique. As the old saying goes:

"With great power comes great responsibility."

Summary

In this chapter, we have learned how to create our own web browser and make it interact with the native code. Qt provides us with the web channel technology that makes Qt a very powerful platform for software development.

It takes advantage of both the power of Qt and the beauty of web technology, which means you can have a lot more options when it comes to development and not just be limited to Qt's methods. I'm really excited and can't wait to see what you can achieve with this!

Join us in the next chapter to learn how to create a map viewer similar to Google Maps, using Qt!

7
Map Viewer

User location and map display are two features that have become more common these days and have been used in various types of applications. They are commonly used for both backend analytics and frontend display purposes.

The map viewer can be used for navigation, nearby point-of-interest lookup, location-based services (such as calling for a taxi), and so on. You can use Qt to achieve most of it but you will require an advanced database system, if you're going for something more complex.

In the previous chapter, we learned how to embed a web browser into your application. In this chapter, we will try something more fun, which covers the following topics:

- Creating a map display
- Marker and shape display
- Obtaining a user's location
- Geo Routing Request

Let's proceed to create our own map viewer!

Map display

The **Qt Location** module provides developer access to geocoding and navigation information. It can also allow the user to do a place search for which the data needs to be retrieved, either from a server or from the user's device.

At the moment, Qt's map view does not support C++, only QML. This means that we can only use QML script to alter anything related to the visual—displaying a map, adding a marker, and so on; on the other hand, we can use the C++ classes provided by the module to obtain information from a database or from a service provider, before displaying it to the user via QML.

Just a quick note, **QML (Qt Modeling Language)** is a user interface markup language for Qt Quick applications. Since QML is powered by the JavaScript framework, its coding syntax is almost similar to the JavaScript. If you need an in-depth learning on QML and Qt Quick, please proceed to `Chapter 14`, *Qt Quick and QML,* as it is an entire chapter dedicated to it.

There are many tutorials out there that teach you how to create a fully fledged map viewer using Qt Quick and QML language, but there isn't a lot that teaches you how to combine C++ with QML. Let's get started!

Setting up the Qt location module

1. First, create a new Qt Widgets Application project.
2. After that, open up your project file (`.pro`) and add the following modules to your Qt project:

```
QT += core gui location qml quickwidgets
```

Besides the `location` module, we also added `qml` and `quickwidgets` modules, which are required by the map display widget in the next section. That is all we need to do for enabling the `Qt Location` module in our project. Next, we will proceed to add the map display widget to our project.

Creating a map display

Once you are ready, let's open up `mainwindow.ui` and remove the **menuBar, toolBar,** and **statusBar** as we don't need any of those in this project:

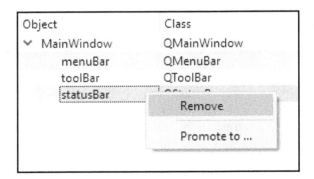

After that, drag a **QQuickWidget** from the **widget box** to the UI canvas. Then, click on the **Lay Out Horizontally** button located at the top of the canvas to add layout properties to it:

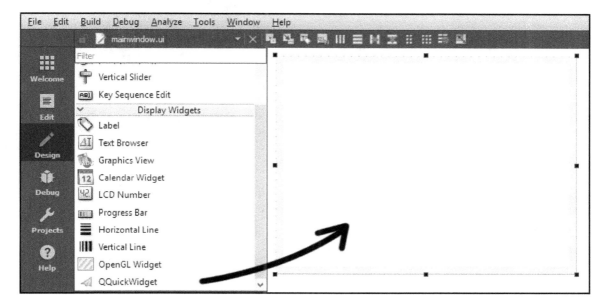

Then, set all the **margin** properties of the **central widget** to 0:

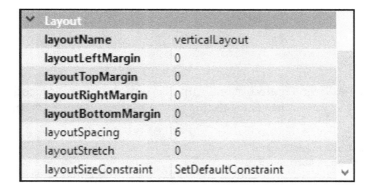

Next, we need to create a new file called `mapview.qml` by going to **File | New File or Project....** After that, select **Qt** category and follow **QML File (Qt Quick 2):**

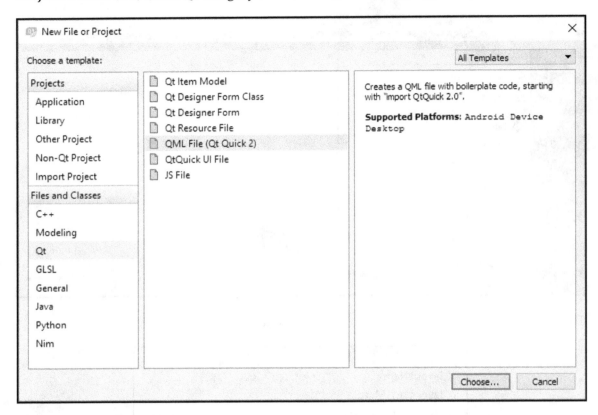

Once the QML file has been created, open it up and add the following code to include the `location` and `positioning` modules to this file so that we can use its functions later:

```
import QtQuick 2.0
import QtLocation 5.3
import QtPositioning 5.0
```

After that, we create a `Plugin` object and name it **osm (Open Street Map)**, we then create a **Map** object and apply the plugin to its `plugin` property. We also set the starting coordinates to (40.7264175, -73.99735), which is somewhere in New York. Other than that, the default `zoom level` is set to `14`, which is enough to have a good view of the city:

```
Item
{
    Plugin
    {
        id: mapPlugin
        name: "osm"
    }

    Map
    {
        id: map
        anchors.fill: parent
        plugin: mapPlugin
        center: QtPositioning.coordinate(40.7264175,-73.99735)
        zoomLevel: 14
    }
}
```

Before we're able to display the map on our application, we must first create a **resource** file and add the QML file to it. This can be done by going to **File | Create New File or Project....** Then, select **Qt** category and pick **Qt Resource File.**

Once the resource file has been created, add a prefix called `qml`, and add the QML file to the prefix, like so:

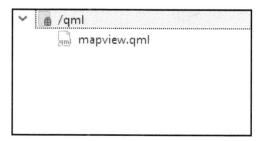

We can now open up `mainwindow.ui` and set the `source` property of the QQuickWidget to `qrc:/qml/mapview.qml`. You may also click the button behind the source property to select the QML file straight from the resources.

Once you're done, let's compile and run our project and see what we've got! You can try panning around and zooming in and out from the map using the mouse, too:

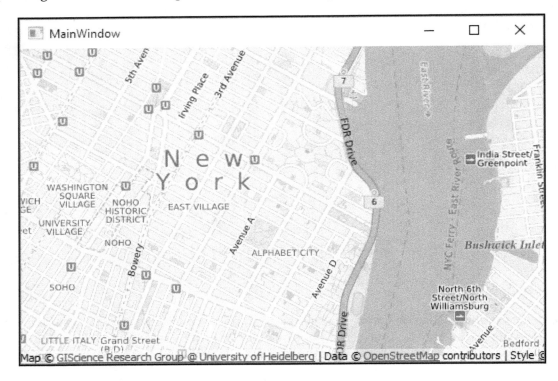

Even though we can achieve the same result by using the web view widget, it will make us write a ton of JavaScript code just to display a map like this. By using Qt Quick, we only need to write a few simple lines of QML code and that's it.

Marker and shape display

In the previous section, we successfully created a map display, but that is just the beginning of this project. We need to be able to display custom data in the form of markers or shapes layered on top of the map, so that the user can understand the data.

Displaying position markers on a map

If I tell you my favorite restaurant is located at (40.7802655, −74.108644), you won't be able to make sense of it. However, if those coordinates are being displayed on the map view in the form of a location marker, instantly, you will have an idea of where it is. Let's see how we can add position markers to our map view!

First of all, we need a marker image that should look something like this, or even better, design your own marker:

After that, we need to register this image to our project's resource file. Open up `resource.qrc` with Qt Creator and create a new prefix called `images`. Then, add the marker image to the newly created prefix. Do make sure that the image has a transparent background to look good on the map:

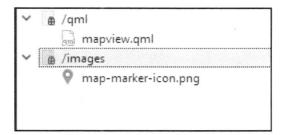

Next, open up `mapview.qml` and replace the code with the following:

```
Item
{
    id: window

    Plugin
    {
        id: mapPlugin
        name: "osm"
    }
}
```

```qml
Image
{
    id: icon
    source: "qrc:///images/map-marker-icon.png"
    sourceSize.width: 50
    sourceSize.height: 50
}

MapQuickItem
{
    id: marker
    anchorPoint.x: marker.width / 4
    anchorPoint.y: marker.height
    coordinate: QtPositioning.coordinate(40.7274175,-73.99835)

    sourceItem: icon
}

Map
{
    id: map
    anchors.fill: parent
    plugin: mapPlugin
    center: QtPositioning.coordinate(40.7264175,-73.99735)
    zoomLevel: 14

    Component.onCompleted:
    {
        map.addMapItem(marker)
    }
}
}
```

In the preceding code, we first added an image object that will be used as the marker's image. Since the original image is really huge, we have to resize it by setting the sourceSize property to 50x50. We must also set the anchor point of the marker image to the center-bottom of the image because that is where the tip of the marker is located.

After that, we create a `MapQuickItem` object that will be served as the marker itself. Set the marker image as the `sourceItem` of the `MapQuickItem` object, then add the marker to the map by calling `map.addMapItem()`. This function must be called after the map has been created and is ready to be displayed, which means we can only call it after the `Component.onCompleted` event has been triggered.

Now that we're done with the code, let's compile and look at the result:

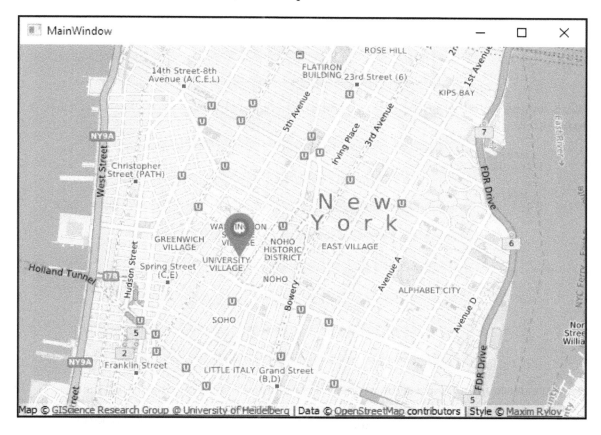

Even though it's now looking all good, we don't want to hardcode the marker in QML. Imagine adding hundreds of markers to the map, it's simply impossible to manually add each marker using a distinct set of code.

In order to create a function that allows us to dynamically create position markers, we need to first separate the marker QML code from `mapview.qml` to a new QML file. Let's create a new QML file called `marker.qml` and add it to the resource file:

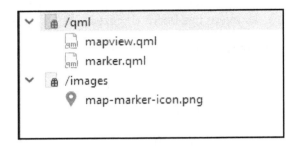

Next, remove both the `MapQuickItem` and `Image` objects from `mapview.qml` and move it to `marker.qml`:

```
import QtQuick 2.0
import QtLocation 5.3

MapQuickItem
{
    id: marker
    anchorPoint.x: marker.width / 4
    anchorPoint.y: marker.height
    sourceItem: Image
    {
        id: icon
        source: "qrc:///images/map-marker-icon.png"
        sourceSize.width: 50
        sourceSize.height: 50
    }
}
```

As you can see from the preceding code, I have merged the `Image` object with the `MapQuickItem` object. The coordinate property has also been removed as we will only set it when putting the marker on the map.

Now, open up `mapview.qml` again, and add this function to the `Item` object:

```
Item
{
    id: window

    Plugin
    {
        id: mapPlugin
        name: "osm"
    }

    function addMarker(latitude, longitude)
    {
        var component = Qt.createComponent("qrc:///qml/marker.qml")
        var item = component.createObject(window, { coordinate:
        QtPositioning.coordinate(latitude, longitude) })
        map.addMapItem(item)
    }
}
```

From the preceding code, we first created a component by loading the `marker.qml` file. Then, we created an object/item from the component by calling `createObject()`. In the `createObject()` function, we made the window object as its parent and set its position to the coordinate supplied by the `addMarker()` function. Finally, we added the item to the map for it to be rendered.

Whenever we want to create a new position marker, we'll just have to call this `addMarker()` function. To demonstrate this, let's create three different markers by calling `addMarker()` three times:

```
Map
{
    id: map
    anchors.fill: parent
    plugin: mapPlugin
    center: QtPositioning.coordinate(40.7264175,-73.99735)
    zoomLevel: 14

    Component.onCompleted:
    {
        addMarker(40.7274175,-73.99835)
        addMarker(40.7276432,-73.98602)
        addMarker(40.7272175,-73.98935)
    }
}
```

Build and run the project again, and you should be able to see something like this:

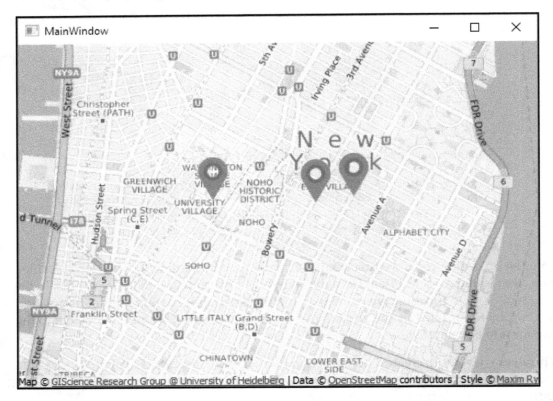

We can go even further by adding a text label to each of the markers. To do that, first open up marker.qml, then add another module called QtQuick.Controls:

```
import QtQuick 2.0
import QtQuick.Controls 2.0
import QtLocation 5.3
```

After that, add a custom property to the MapQuickItem object called labelText:

```
MapQuickItem
{
    id: marker
    anchorPoint.x: marker.width / 4
    anchorPoint.y: marker.height
    property string labelText
```

Once you're done, change its `sourceItem` property into this:

```
sourceItem: Item
{
        Image
        {
            id: icon
            source: "qrc:///images/map-marker-icon.png"
            sourceSize.width: 50
            sourceSize.height: 50
        }

        Rectangle
        {
            id: tag
            anchors.centerIn: label
            width: label.width + 4
            height: label.height + 2
            color: "black"
        }

        Label
        {
            id: label
            anchors.centerIn: parent
            anchors.horizontalCenterOffset: 20
            anchors.verticalCenterOffset: -12
            font.pixelSize: 16
            text: labelText
            color: "white"
        }
    }
```

From the preceding code, we created an `Item` object to group multiple objects together. Then, we created a `Rectangle` object to serve as the label background and a `Label` object for the text. The `text` property of the `Label` object will get linked to the `labelText` property of the `MapQuickItem` object. We can add another input to the `addMarker()` function for setting the `labelText` property, like so:

```
function addMarker(name, latitude, longitude)
{
        var component = Qt.createComponent("qrc:///qml/marker.qml")
        var item = component.createObject(window, { coordinate:
QtPositioning.coordinate(latitude, longitude), labelText: name })
        map.addMapItem(item)
}
```

Therefore, when we create the markers, we can call the `addMarker()` function like this:

```
Component.onCompleted:
{
    addMarker("Restaurant", 40.7274175,-73.99835)
    addMarker("My Home", 40.7276432,-73.98602)
    addMarker("School", 40.7272175,-73.98935)
}
```

Build and run the project again and you should see this:

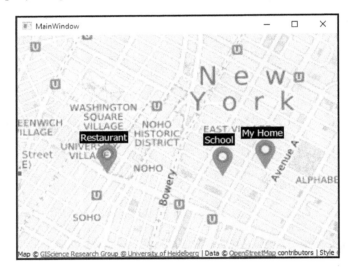

Pretty awesome isn't it? However, we're not done yet. Since we're most likely using C++ to obtain data from the database through Qt's SQL module, we need to find a way to call the QML function from C++.

To achieve that, let's comment out the three `addMarker()` functions in `mapview.qml` and open up `mainwindow.h` and the following headers:

```
#include <QQuickItem>
#include <QQuickView>
```

After that, open up `mainwindow.cpp` and call the `QMetaObject::invokeMethod()` function, like this:

```
MainWindow::MainWindow(QWidget *parent) :
    QMainWindow(parent),
    ui(new Ui::MainWindow)
{
```

```
    ui->setupUi(this);

    QObject* target =
qobject_cast<QObject*>(ui->quickWidget->rootObject());
    QString functionName = "addMarker";

    QMetaObject::invokeMethod(target, functionName, Qt::AutoConnection,
Q_ARG(QVariant, "Testing"), Q_ARG(QVariant, 40.7274175),
Q_ARG(QVariant, -73.99835));
    }
```

The preceding code might seem complex, but it's actually really simple if we dissect it and analyze each of its arguments. The first argument of the preceding function is the object that we want to call the function from, and in this case, it is the root object (the `Item` object in `mapview.qml`) of the map view widget. Next, we want to tell which function name we want to call, and it is the `addMarker()` function. After that, the third argument is the connection type used by the signal and slot system to invoke this method. For this, we'll just let it be the default setting, which is `Qt::AutoConnection`. The rest are the arguments that are needed by the `addMarker()` function. We used the `Q_ARG` macro for indicating the type and value of the data.

Finally, build and run the application again. You will see a marker with the label has been added to the map, but this time, it's called from our C++ code instead of QML:

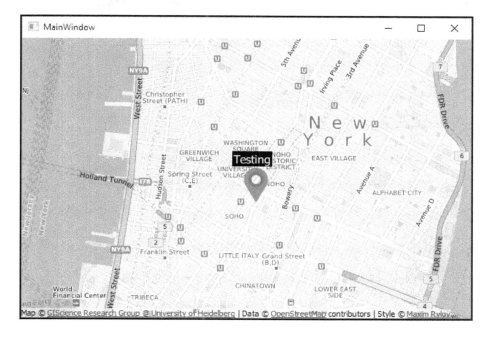

Displaying shapes on a map

Besides adding markers to the map, we can also draw different types of shapes on the map to indicate an area of interest or serve as geofences, which give out warnings whenever a target is entering or leaving the area covered by the shape. A geofence is a polygonal shape that defines an area of interest or virtual geographic boundary on a map for location-based services. Usually, geofences are used to trigger an alarm when a device is entering and/or exiting a geofence. A good example of using a geofence is when you need a shopping reminder, you can draw a geofence around the supermarket and attach a shopping list along with the geofence. When you (and your phone) are entering the area of the geofence, you will get a notification on your phone that reminds you what to buy. Wouldn't that be great?

For more information about geofences, please visit: https://en.wikipedia.org/wiki/Geo-fence

We won't be creating a functional geofence in this chapter as it is quite an advanced topic, and it usually runs as a server-side service for checking and triggering an alarm. We will only use Qt to draw the shape and display it visually on the screen.

To draw shapes on the map view widget, we'll create a few more QML files for each type of shape and add them to the program's resources:

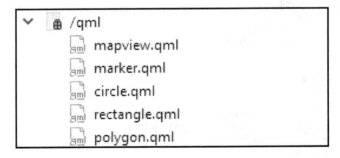

For each of the newly created QML files, we'll do something similar to the position marker. For `circle.qml`, it looks like this:

```
import QtQuick 2.0
import QtLocation 5.3

MapCircle
{
```

```
        property int borderWidth
        border.width: borderWidth
    }
```

We only declare `borderWidth` in this file because we can directly set the other properties later, when calling the `createCircle()` function. The same goes for `rectangle.qml`:

```
import QtQuick 2.0
import QtLocation 5.3

MapRectangle
{
    property int borderWidth
    border.width: borderWidth
}
```

Repeat a similar step for `polygon.qml`:

```
import QtQuick 2.0
import QtLocation 5.3

MapPolygon
{
    property int borderWidth
    border.width: borderWidth
}
```

You can set other properties if you want, but for the sake of demonstration, we only change a few of the properties such as color, shape, and border width. Once you're done, let's open up `mapview.qml` and define a few functions for adding the shapes:

```
Item
{
    id: window

    Plugin
    {
        id: mapPlugin
        name: "osm"
    }

    function addCircle(latitude, longitude, radius, color, borderWidth)
    {
        var component = Qt.createComponent("qrc:///qml/circle.qml")
        var item = component.createObject(window, { center:
        QtPositioning.coordinate(latitude, longitude), radius: radius,
        color: color, borderWidth: borderWidth })
```

```
    map.addMapItem(item)
}

function addRectangle(startLat, startLong, endLat, endLong, color,
borderWidth)
{
    var component = Qt.createComponent("qrc:///qml/rectangle.qml")
    var item = component.createObject(window, { topLeft:
QtPositioning.coordinate(startLat, startLong), bottomRight:
QtPositioning.coordinate(endLat, endLong), color: color,
borderWidth: borderWidth })
    map.addMapItem(item)
}

function addPolygon(path, color, borderWidth)
{
    var component = Qt.createComponent("qrc:///qml/polygon.qml")
    var item = component.createObject(window, { path: path, color:
color, borderWidth: borderWidth })
    map.addMapItem(item)
}
```

These functions are very similar to the `addMarker()` function, except it takes in different arguments that are later passed to the `createObject()` function. After that, let's try and create the shapes using the preceding function:

```
addCircle(40.7274175,-73.99835, 250, "green", 3);
addRectangle(40.7274175,-73.99835, 40.7376432, -73.98602, "red", 2)
var path = [{ latitude: 40.7324281, longitude: -73.97602 },
            { latitude: 40.7396432, longitude: -73.98666 },
            { latitude: 40.7273266, longitude: -73.99835 },
            { latitude: 40.7264281, longitude: -73.98602 }];
addPolygon(path, "blue", 3);
```

The following are the shapes created using the functions we have just defined. I have called each of the functions separately to demonstrate its outcome, hence the three different windows:

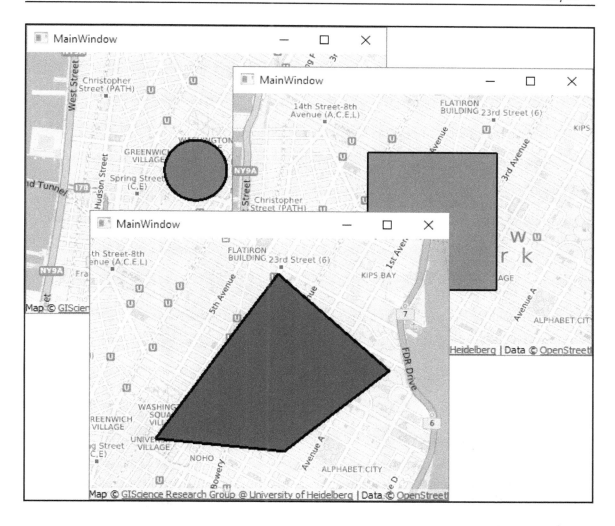

Obtaining a user's location

Qt provides us with a set of functions to retrieve a user's location information, but it will only work if the user's device supports geopositioning. This should work on all modern smartphones and might work on some of the modern computers as well.

To obtain the user's location using the `Qt Location` module, first let's open up `mainwindow.h` and add the following header files:

```
#include <QDebug>
#include <QGeoPositionInfo>
#include <QGeoPositionInfoSource>
```

After that, declare the following `slot` function in the same file:

```
private slots:
    void positionUpdated(const QGeoPositionInfo &info);
```

Right after that, open up `mainwindow.cpp` and add the following code to the place where you want it to start getting the user's location. For demonstration purposes, I'll just call it within the `MainWindow` constructor:

```
QGeoPositionInfoSource *source =
QGeoPositionInfoSource::createDefaultSource(this);
if (source)
{
    connect(source, &QGeoPositionInfoSource::positionUpdated,
            this, &MainWindow::positionUpdated);
    source->startUpdates();
}
```

Then, implement the `positionUpdated()` function we declared earlier, like this:

```
void MainWindow::positionUpdated(const QGeoPositionInfo &info)
{
    qDebug() << "Position updated:" << info;
}
```

If you build and run the application now, you may or may not get any location information, depending on the device you use to run the test. If you get debug messages like these:

```
serialnmea: No serial ports found
Failed to create Geoclue client interface. Geoclue error:
org.freedesktop.DBus.Error.Disconnected
```

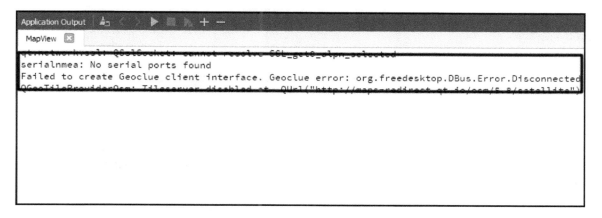

Then you probably need to find some other devices for the test. Otherwise, you may get a result similar to this:

```
Position updated: QGeoPositionInfo(QDateTime(2018-02-22 19:13:05.000 EST
Qt::TimeSpec(LocalTime)), QGeoCoordinate(45.3333, -75.9))
```

I will leave you an assignment here which you can try and do by making use of the functions that we have created thus far. Since you can now obtain the coordinates of your location, try and further enhance your application by adding a marker to the map display to show where you are currently located. That should be fun to work with!

Geo Routing Request

There is another important feature called **Geo Routing Request**, which is a set of functions that help you plot out the route (often the shortest route) from point A to point B. This feature requires a service provider; in this case, we will be using **Open Street Map (OSM)** as it is completely free.

Do note that OSM is an online collaborative project, which means that if no one from your area contributed the route data to the OSM server, then you won't be able to get an accurate result. Optionally, you can also use paid services such as Mapbox or ESRI.

Let's see how we can implement Geo Routing Request in Qt! First, include the following headers to our `mainwindow.h` file:

```
#include <QGeoServiceProvider>
#include <QGeoRoutingManager>
#include <QGeoRouteRequest>
#include <QGeoRouteReply>
```

After that, add two slot functions to `MainWindow` class, namely, `routeCalculated()` and `routeError()`:

```
private slots:
    void positionUpdated(const QGeoPositionInfo &info);
    void routeCalculated(QGeoRouteReply *reply);
    void routeError(QGeoRouteReply *reply, QGeoRouteReply::Error error,
const QString &errorString);
```

Once you're done, open up `mainwindow.cpp` and create a service provider object in the `MainWindow` constructor method. We will be using the OSM service so we'll place the acronym "`osm`" when initiating the `QGeoServiceProvider` class:

```
QGeoServiceProvider* serviceProvider = new QGeoServiceProvider("osm");
```

Right after that, we'll get the pointer of the routing manager from the service provider object we just created:

```
QGeoRoutingManager* routingManager = serviceProvider->routingManager();
```

Then, connect the `finished()` signal and `error()` signal from the routing manager with the `slot` functions we just defined:

```
connect(routingManager, &QGeoRoutingManager::finished, this,
&MainWindow::routeCalculated);
connect(routingManager, &QGeoRoutingManager::error, this,
&MainWindow::routeError);
```

These slot functions will be triggered when there is a reply from the service provider upon a successful request, or when the request is failed and returned with an error message instead. The `routeCalculated()` slot function looks something like this:

```
void MainWindow::routeCalculated(QGeoRouteReply *reply)
{
    qDebug() << "Route Calculated";
    if (reply->routes().size() != 0)
    {
        // There could be more than 1 path
        // But we only get the first route
        QGeoRoute route = reply->routes().at(0);
        qDebug() << route.path();
    }
    reply->deleteLater();
}
```

As you can see, the `QGeoRouteReply` pointer contains route information sent by the service provider upon a successful request. Sometimes it comes with more than one route, so in the example, we just obtain the first route and display it through Qt's application output window. Alternatively, you can use these coordinates to draw a path or animate your marker along the route.

As for `routeError()` slot function, we'll just output the error string sent by the service provider:

```
void MainWindow::routeError(QGeoRouteReply *reply,
QGeoRouteReply::Error error, const QString &errorString)
{
    qDebug() << "Route Error" << errorString;
    reply->deleteLater();
}
```

Once you're done with that, let's initiate a Geo Routing Request in the `MainWindow` constructor method and send it to the service provider:

```
QGeoRouteRequest request(QGeoCoordinate(40.675895,-73.9562151),
QGeoCoordinate(40.6833154,-73.987715));
routingManager->calculateRoute(request);
```

Build and run the project now and you should see results like the following:

```
Application Output
MapView
Route Calculated
(QGeoCoordinate(40.67595, -73.95618), QGeoCoordinate(40.67593, -73.95607), QGeoCoordinate(40.67593, -73.95607),
QGeoCoordinate(40.67505, -73.95639), QGeoCoordinate(40.67505, -73.95639), QGeoCoordinate(40.67529, -73.95757),
QGeoCoordinate(40.67539, -73.95801), QGeoCoordinate(40.6755, -73.95852), QGeoCoordinate(40.67576, -73.95976),
QGeoCoordinate(40.6758, -73.95996), QGeoCoordinate(40.67641, -73.96287), QGeoCoordinate(40.67655, -73.96353),
QGeoCoordinate(40.67706, -73.96597), QGeoCoordinate(40.67767, -73.96886), QGeoCoordinate(40.67833, -73.97203),
QGeoCoordinate(40.67861, -73.97333), QGeoCoordinate(40.67868, -73.97354), QGeoCoordinate(40.67875, -73.97376),
QGeoCoordinate(40.67933, -73.97532), QGeoCoordinate(40.68029, -73.97774), QGeoCoordinate(40.68027, -73.97784),
QGeoCoordinate(40.68027, -73.97784), QGeoCoordinate(40.68025, -73.97798), QGeoCoordinate(40.6812, -73.9804),
QGeoCoordinate(40.68125, -73.98052), QGeoCoordinate(40.68125, -73.98052), QGeoCoordinate(40.68077, -73.98085),
QGeoCoordinate(40.68062, -73.98095), QGeoCoordinate(40.67998, -73.98138), QGeoCoordinate(40.67998, -73.98138),
QGeoCoordinate(40.68088, -73.98371), QGeoCoordinate(40.68164, -73.98567), QGeoCoordinate(40.68196, -73.98648),
QGeoCoordinate(40.68211, -73.98687), QGeoCoordinate(40.68244, -73.98773), QGeoCoordinate(40.68249, -73.98786),
QGeoCoordinate(40.68249, -73.98786), QGeoCoordinate(40.68276, -73.98768), QGeoCoordinate(40.68313, -73.98743),
QGeoCoordinate(40.68313, -73.98743), QGeoCoordinate(40.68321, -73.98748), QGeoCoordinate(40.68329, -73.98771),
QGeoCoordinate(40.68329, -73.98771))
```

Here comes another challenging assignment for you—try to put all these coordinates into an array and create an `addLine()` function that takes in the array and draws a series of straight lines that represent the route described by the Geo Routing service.

Geo Routing has been one of the most important features ever since GPS navigator systems were invented. Hopefully, you will be able to create something useful after going through the tutorial!

Summary

In this chapter, we have learned how to create our own map view similar to Google Maps. We have learned how to create a map display, placing markers and shapes on the map, and finally finding a user's location. Do note that you can also use the web view and call Google's JavaScript mapping API to create a similar map display. However, using QML is much simpler, lightweight (we don't have to load the entire web engine module just to use the map), works very well on mobile and touch screens, and it can also be easily ported to other map services. Hopefully, you can make use of this knowledge and create something really awesome and useful.

In the next chapter, we will look into how to display information using graphical items. Let's move on!

8
Graphics View

In the previous chapter, we learned about the importance of visual presentation for the user by displaying coordinate data on a map. In this chapter, we will further explore the possibility of graphics data representation using Qt's Graphics View framework.

In this chapter, we will cover the following topics:

- Graphics View framework
- Moveable graphics items
- Creating an organization chart

At the end of this chapter, you will be able to create an organization chart display using C++ and Qt's API. Let's get started!

Graphics View framework

The Graphics View framework is part of the widgets module in Qt so it is already supported by default, unless you're running Qt console application instead, which does not need the widgets module.

The Graphics View view in Qt works pretty much like a whiteboard, where you can draw anything on it using C/C++ code, such as drawing shapes, lines, text, and even images. This chapter may be a little hard to follow for beginners but it will definitely be a fun project to work with. Let's get started!

Setting up a new project

First, create a new **Qt Widgets Application** project. After that, open `mainwindow.ui` and drag and drop the **Graphics View** widget onto the main window, like this:

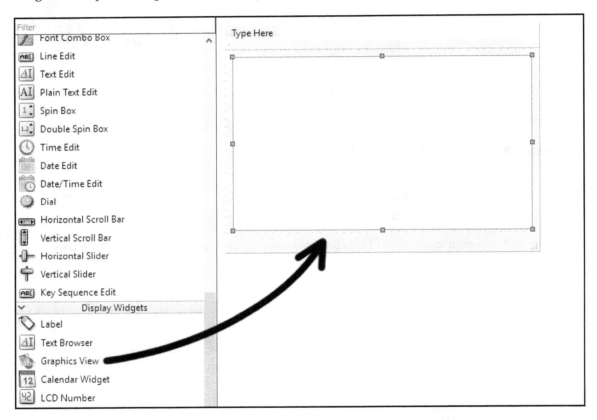

Then, create a layout for the graphics view by clicking on the **Lay Out Vertically** button at the top of the canvas. After that, open up `mainwindow.h` and add the following headers and variables:

```
#include <QGraphicsScene>
#include <QGraphicsRectItem>
#include <QGraphicsEllipseItem>
#include <QGraphicsTextItem>
#include <QBrush>
#include <QPen>
```

```
private:
  Ui::MainWindow *ui;
  QGraphicsScene* scene;
```

After that, open `mainwindow.cpp`. Once it is opened, add the following code:

```
MainWindow::MainWindow(QWidget *parent) :
    QMainWindow(parent),
    ui(new Ui::MainWindow)
{
    ui->setupUi(this);

    scene = new QGraphicsScene(this);
    ui->graphicsView->setScene(scene);

    QBrush greenBrush(Qt::green);
    QBrush blueBrush(Qt::blue);
    QPen pen(Qt::black);
    pen.setWidth(2);

    QGraphicsRectItem* rectangle = scene->addRect(80, 0, 80, 80, pen,
greenBrush);
    QGraphicsEllipseItem* ellipse = scene->addEllipse(0, -80, 200, 60,
pen, blueBrush);
    QGraphicsTextItem* text = scene->addText("Hello World!",
QFont("Times", 25));
}
```

Build and run the program now, and you should see something like this:

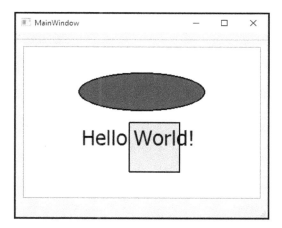

The code is a bit long so let me explain to you what it does and how it draws the graphics onto the screen.

As I said earlier, the **Graphics View** widget is like a canvas or whiteboard that allows you to draw anything you want on it. However, we also need something called Graphics Scene, which is essentially a scene graph that stores all the graphical components in a parent–child hierarchy before displaying them on the **Graphics View,** accordingly. Scene graph hierarchy is something that the image that appears in the previous screenshot, where each object could have a parent or children that link together:

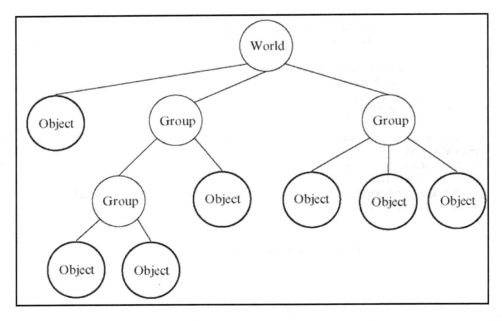

In the preceding code, we first created a QGraphicsScene object and set it as the Graphics Scene for our **Graphics View** widget:

```
scene = new QGraphicsScene(this);
ui->graphicsView->setScene(scene);
```

In this example, however, we don't have to link the graphics items together so we'll just create them independently, like so:

```
QBrush greenBrush(Qt::green);
...
QGraphicsTextItem* text = scene->addText("Hello World!", QFont("Times",
25));
```

The QPen and QBrush classes are used to define the rendering style of these graphics items. QBrush is usually for defining the background color and pattern for the item, while QPen normally affects the outline of the item.

Qt provides many types of graphics items for the most common shapes, including:

- QGraphicsEllipseItem – ellipse item
- QGraphicsLineItem – line item
- QGraphicsPathItem – arbitrary path item
- QGraphicsPixmapItem – pixmap item
- QGraphicsPolygonItem – polygon item
- QGraphicsRectItem – rectangular item
- QGraphicsSimpleTextItem – simple text label item
- QGraphicsTextItem – advanced formatted text item

For more information, please visit this link:
http://doc.qt.io/archives/qt-5.8/qgraphicsitem.html#details.

Movable graphics items

In the previous example, we have successfully drawn some simple shapes and text onto the **Graphics View** widget. However, these graphics items are not interactive and thus don't suit our purpose. What we want is an interactive organization chart where the user can move the items around using mouse. It is actually really easy to make these items movable under Qt; let's see how we can do that by continuing our previous project.

First, make sure you don't change the default **interactive** property of our **Graphics View** widget, which is set to enabled (checkbox is checked):

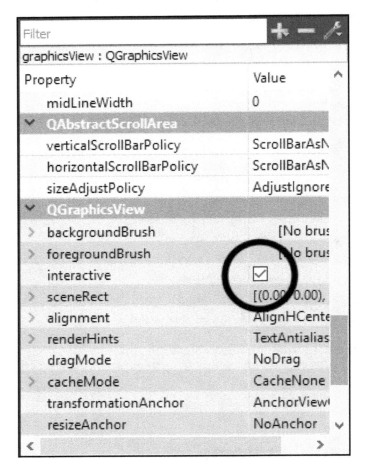

After that, add the following code below each of the graphics items we just created in the previous `Hello World` example:

```
QGraphicsRectItem* rectangle = scene->addRect(80, 0, 80, 80, pen,
greenBrush);
rectangle->setFlag(QGraphicsItem::ItemIsMovable);
rectangle->setFlag(QGraphicsItem::ItemIsSelectable);

QGraphicsEllipseItem* ellipse = scene->addEllipse(0, -80, 200, 60, pen,
blueBrush);
ellipse->setFlag(QGraphicsItem::ItemIsMovable);
```

```
ellipse->setFlag(QGraphicsItem::ItemIsSelectable);

QGraphicsTextItem* text = scene->addText("Hello World!", QFont("Times",
25));
text->setFlag(QGraphicsItem::ItemIsMovable);
text->setFlag(QGraphicsItem::ItemIsSelectable);
```

Build and run the program again, and this time you should be able to select and move the items around the Graphics View. Do note that ItemIsMovable and ItemIsSelectable both give you a different behavior—the former flag will make the item movable by mouse, and the latter makes the item selectable, which typically gives it a visual indication using dotted outline when selected. Each of the flags works independently and will not affect the other.

We can test out the effect of ItemIsSelectable flag by using the signal and slot mechanism in Qt. Let's go back to our code and add the following line:

```
ui->setupUi(this);
scene = new QGraphicsScene(this);
ui->graphicsView->setScene(scene);
connect(scene, &QGraphicsScene::selectionChanged, this,
&MainWindow::selectionChanged);
```

The selectionChanged() signal will be triggered whenever you selected an item on the Graphics View widget and the selectionChanged() slot function under our MainWindow class will then be called (which we need to write). Let's open up mainwindow.h and add in another header for displaying debug messages:

```
#include <QDebug>
```

Then, we declare the slot function, like this:

```
private:
    Ui::MainWindow *ui;

public slots:
    void selectionChanged();
```

After that open `mainwindow.cpp` and define the slot function, like this:

```
void MainWindow::selectionChanged()
{
    qDebug() << "Item selected";
}
```

Now try and run the program again; you should see a line of debug messages that say **Item selection** which appears whenever a graphics item has been clicked. It's really simple, isn't it?

As for the `ItemIsMovable` flag, we won't be able to test it using the signal and slot method. This is because all classes inherited from `QGraphicsItem` class are not inherited from the `QObject` class, and therefore the signal and slot mechanism doesn't work on these classes. This is intentionally done by Qt developers to make it lightweight, which improves the performance, especially when rendering thousands of items on the screen.

Even though signal and slot is not an option for this, we can still use the event system, which requires an override to the `itemChange()` virtual function, which I will demonstrate in the next section.

Creating an organization chart

Let's proceed to learn how to create an organization chart using Graphics View. An organization chart is a diagram that shows the structure of an organization and the relationship hierarchy of its employee positions. It is easy to understand a company's structure by using graphical representation; therefore it's best to use Graphics View instead of, say, a table.

This time, we need to create our own classes for the graphics items so that we can make use of Qt's event system, as well as have more control of how it's grouped and displayed.

First, create a C/C++ class by going to **File** | **New File or Project**:

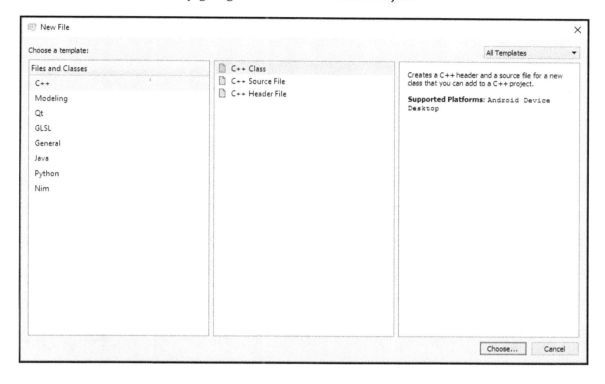

Next, name our class as `profileBox` before clicking the **Next** and **Finish** button:

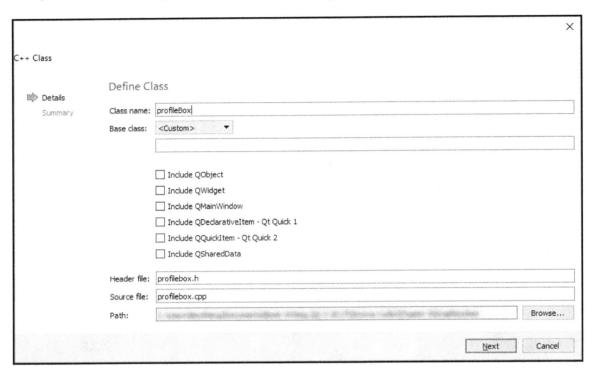

After that, open `mainwindow.h` and add in these headers:

```
#include <QWidget>
#include <QDebug>
#include <QBrush>
#include <QPen>
#include <QFont>
#include <QGraphicsScene>
#include <QGraphicsItemGroup>
#include <QGraphicsItem>
#include <QGraphicsRectItem>
#include <QGraphicsTextItem>
#include <QGraphicsPixmapItem>
```

Then, open `profilebox.h` and make our `profileBox` class inherit `QGraphicsItemGroup` instead:

```
class profileBox : public QGraphicsItemGroup
{
public:
    explicit profileBox(QGraphicsItem* parent = nullptr);
```

After that, open `profilebox.cpp` and at the constructor of the class, set up `QBrush`, `QPen` and `QFont`, which will be used for rendering in a moment:

```
profileBox::profileBox(QGraphicsItem *parent) :
QGraphicsItemGroup(parent)
{
    QBrush brush(Qt::white);
    QPen pen(Qt::black);
    QFont font;
    font.setFamily("Arial");
    font.setPointSize(12);
}
```

After that, also in the constructor, create a `QGraphicsRectItem`, `QGraphicsTextItem` and a `QGraphicsPixmapItem`:

```
QGraphicsRectItem* rectangle = new QGraphicsRectItem();
rectangle->setRect(0, 0, 90, 100);
rectangle->setBrush(brush);
rectangle->setPen(pen);

nameTag = new QGraphicsTextItem();
nameTag->setPlainText("");
nameTag->setFont(font);

QGraphicsPixmapItem* picture = new QGraphicsPixmapItem();
QPixmap pixmap(":/images/person-icon-blue.png");
picture->setPixmap(pixmap);
picture->setPos(15, 30);
```

Then, add these items to the group, which is the current class, since this class is inherited from the `QGraphicsItemGroup` class:

```
this->addToGroup(rectangle);
this->addToGroup(nameTag);
this->addToGroup(picture);
```

Finally, set three flags for the current class, which are `ItemIsMovable`, `ItemIsSelectable` and `ItemSendsScenePositionChanges`:

```
this->setFlag(QGraphicsItem::ItemIsMovable);
this->setFlag(QGraphicsItem::ItemIsSelectable);
this->setFlag(QGraphicsItem::ItemSendsScenePositionChanges);
```

These flags are very important because they are all disabled by default for performance reasons. We have covered both `ItemIsMovable` and `ItemIsSelectable` in the previous section, while `ItemSendsPositionChanges` is something new. This flag makes the graphics item notify Graphics Scene when it's being moved by the user, hence the name.

Next, create another function called `init()` for setting up the employee profile. For the sake of simplicity, we only set the employee name, however, you can do more if you wish, such as setting a different background color based on the rank, or changing their profile picture:

```
void profileBox::init(QString name, MainWindow *window, QGraphicsScene*
scene)
{
    nameTag->setPlainText(name);
    mainWindow = window;
    scene->addItem(this);
}
```

Do notice that we also set the main window and Graphics Scene pointers here so that we can use them later on. We must add the `QGraphicsItem` to a scene before it will render on screen. In this case, we group all the graphics items into a `QGraphicsItemGroup` so we only need to add the group to the scene instead of an individual item.

Do note that you must do a forward declaration for the `MainWindow` class in `profilebox.h` after `#include "mainwindow.h"` to avoid the error that says recursive header inclusion. At the same time, we also placed the `MainWindow` and `QGraphicsTextItem` pointers in `profilebox.h` so that we can call them later:

```
#include "mainwindow.h"

class MainWindow;

class profileBox : public QGraphicsItemGroup
{
public:
    explicit profileBox(QGraphicsItem* parent = nullptr);
    void init(QString name, MainWindow* window, QGraphicsScene* scene);
```

```
private:
    MainWindow* mainWindow;
    QGraphicsTextItem* nameTag;
```

You will also notice that I have used an icon in the `QGraphicsPixmapItem` as a decorative icon:

This icon is a PNG image that is stored within the resource file. You can get this image from our sample project files on our GitHub page: `http://github.com/PacktPublishing/Hands-On-GUI-Programming-with-C-QT5`

Let's create a resource file for your project. Go to **File** | **New File or Project** and select the **Qt Resource File** option under **Qt category**:

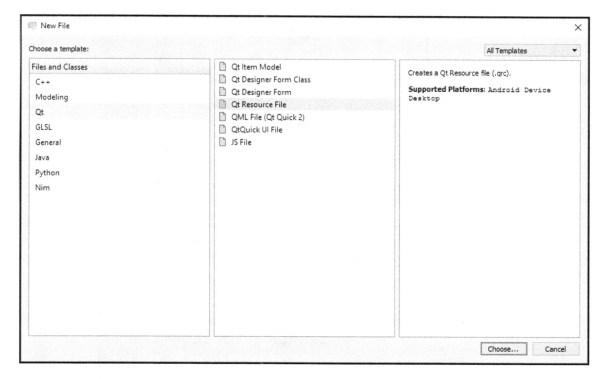

After you have created an empty resource file, add a new prefix by going to **Add** | **AddPrefix**. We will just call this prefix images:

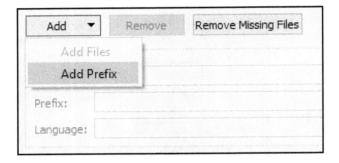

Then, select the newly created images prefix and click **Add** | **Add Files**. Add the icon image to your resource file and save. You have now successfully added the image to your project.

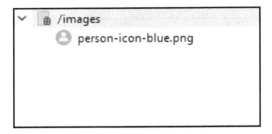

 If your prefix name or filename is different than the prefix name or filename in this book, you may right-click on your image in the resource file and select **Copy Resource Path to Clipboard** and replace the one in the code with your path.

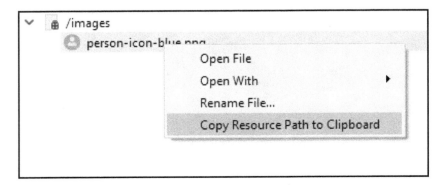

After that, open `mainwindow.h` and add in:

```
#include "profilebox.h"
```

Then, open `mainwindow.cpp` and add the following code to create a profile box manually:

```
MainWindow::MainWindow(QWidget *parent) :
    QMainWindow(parent),
    ui(new Ui::MainWindow)
{
    ui->setupUi(this);

    scene = new QGraphicsScene(this);
    ui->graphicsView->setScene(scene);

    connect(scene, &QGraphicsScene::selectionChanged, this,
&MainWindow::selectionChanged);

    profileBox* box = new profileBox();
    box->init("John Doe", this, scene);
}
```

Build and run the project now and you should see something like this:

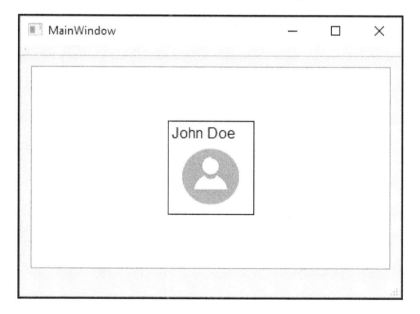

Looks neat; but we're far from done. There are a few things left to be done—we must allow the user to add or delete profile boxes with a user interface, and not by using code. At the same time, we also need to add lines that connect different profile boxes to showcase the relationship between different employees and their position within the company.

Let's start with the easy part. Open `mainwindow.ui` again and add a push button to the bottom of the **Graphics View** widget and name it `addButton`:

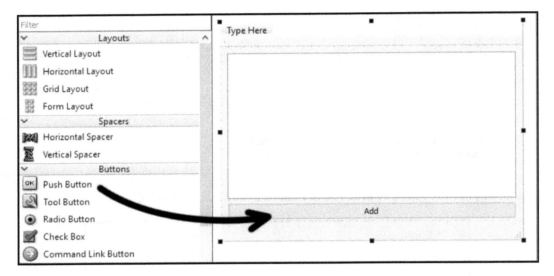

Then, right-click on the push button and select **Go to slot...** After that, select the clicked option and click **Ok**. A new slot function will be created for you automatically, called `on_addButton_clicked()`. Add the following code to allow the user to create a profile box when they click the **Add** button:

```
void MainWindow::on_addButton_clicked()
{
    bool ok;
    QString name = QInputDialog::getText(this, tr("Employee Name"),
    tr("Please insert employee's full name here:"), QLineEdit::Normal,
    "John Doe", &ok);
    if (ok && !name.isEmpty())
    {
        profileBox* box = new profileBox();
        box->init(name, this, scene);
    }
}
```

Instead of creating each profile box using code, users can now easily create any number of profile boxes they want by clicking the **Add** button. A message box will also appear and let the user type in the employee name before creating the profile box:

Next, we'll create another class called `profileLine`. This time, we will make this class inherit `QGraphicsLineItem`. The `profileline.h` basically looks like this:

```
#include <QWidget>
#include <QGraphicsItem>
#include <QPen>

class profileLine : public QGraphicsLineItem
{
public:
    profileLine(QGraphicsItem* parent = nullptr);
    void initLine(QGraphicsItem* start, QGraphicsItem* end);
    void updateLine();

    QGraphicsItem* startBox;
    QGraphicsItem* endBox;

private:
};
```

Similar to `profileBox` class, we also create an `init` function for `profileLine` class, called the `initLine()` function. This function takes in two `QGraphicsItem` objects as the starting point and ending point for rendering the line. Besides that, we also create an `updateLine()` function to redraw the line whenever the profile boxes move.

Next, open `profileline.cpp` and add the following code to the constructor:

```
profileLine::profileLine(QGraphicsItem *parent) :
QGraphicsLineItem(parent)
{
    QPen pen(Qt::black);
    pen.setWidth(2);
    this->setPen(pen);

    this->setZValue(-999);
}
```

We used `QPen` to set the color of the line to be black and its width to be 2. After that, we also set the `Zvalue` of the line to be `-999` so that it will always remain at the back of the profile boxes.

After that, add the following code to our `initLine()` function so that it looks something like this:

```
void profileLine::initLine(QGraphicsItem* start, QGraphicsItem* end)
{
    startBox = start;
    endBox = end;

    updateLine();
}
```

What it does is basically set the boxes for it to position its starting point and ending point. After that, call `updateLine()` function to render the line.

Finally, the `updateLine()` function looks like this:

```
void profileLine::updateLine()
{
    if (startBox != NULL && endBox != NULL)
    {
        this->setLine(startBox->pos().x() +
startBox->boundingRect().width() / 2, startBox->pos().y() +
startBox->boundingRect().height() / 2, endBox->pos().x() +
endBox->boundingRect().width() / 2, endBox->pos().y() +
endBox->boundingRect().height() / 2);
    }
}
```

The preceding code looks a little complicated, but it's really simple if I put it this way:

```
this->setLine(x1, y1, x2, y2);
```

The values x1 and y1 are basically the center position of the first profile box while x2 and y2 are the center position of the second profile box. Since the position value we get from calling pos() starts from the top-left corner, we must get the bounding size of the profile box and divide it by two to get its center position. Then, add that value to the top-left corner position to offset it to the center.

Once you're done, let's open mainwindow.cpp again and add the following code to the on_addButton_clicked() function:

```
void MainWindow::on_addButton_clicked()
{
    bool ok;
    QString name = QInputDialog::getText(this, tr("Employee Name"),
tr("Please insert employee's full name here:"), QLineEdit::Normal,
"John Doe", &ok);
    if (ok && !name.isEmpty())
    {
        profileBox* box = new profileBox();
        box->init(name, this, scene);

        if (scene->selectedItems().size() > 0)
        {
            profileLine* line = new profileLine();
            line->initLine(box, scene->selectedItems().at(0));
            scene->addItem(line);

            lines.push_back(line);
        }
    }
}
```

In the preceding code, we check whether there is any profile box selected by the user. If there is none, we don't have to create any line. Otherwise, create a new profileLine object and set the newly created profile box and the currently selected profile box as the startBox and endBox properties.

After that, add the line to our Graphics Scene so that it will appear on the screen. Lastly, store this profileLine object to a QList array so that we can use it later. The array declaration looks like this in mainwindow.h:

```
private:
    Ui::MainWindow *ui;
    QGraphicsScene* scene;
    QList<profileLine*> lines;
```

Build and run the project now. You should be able to see the line appear when you created the second profile box by clicking on the Add button, entering a name, and selecting OK while the first box remains selected. However, you may notice a problem whenever you move the profile box away from its original position—the lines simply won't update themselves!:

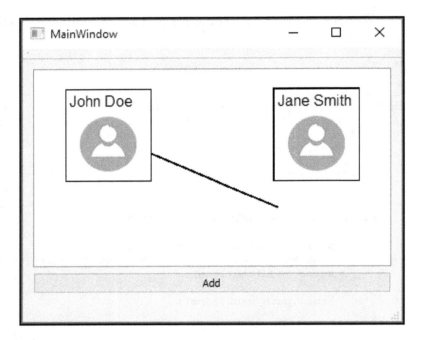

That is the main reason we put the lines into a QList array, so that we can update these lines whenever a profile box has been moved by the user.

To do that, first, we need to override the virtual function in the profileBox class called itemChanged(). Let's open profilebox.h and add the following line of code:

```
class profileBox : public QGraphicsItemGroup
{
public:
    explicit profileBox(QGraphicsItem* parent = nullptr);
    void init(QString name, MainWindow* window, QGraphicsScene* scene);
    QVariant itemChange(GraphicsItemChange change, const QVariant
    &value) override;
```

Then, open `profilebox.cpp` and add the code for `itemChanged()`:

```
QVariant profileBox::itemChange(GraphicsItemChange change, const
QVariant &value)
{
    if (change == QGraphicsItem::ItemPositionChange)
    {
        qDebug() << "Item moved";

        mainWindow->updateLines();
    }

    return QGraphicsItem::itemChange(change, value);
}
```

The `itemChanged()` function is a virtual function in `QGraphicsItem` class which will automatically be called by Qt's event system when something has changed in the graphics item, be it position change, visibility change, parent change, selection change, and so on.

Therefore, all we need to do is to override the function and add in our own custom behavior to the function. In the preceding sample code, all we did was to call the `updateLines()` function in our main window class.

Next, open `mainwindow.cpp` and define the `updateLines()` function. As the function name implies, what you're going to do in this function is to loop through all the profile line objects stored in the lines array and update every single one of them, like so:

```
void MainWindow::updateLines()
{
    if (lines.size() > 0)
    {
        for (int i = 0; i < lines.size(); i++)
        {
            lines.at(i)->updateLine();
        }
    }
}
```

Once you're done, build and run the project again. This time, you should be able to create an organization chart, such as the following:

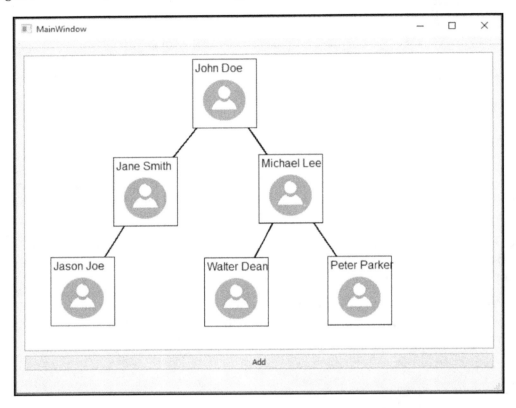

This is just a simpler version that shows you how you can make use of Qt's powerful Graphics View system to display graphical representation of a set of data that can be easily understood by an average Joe.

One last thing before it's done–we have yet to cover how to delete the profile box yet. It's actually pretty simple, let's open `mainwindow.h` and add the `keyReleaseEvent()` function, which looks like this:

```
public:
    explicit MainWindow(QWidget *parent = 0);
    ~MainWindow();

    void updateLines();
    void keyReleaseEvent(QKeyEvent* event);
```

This virtual function will also get called by Qt's event system automatically when a keyboard button is being pressed and released. The content of the function looks like this in `mainwindow.cpp`:

```
void MainWindow::keyReleaseEvent(QKeyEvent* event)
{
    qDebug() << "Key pressed: " + event->text();

    if (event->key() == Qt::Key_Delete)
    {
        if (scene->selectedItems().size() > 0)
        {
            QGraphicsItem* item = scene->selectedItems().at(0);
            scene->removeItem(item);

            for (int i = lines.size() - 1; i >= 0; i--)
            {
                profileLine* line = lines.at(i);

                if (line->startBox == item || line->endBox ==
                item)
                {
                    lines.removeAt(i);
                    scene->removeItem(line);
                    delete line;
                }
            }
            delete item;
        }
    }
}
```

What we did in this function is first to detect the keyboard button that's being pressed by the user. If the button is Qt::Key_Delete (delete button), then we'll check if the user has selected any profile box by checking whether scene->selectedItems().size() is empty. If the user has indeed selected a profile box, then remove that item from the Graphics Scene. After that, loop through the lines array and check whether any profile line has connected to the profile box that has been deleted. Remove any lines that are connected to the profile box from the scene and we're done:

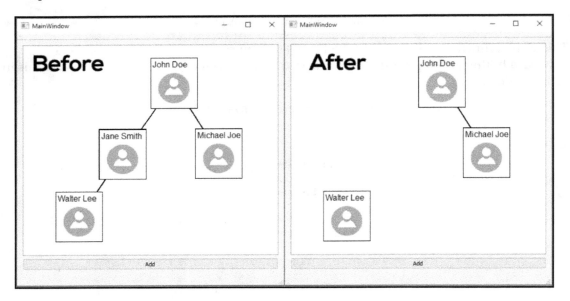

This screenshot shows the result of deleting the Jane Smith profile box from the organization chart. Notice that the lines connecting the profile box have been correctly removed. That's it for this chapter; I hope you found this interesting and will perhaps go on to create something even better than this!

Summary

In this chapter, we have learned how to create an application using Qt that allows the user to easily create and edit an organization chart. We have learned about classes such as QGraphicsScene, QGrapicsItem, QGraphicsTextItem, QGraphicsPixmapItem and so on that help us to create an interactive organization chart in a short period of time. In the upcoming chapter, we will learn how to capture images using our webcam!

9
The Camera Module

After working your way through so many chapters with increasing difficulty, let's try out something simpler and more fun for this chapter instead! We will learn how to access our camera through Qt's multimedia module and take photos using it.

In this chapter, we will cover the following topics:

- The Qt multimedia module
- Connecting to the camera
- Capturing a camera image to file
- Recording a camera video to file

You can use this to create a video conference app, a security camera system, and more. Let's get started!

The Qt multimedia module

The multimedia module in Qt is the module that handles a platform's multimedia capabilities, such as media playback and the use of camera and radio devices. This module covers a wide range of topics, but we will just focus on the camera for this chapter.

Setting up a new project

First, create a new Qt Widgets Application project.

Then, the first thing we need to do is to open up the project file (.pro) and add two keywords—multimedia and multimediawidgets:

```
QT += core gui multimedia multimediawidgets
```

By detecting these keywords in the project file, Qt will include the multimedia module and all the widgets that are related to multimedia into your project when it compiles. The multimedia module includes four major components which are listed as follows:

- Audio
- Video
- Camera
- Radio

Each component includes a range of classes that provide respective functionality. By using this module, you no longer have to implement low-level, platform-specific code yourself. Let Qt do the job for you. It's really that easy.

After you have finished adding the multimedia module, let's open `mainwindow.ui` and drag and drop a **Horizontal Layout** on to the main window, shown as follows:

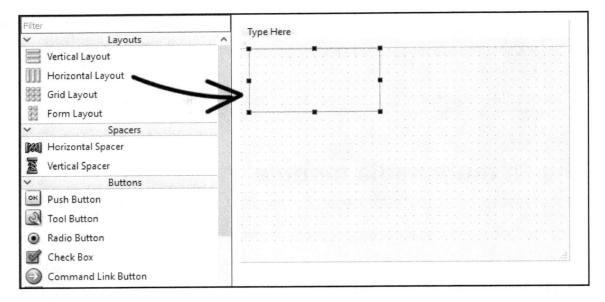

Then, add a **Label**, **Combo Box** (name it `deviceSelection`), and a **Push Button** into the **Horizontal Layout** we just added in the previous step. After that, add a **Horizontal Spacer** between the combo box and a push button to push them apart from each other. Once you're done, select the central widget and click on the **Layout Vertically** button located above the workspace.

Then, add another **Horizontal Layout** to the bottom of the previous horizontal layout and right-click on it and select **Morph into | QFrame**. After that, set its **sizePolicy (Horizontal Policy** and **Vertical Policy)** settings to **Expanding**. Refer the following screenshot:

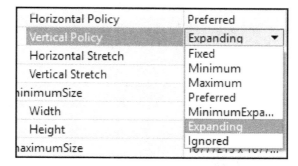

Your program's user interface should look something like this by now:

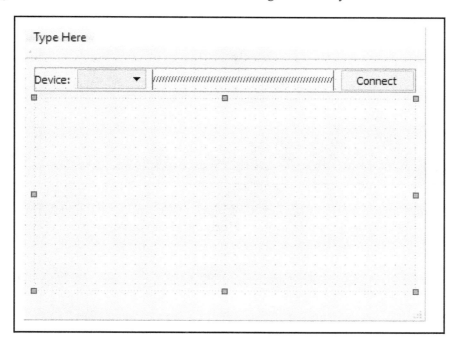

The reason we convert the layout to a frame is so that we can set the **sizePolicy** (both **Horizontal policy** and **Vertical policy)** to **Expanding**. However, if we just add a **Frame widget** (which is essentially a **QFrame**) from the widget box, we don't get the layout component on it which is needed for attaching the viewfinder later.

Next, right click on the **QFrame** again and select **Change styleSheet**. A window will pop up for setting the style sheet of that widget. Add the following style sheet code to make the background black:

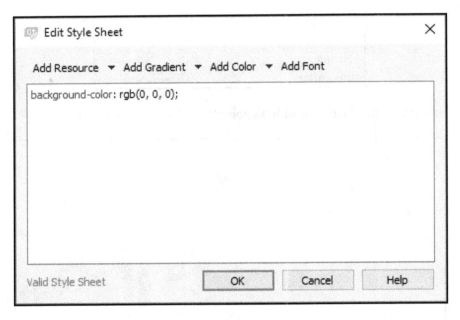

This step is optional; we made its background black just to indicate the viewfinder's location. Once this is done, let's put another **Horizontal Layout** above the **QFrame**, such as the following:

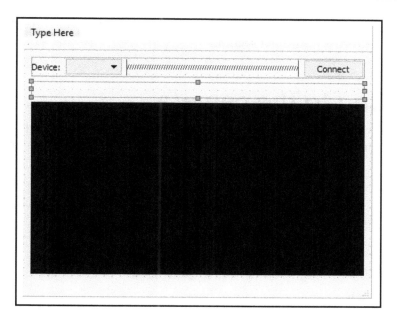

After that, add two **Push Buttons** to the **Horizontal Layout** and a **Horizontal Spacer** to keep them aligned to the right:

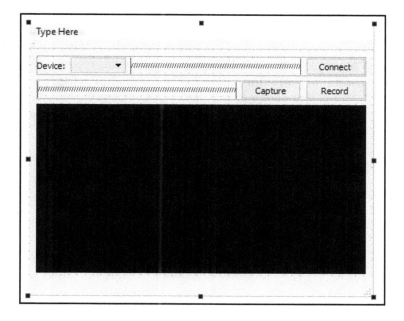

That's it; we have finished setting up our project with the multimedia module and laid out the user interface nicely for our next sections.

Connecting to the camera

Here comes the most exciting part. We are going to learn how to access our camera(s) using Qt's multimedia module! First, open `mainwindow.h` and add the following headers:

```
#include <QMainWindow>
#include <QDebug>
#include <QCameraInfo>
#include <QCamera>
#include <QCameraViewfinder>
#include <QCameraImageCapture>
#include <QMediaRecorder>
#include <QUrl>
```

Next, add the following variable, as shown here:

```
private:
    Ui::MainWindow *ui;
    QCamera* camera;
    QCameraViewfinder* viewfinder;
    bool connected;
```

Then, open up `mainwindow.cpp` and add the following code to the class constructor to initiate the `QCamera` object. We then use the `QCameraInfo` class to retrieve a list of connected cameras and fill in that information in the combo box widget:

```
MainWindow::MainWindow(QWidget *parent) :
    QMainWindow(parent),
    ui(new Ui::MainWindow)
{
    ui->setupUi(this);

    connected = false;
    camera = new QCamera();

    qDebug() << "Number of cameras found:" <<
QCameraInfo::availableCameras().count();

    QList<QCameraInfo> cameras = QCameraInfo::availableCameras();
    foreach (const QCameraInfo &cameraInfo, cameras)
    {
        qDebug() << "Camera info:" << cameraInfo.deviceName() <<
```

```
        cameraInfo.description() << cameraInfo.position();

        ui->deviceSelection->addItem(cameraInfo.description());
    }
}
```

Let's build and run the project now. After that, check the debug output for any detected cameras on your computer. The cameras that have been detected should also be displayed in the drop-down box. If you are running on a laptop with a supported camera, you should see it listed. If you're running a system with no built-in camera, then the debug output may not display anything and the drop-down box will remain empty as well. If that's the case, try plugging in an inexpensive USB camera and run the program again:

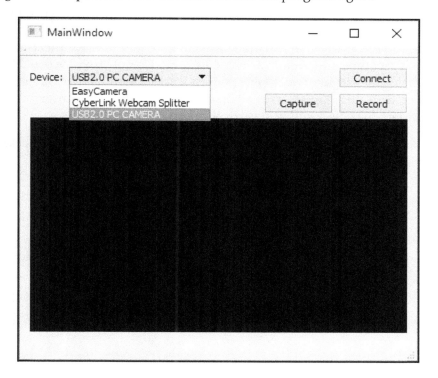

After that, open up `mainwindow.ui` and right click on the **Connect** button, and select **Go to slot....** Select the `clicked()` option and click **OK**. Qt Creator will automatically create a `slot` function for you; add the following code into the function, like so:

```
void MainWindow::on_connectButton_clicked()
{
    if (!connected)
```

```
        {
                connectCamera();
        }
        else
        {
                camera->stop();
                viewfinder->deleteLater();
                ui->connectButton->setText("Connect");
                connected = false;
        }
    }
```

When the **Connect** button is being clicked, we first check whether the camera is already connected by checking the connect variable. If it's not connected yet, we run the connectCamera() function which we will define in the next step. If the camera is already connected, we stop the camera, delete the viewfinder and set the **Connect** button's text to Connect. Finally, set the connected variable to false. Do note that we're using deleteLater() here instead of delete(), which is the recommended way to delete a memory pointer. deleteLater() is called on an object that lives in a thread with no running event loop, the object will be destroyed when the thread finishes.

Next, we will add a new function in our MainWindow class called connectCamera(). The function looks like the following code block:

```
void MainWindow::connectCamera()
{
    QList<QCameraInfo> cameras = QCameraInfo::availableCameras();
    foreach (const QCameraInfo &cameraInfo, cameras)
    {
            qDebug() << cameraInfo.description() << ui->deviceSelection-
            >currentText();

            if (cameraInfo.description() == ui->deviceSelection-
            >currentText())
            {
                    camera = new QCamera(cameraInfo);
                    viewfinder = new QCameraViewfinder(this);
                    camera->setViewfinder(viewfinder);
                    ui->webcamLayout->addWidget(viewfinder);

                    connected = true;
                    ui->connectButton->setText("Disconnect");

                    camera->start();

                    return;
```

```
        }
      }
    }
```

In the `connectCamera()` function, we repeat what we did in the construction and get the current list of connected cameras. Then, we loop through the list and compare the name of the camera (stored in the `description` variable) with the currently selected device name on the combo box widget.

If there's a matching name, it means the user is intending to connect to that particular camera, and thus we will proceed to connect to that camera by initializing a `QCamera` object and a new `QCameraViewFinder` object. We then link the `viewfinder` to the `camera` and add the `viewfinder` to the layout with the black color background. Then, we set the `connected` variable to `true` and set the **Connect** button's text to `Disconnect`. Finally, call the `start()` function to start running the camera.

Build and run the project now. Select the camera you are intending to connect to and click the **Connect** button. You should be able to connect to your camera and see yourself in the program:

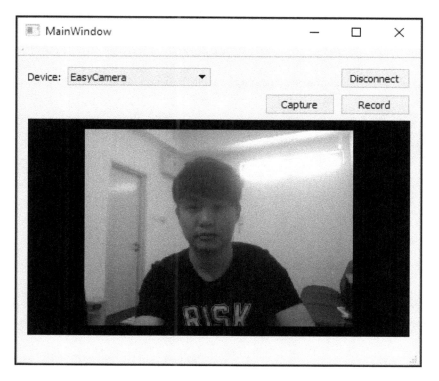

If your camera is unable to connect, do the following steps to display any errors returned by the operating system. First, open up `mainwindow.h` and add in the following `slot` function:

```
private slots:
    void cameraError(QCamera::Error error);
```

After that, open `mainwindow.cpp` and add the following code to `connectCamera()` function to connect the `error()` signal to the `cameraError()`, `slot` function:

```
void MainWindow::connectCamera()
{
    QList<QCameraInfo> cameras = QCameraInfo::availableCameras();
    foreach (const QCameraInfo &cameraInfo, cameras)
    {
        qDebug() << cameraInfo.description() << ui->deviceSelection-
        >currentText();

        if (cameraInfo.description() == ui->deviceSelection-
        >currentText())
        {
            camera = new QCamera(cameraInfo);
            viewfinder = new QCameraViewfinder(this);
            camera->setViewfinder(viewfinder);
            ui->webcamLayout->addWidget(viewfinder);

            connect(camera, SIGNAL(error(QCamera::Error)), this,
            SLOT(cameraError(QCamera::Error)));

            connected = true;
            ui->connectButton->setText("Disconnect");

            camera->start();

            return;
        }
    }
}
```

The `cameraError()` slot function looks like this:

```
void MainWindow::cameraError(QCamera::Error error)
{
    qDebug() << "Camera error:" << error;

    connected = false;
    camera->stop();
```

```
ui->connectButton->setText("Connect");
}
```

In the preceding code, we display the error message and make sure the camera has completely stopped, just in case. By looking at the error message, you should be able to debug the problem more easily.

Capturing a camera image to file

We have learned how to connect to our camera using Qt's multimedia module in the previous section. Now, we will try and capture a still image from the camera and save it into a JPEG file. It's actually very very simple with Qt.

First, open `mainwindow.h` and add the following variable:

```
private:
    Ui::MainWindow *ui;
    QCamera* camera;
    QCameraViewfinder* viewfinder;
    QCameraImageCapture* imageCapture;
    bool connected;
```

Then, right-click on the **Capture** button in `mainwindow.ui` and select **Go to slot....** Then, select `clicked()` and press **OK**. Now, a new `slot` function will be created for you in `mainwindow.cpp`. Add the following code to capture an image from the camera:

```
void MainWindow::on_captureButton_clicked()
{
    if (connected)
    {
        imageCapture = new QCameraImageCapture(camera);
        camera->setCaptureMode(QCamera::CaptureStillImage);
        camera->searchAndLock();
        imageCapture->capture(qApp->applicationDirPath());
        camera->unlock();
    }
}
```

What we did in the preceding code is basically create a new `QCameraImageCapture` object and set its media object as the active camera. Then, set its capture mode as a still image. Before we ask the `QCameraImageCapture` object to capture an image, we must lock the camera so that the settings remain unchanged during the process of capturing the image. You may unlock it by calling `camera->unlock()` after you have successfully captured the image.

We used `qApp->applicationDirPath()` to get the application directory so that the image will be saved alongside the executable file. You can change this to whatever directory you want. You can also put your desired filename behind the directory path; otherwise, it will save the images sequentially using the default filename format starting with `IMG_00000001.jpg`, `IMG_00000002.jpg`, and so on.

Recording a camera video to file

After we have learned how to capture a still image from our camera, let's proceed to learn how to record videos as well. First, open `mainwindow.h` and add the following variables:

```
private:
    Ui::MainWindow *ui;
    QCamera* camera;
    QCameraViewfinder* viewfinder;
    QCameraImageCapture* imageCapture;
    QMediaRecorder* recorder;

    bool connected;
    bool recording;
```

Next, open `mainwindow.ui` again and right-click on the **Record** button. Choose **Go to slot...** from the menu and select the `clicked()` option, then, click the **OK** button. A `slot` function will be created for you; then proceed to add the following code into the `slot` function:

```
void MainWindow::on_recordButton_clicked()
{
    if (connected)
    {
        if (!recording)
        {
            recorder = new QMediaRecorder(camera);
            camera->setCaptureMode(QCamera::CaptureVideo);
            recorder->setOutputLocation(QUrl(qApp-
            >applicationDirPath()));
```

```
                recorder->record();
                recording = true;
        }
        else
        {
                recorder->stop();
                recording = false;
        }
    }
}
```

This time, we use a QMediaRecorder for recording video instead. We must also set the camera's capture mode to QCamera::CaptureVideo before calling recorder->record().

To check the error message produced by the media recorder during the recording stage, you may connect the error() signal of the media recorder to a slot function like this:

```
void MainWindow::on_recordButton_clicked()
{
    if (connected)
    {
        if (!recording)
        {
            recorder = new QMediaRecorder(camera);
            connect(recorder, SIGNAL(error(QMediaRecorder::Error)),
            this, SLOT(recordError(QMediaRecorder::Error)));
            camera->setCaptureMode(QCamera::CaptureVideo);
            recorder->setOutputLocation(QUrl(qApp-
            >applicationDirPath()));
            recorder->record();
            recording = true;
        }
        else
        {
            recorder->stop();
            recording = false;
        }
    }
}
```

Then, simply display the error message in the `slot` function:

```
void MainWindow::recordError(QMediaRecorder::Error error)
{
    qDebug() << errorString();
}
```

Do note that, at the time of writing this chapter, the `QMediaRecorder` class only supports video recording on macOS, Linux, mobile platforms and Windows XP. It doesn't work on Windows 8 and Windows 10 at the moment, but it will be ported over in one of the upcoming versions. The main reason is that Qt is using Microsoft's `DirectShow` API to record video on the Windows platform, but it has since been deprecated from the Windows operating system. Hopefully, by the time you're reading this book, this feature has been completely implemented in Qt for Windows 8 and 10.

If it hasn't, you may use third-party plugins that use `OpenCV` API for recording video, such as the **Qt Media Encoding Library** (**QtMEL**) API, as a temporary solutions. Do note that the code used in QtMEL is completely different than the one we're showing here in this chapter.

 For more information about **QtMEL**, please check out the following link: `http://kibsoft.ru`.

Summary

In this chapter, we have learned how to connect to our camera using Qt. We have also learned how to capture an image or record a video from the camera. In the next chapter, we will learn about the networking module and try and make an instant messenger using Qt!

10
Instant Messaging

One important feature of corporate software is the ability to communicate with staff. Thus, an internal instant messaging system is a crucial part of the software. By incorporating the networking module in Qt, we can easily create a chat system out of it.

In this chapter, we will cover the following topics:

- Qt networking module
- Creating an instant messaging server
- Creating an instant messaging client

Creating an instant messaging system using Qt is a lot easier than you think. Let's get started!

The Qt networking module

In the following section, we will learn about the Qt networking module and how it can help us to achieve server-client communication via the TCP or UDP connection protocols.

Connection protocols

The networking module in Qt is the module that offers both low-level networking functionality, such as TCP and UDP sockets, as well as high-level networking classes for web integration and network communication.

In this chapter, we will use the **TCP** (**Transmission Control Protocol**) internet protocol for our program instead of the **UDP** (**User Datagram Protocol**) protocol. The main difference is that TCP is a connection-oriented protocol that requires all clients to establish a connection to the server before they are able to communicate with each other.

UDP on the other hand is a connectionless protocol that does not require a connection. The client will just send whatever data it needs to send to the destination, without checking if the data has been received by the other end. There are pros and cons for both protocols, but TCP is much more suitable for our sample project. We want to make sure every chat message is being received by the recipient, don't we?

The differences between both protocols are as follows:

- TCP:
    - Connection-oriented protocol
    - Suitable for applications that require high reliability, and it is less critical toward its data transmission time
    - The speed for TCP is slower than UDP
    - Requires acknowledgment of receipt from the receiving client before sending the next data
    - There is an absolute guarantee that the data transferred remains intact and arrives in the same order in which it was sent

- UDP:
    - Connectionless protocol
    - Suitable for applications that need fast, efficient transmission, such as games and VOIP
    - UDP is lightweight and faster than TCP because error recovery is not attempted
    - Also suitable for servers that answer small queries from huge numbers of clients
    - There is no guarantee that the data sent reaches its destination at all as there is no tracking connections and no need for any acknowledgment from the receiving client

Since we are not going for the peer-to-peer connection approach, our chat system will require two different pieces of software—the server program and the client program. The server program will act as the middleman (just like a postman) who receives all the messages from all the users and sends them to the targeted recipients accordingly. The server program will be locked away from the normal users in one of the computers in the server room.

The client program, on the other hand, is the instant messaging software that is used by all the users. This program is the one that is being installed on the users' computers. Users can send their messages using this client program and see the messages sent by others as well. The overall architecture of our messaging system looks something like this:

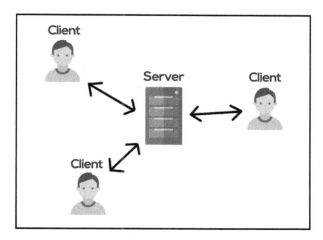

Let's proceed to setting up our project and enabling Qt's networking module! For this project, we will start on the server program before working on the client program.

Setting up a new project

First, create a new **Qt Console Application** project. Then, open up the project file (.pro) and add in the following module:

```
QT += core network
Qt -= gui
```

You should have noticed that this project doesn't have any gui module (we make sure it's explicitly removed) as we don't need any user interface for the server program. That is also the reason why we chose **Qt Console Application** instead of the usual **Qt Widgets Application**.

Actually, that's it—you have successfully added the networking module to your project. In the next section, we will learn how to create the server program for our chat system.

Creating an instant messaging server

In the following section, we will learn how to create an instant messaging server that receives messages sent by the users and redistributes them to their respective recipients.

Creating TCP Server

In this section, we will learn how to create a TCP server that constantly listens to a specific port for incoming messages. For the sake of simplicity, we will just create a global chat room in which every user can see the messages sent by each and every user within the chat room, instead of a one-to-one messaging system with a friend list. You can easily improvise this system to the latter once you have understood how a chat system functions.

First, go to **File** | **New File or Project** and choose **C++ Class** under the **C++** category. Then, name the class as server and select **QObject** as the base class. Make sure the **Include QObject** option is ticked before proceeding to create the custom class. You should have also noticed the absence of mainwindow.ui, mainwindow.h, and mainwindow.cpp. This is because there is no user interface in a console application project.

Once the server class has been created, let's open up server.h and add in the following headers, variables and functions:

```cpp
#ifndef SERVER_H
#define SERVER_H

#include <QObject>
#include <QTcpServer>
#include <QTcpSocket>
#include <QDebug>
#include <QVector>

private:
    QTcpServer* chatServer;
    QVector<QTcpSocket*>* allClients;

public:
    explicit server(QObject *parent = nullptr);
    void startServer();
    void sendMessageToClients(QString message);

public slots:
    void newClientConnection();
    void socketDisconnected();
```

```
void socketReadyRead();
void socketStateChanged(QAbstractSocket::SocketState state);
```

Next, create a function called `startServer()` and add the following code to the function definition in `server.cpp`:

```
void server::startServer()
{
    allClients = new QVector<QTcpSocket*>;

    chatServer = new QTcpServer();
    chatServer->setMaxPendingConnections(10);
    connect(chatServer, SIGNAL(newConnection()), this,
    SLOT(newClientConnection()));

    if (chatServer->listen(QHostAddress::Any, 8001))
    {
        qDebug() << "Server has started. Listening to port 8001.";
    }
    else
    {
        qDebug() << "Server failed to start. Error: " + chatServer-
        >errorString();
    }
}
```

We created a `QTcpServer` object called `chatServer` and made it constantly listen to port `8001`. You can choose any unused port number ranging from `1024` to `49151`. Other numbers outside of this range are usually reserved for common systems, such as HTTP or FTP services, so we better not use them to avoid conflicts. We also created a `QVector` array called `allClients` to store all the connected clients so that we can make use of it later to redirect incoming messages to all users.

We also used the `setMaxPendingConnections()` function to limit the maximum pending connections to 10 clients. You can use this method to keep the number of active clients to a specific amount so that your server's bandwidth is always within its limit. This can ensure good service quality and maintain a positive user experience.

Listening to clients

The `chatServer` will trigger the `newConnection()` signal whenever a client has connected to the server, so we connect that signal to our custom slot function called `newClientConnection()`. The slot function looks like this:

```
void server::newClientConnection()
{
    QTcpSocket* client = chatServer->nextPendingConnection();
    QString ipAddress = client->peerAddress().toString();
    int port = client->peerPort();

    connect(client, &QTcpSocket::disconnected, this,
&server::socketDisconnected);
    connect(client, &QTcpSocket::readyRead, this,
&server::socketReadyRead);
    connect(client, &QTcpSocket::stateChanged, this,
&server::socketStateChanged);

    allClients->push_back(client);

    qDebug() << "Socket connected from " + ipAddress + ":" +
QString::number(port);
}
```

Every new client connected to the server is a `QTcpSocket` object, which can be obtained from the `QTcpServer` object by calling `nextPendingConnection()`. You can obtain information about the client such as its IP address and port number by calling `peerAddress()` and `peerPort()`, respectively. We then store each new client into the `allClients` array for future use. We also connect the client's `disconnected()`, `readyRead()` and `stateChanged()` signals to its respective slot function.

When a client is disconnected from the server, the `disconnected()` signal will be triggered, and subsequently the `socketDisconnected()`, `slot` function will be called. What we are doing in this function is just displaying the message on the server console whenever it happens, and nothing more. You can do anything you like here such as saving the user's offline state to the database and so on. For the sake of simplicity, we will just print out the message on the console window:

```
void server::socketDisconnected()
{
    QTcpSocket* client = qobject_cast<QTcpSocket*>(QObject::sender());
    QString socketIpAddress = client->peerAddress().toString();
    int port = client->peerPort();
```

```
qDebug() << "Socket disconnected from " + socketIpAddress + ":" +
QString::number(port);
}
```

Next, whenever a client is sending in a message to the server, the `readyRead()` signal will be triggered. We have connected the signal to a slot function called `socketReadyRead()` and it looks something like this:

```
void server::socketReadyRead()
{
    QTcpSocket* client = qobject_cast<QTcpSocket*>(QObject::sender());
    QString socketIpAddress = client->peerAddress().toString();
    int port = client->peerPort();

    QString data = QString(client->readAll());

    qDebug() << "Message: " + data + " (" + socketIpAddress + ":" +
    QString::number(port) + ")";

    sendMessageToClients(data);
}
```

In the preceding code, we simply redirect the message to a custom function called `sendMessageToClients()`, which handles passing the message to all connected clients. We will look at how this function works in a minute. We use `QObject::sender()` to get the pointer of the object that emitted the `readyRead` signal and convert it to the `QTcpSocket` class so that we can access its `readAll()` function.

After that, we also connected another signal called `stateChanged()` to the `socketStateChanged()` slot function. The slow function looks like this:

```
void server::socketStateChanged(QAbstractSocket::SocketState state)
{
    QTcpSocket* client = qobject_cast<QTcpSocket*>(QObject::sender());
    QString socketIpAddress = client->peerAddress().toString();
    int port = client->peerPort();

    QString desc;

    if (state == QAbstractSocket::UnconnectedState)
        desc = "The socket is not connected.";
    else if (state == QAbstractSocket::HostLookupState)
        desc = "The socket is performing a host name lookup.";
    else if (state == QAbstractSocket::ConnectingState)
        desc = "The socket has started establishing a connection.";
    else if (state == QAbstractSocket::ConnectedState)
```

```
        desc = "A connection is established.";
    else if (state == QAbstractSocket::BoundState)
        desc = "The socket is bound to an address and port.";
    else if (state == QAbstractSocket::ClosingState)
        desc = "The socket is about to close (data may still be
        waiting to be written).";
    else if (state == QAbstractSocket::ListeningState)
        desc = "For internal use only.";

    qDebug() << "Socket state changed (" + socketIpAddress + ":" +
    QString::number(port) + "): " + desc;
}
```

This function gets triggered whenever a client's network state has changed, such as connected, disconnected, listening, and so on. We will simply print out a relevant message according to its new state so that we can debug our program more easily.

Now, let's look at what the sendMessageToClients() function looks like:

```
void server::sendMessageToClients(QString message)
{
    if (allClients->size() > 0)
    {
        for (int i = 0; i < allClients->size(); i++)
        {
            if (allClients->at(i)->isOpen() && allClients->at(i)-
            >isWritable())
            {
                allClients->at(i)->write(message.toUtf8());
            }
        }
    }
}
```

In the preceding code, we simply loop through the allClients array and pass the message data to all the connected clients.

Lastly, open up main.cpp and add the following code to start our server:

```
#include <QCoreApplication>
#include "server.h"

int main(int argc, char *argv[])
{
    QCoreApplication a(argc, argv);

    server* myServer = new server();
```

```
    myServer->startServer();

    return a.exec();
}
```

Build and run the program now, and you should see something like this:

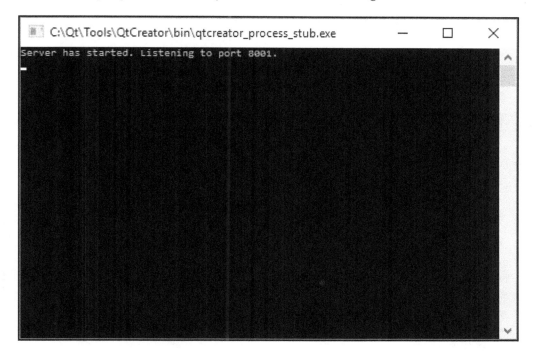

It doesn't look like anything is happening except showing that the server is listening to port `8001`. Don't worry, because we haven't created the client program yet. Let's proceed!

Creating an instant messaging client

In the following section, we will proceed to create our instant messaging client, which the users will be using to send and receive messages.

Designing the user interface

In this section, we will learn how to design the user interface for the instant messaging client and create functionality for it:

1. First, create another Qt project by going to **File | New File or Project**. Then select **Qt Widget Application** under the **Application** category.
2. After the project has been created, open up `mainwindow.ui` and drag a **Line Edit** and **Text Browser** to the window canvas. Then, select the central widget and click the **Lay Out Vertically** button, located on the widget bar above, to apply the vertical layout effect to the widgets:

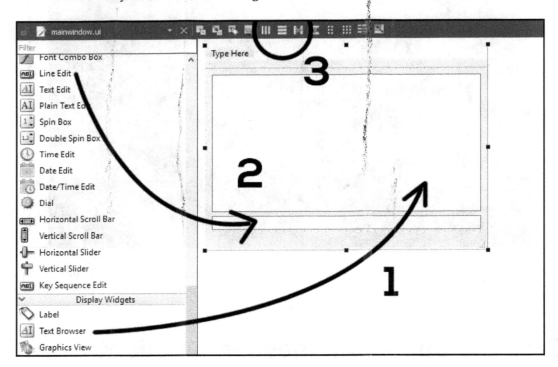

3. After that, place a **Horizontal Layout** at the bottom and put the **Line Edit** into the layout. Then, pull a **Push Button** from the widget box into the **Horizontal Layout** and name it as `sendButton`; we also set its label as `Send`, like this:

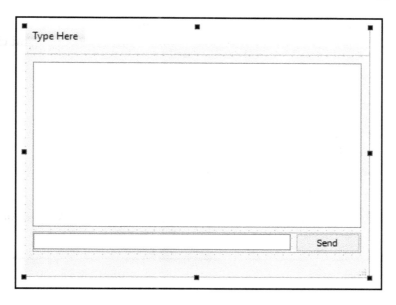

4. Once you're finished, drag and drop another **Horizontal Layout** and place it on top of the text browser. After that, place a **Label**, **Line Edit**, and a **Push Button** into the horizontal layout, like this:

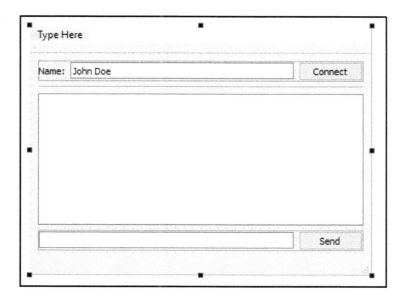

We call the line edit widget `nameInput` and set a default text for it as `John Doe`, just so the user has a default name. Then, we call the push button `connectButton` and change its label to `Connect`.

We have completed the user interface design for a very simple instant messaging program, which will do the following tasks:

1. Connect to a server
2. Let a user set their name
3. Can see messages sent by all users
4. A user can type and send their messages for all to see

Compile and run the project now, you should see your program looking something like this:

Do note that I also changed the window title to `Chat Client` so that it looks slightly more professional. You can do so by selecting the `MainWindow` object at the hierarchy window and change its `windowTitle` property.

In the next section, we will start working on the programming part and implement the features mentioned in the list above.

Implementing chat features

Before we start writing any code, we must first enable the networking module by opening our project file (`.pro`) and add the `network` keyword there:

```
QT += core gui network
```

Next, open up `mainwindow.h` and add the following headers and variables:

```
#ifndef MAINWINDOW_H
#define MAINWINDOW_H

#include <QMainWindow>
#include <QDebug>
#include <QTcpSocket>

private:
    Ui::MainWindow *ui;
    bool connectedToHost;
    QTcpSocket* socket;
```

We set the `connectedToHost` variable to `false` by default in `mainwindow.cpp`:

```
MainWindow::MainWindow(QWidget *parent) :
    QMainWindow(parent),
    ui(new Ui::MainWindow)
{
    ui->setupUi(this);
    connectedToHost = false;
}
```

Once this is done, the first feature we need to implement is the server connection. Open up `mainwindow.ui`, right-click on the **Connect** button, then choose **Go to slot...**, and pick `clicked()`. After that, a slot function will be created for you automatically. Add in the following code to the `SLOT` function:

```
void MainWindow::on_connectButton_clicked()
{
    if (!connectedToHost)
    {
        socket = new QTcpSocket();

        connect(socket, SIGNAL(connected()), this,
        SLOT(socketConnected()));
        connect(socket, SIGNAL(disconnected()), this,
        SLOT(socketDisconnected()));
        connect(socket, SIGNAL(readyRead()), this,
        SLOT(socketReadyRead()));

        socket->connectToHost("127.0.0.1", 8001);
    }
    else
    {
        QString name = ui->nameInput->text();
        socket->write("<font color="Orange">" + name.toUtf8() + " has
        left the chat room.</font>");

        socket->disconnectFromHost();
    }
}
```

What we did in the preceding code was basically check for the `connectedToHost` variable. If the variable is `false` (meaning the client is not connected to the server), create a `QTcpSocket` object called `socket` and make it connect to a host at `127.0.0.1` on port `8801`. The IP address `127.0.0.1` stands for a localhost. Since this is only for testing purposes, we will connect the client to our test server, which is located on the same computer. If you're running the server on another computer, you may change the IP address to a LAN or WAN address, depending on your need.

We also connected the `socket` object to its respective slot functions when `connected()`, `disconnected()`, and `readReady()` signals were triggered. This is exactly the same as the server code, which we did previously. If the client is already connected to the server and the **Connect** (now labeled `Disconnect`) button is clicked, then send a disconnection message to the server and terminate the connection.

Next, we will look at the slot functions, which we connected to the `socket` object in the previous step. The first one is the `socketConnected()` function, which will be called when the client has successfully connected to the server:

```
void MainWindow::socketConnected()
{
    qDebug() << "Connected to server.";

    printMessage("<font color=\"Green\">Connected to server.</font>");

    QString name = ui->nameInput->text();
    socket->write("<font color=\"Purple\">" + name.toUtf8() + " has joined
    the chat room.</font>");

    ui->connectButton->setText("Disconnect");
    connectedToHost = true;
}
```

First, the client will display a `Connected to server.` message on both the application output and the text browser widget. We will see what the `printMessage()` function looks like in a minute. Then, we take the user's name from the input field and incorporate it into a text message and send it to the server so that all users are being notified. Finally, set the **Connect** button's label to `Disconnect`, and set the `connectedToHost` variable to `true`.

After this, let's look at `socketDisconnected()`, which as its name implies, will be called whenever the client is disconnected from the server:

```
void MainWindow::socketDisconnected()
{
    qDebug() << "Disconnected from server.";

    printMessage("<font color=\"Red\">Disconnected from server.</font>");

    ui->connectButton->setText("Connect");
    connectedToHost = false;
}
```

The preceding code is quite straightforward. All it does is show disconnected messages on both the application output and text browser widget, then sets the **Disconnect** button's label to `Connect` and the `connectedToHost` variable to `false`. Do note that since this function will only be called after the client has been disconnected from the server, we can no longer send any message to the server at that point to notify it of the disconnection. You should check for the disconnection at the server side and notify all users accordingly.

Then, there is the `socketReadyRead()` function, which will be triggered whenever the server is sending data to the client. This function is even simpler than the previous ones, as all it does is pass the incoming data to the `printMessage()` function and nothing else:

```
void MainWindow::socketReadyRead()
{
    ui->chatDisplay->append(socket->readAll());
}
```

Finally, let's look at what the `printMessage()` function looks like. Actually, it is just as simple. All it does is to append the message to the text browser and it is done:

```
void MainWindow::printMessage(QString message)
{
    ui->chatDisplay->append(message);
}
```

Last but not least, let's check out how to implement the function for sending messages to the server. Open up `mainwindow.ui`, right-click on the **Send** button, select **Go to slot...**, and choose the `clicked()` option. Once the slot function has been created for you, add the following code to the function:

```
void MainWindow::on_sendButton_clicked()
{
    QString name = ui->nameInput->text();
    QString message = ui->messageInput->text();
    socket->write("<font color="Blue">" + name.toUtf8() + "</font>: " +
    message.toUtf8());

    ui->messageInput->clear();
}
```

First, we take the user's name and combine it with the message. Then, we set the name to a blue color before sending the entire thing to the server by calling `write()`. After that, clear the message input field, and we're done. Since the text browser accepts rich text by default, we can use that to color our text by placing the text within the `<font>` tags.

Compile and run the project now; you should be able to chat among yourselves on different clients! Don't forget to turn on the server before connecting the clients. If everything goes right, you should see something like this:

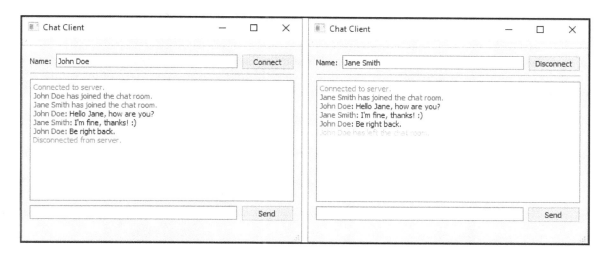

Meanwhile, you should also see all the activities on the server side as well:

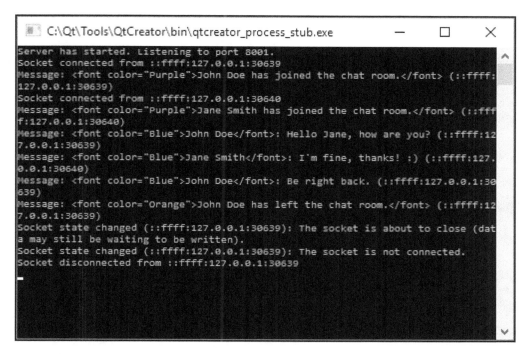

That's it! We have successfully created a simple chat system using Qt. You are welcome to improvise on this and create a fully fledged messaging system!

Summary

In this chapter, we learned how to create an instant messaging system using Qt's networking module. In the following chapter, we will dive into the wonders of graphics rendering using Qt.

11
Implementing a Graphics Editor

Qt provides us with low-level graphics rendering using the `QPainter` class. Qt is capable of rendering both bitmap and vector images. In this chapter, we will learn how to draw shapes using Qt, and finally, create a paint program of our own.

In this chapter, we will cover the following topics:

- Drawing vector shapes
- Saving vector images to an SVG file
- Creating a paint program

Are you ready? Let's get started!

Drawing vector shapes

In the following section, we will learn how to render vector graphics on our Qt application using the QPainter class.

Vector versus bitmap

There are two types of format in computer graphics—bitmap and vector. Bitmap images (also known as raster images) are images that are stored as a series of tiny dots called **pixels**. Each pixel will be assigned a color and gets displayed on screen exactly how it's stored—a one-to-one correspondence between the pixels and what is displayed on the screen.

On the other hand, vector images are not based on bitmap patterns but rather use mathematical formulas to represent lines and curves that can be combined to create geometrical shapes.

The main characteristics of both formats are listed here:

- Bitmap:
    - Usually a larger file size
    - Cannot be enlarged into a higher resolution as the image quality will be affected
    - Used to display complex images with many colors, such as photographs
- Vector:
    - Very small in file size
    - Graphics can be resized without affecting the image quality
    - Only a limited amount of color can be applied to each shape (single color, gradient, or pattern)
    - Complex shapes require high-processing power to be generated

The diagram here compares bitmap and vector graphics:

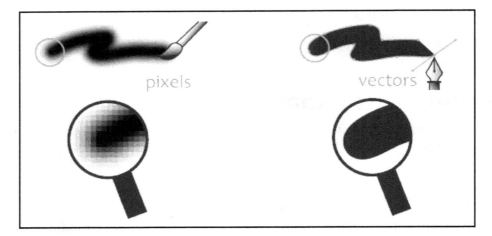

We will focus on learning how to draw vector graphics using Qt in this section, but we will also cover bitmap graphics later in this chapter.

Drawing vector shapes using QPainter

First, create another Qt project by going to **File | New File or Project**. Then select Qt Widget Application under the **Application** category. After the project has been created, open up mainwindow.h and add in the QPainter header:

```
#include <QMainWindow>
#include <QPainter>
```

After that, we also declare a virtual function called paintEvent(), which is a standard event handler in Qt that gets called whenever there is something that needs to be painted, be it a GUI update, a window resize, or when the update() function is being called manually:

```
public:
    explicit MainWindow(QWidget *parent = 0);
    ~MainWindow();
    virtual void paintEvent(QPaintEvent *event);
```

Then, open up mainwindow.cpp and add the paintEvent() function:

```
void MainWindow::paintEvent(QPaintEvent *event)
{
    QPainter painter;
    painter.begin(this);

    // Draw Line
    painter.drawLine(QPoint(50, 60), QPoint(100, 100));

    // Draw Rectangle
    painter.setBrush(Qt::BDiagPattern);
    painter.drawRect(QRect(40, 120, 80, 30));

    // Draw Ellipse
    QPen ellipsePen;
    ellipsePen.setColor(Qt::red);
    ellipsePen.setStyle(Qt::DashDotLine);
    painter.setPen(ellipsePen);
    painter.drawEllipse(QPoint(80, 200), 50, 20);

    // Draw Rectangle
    QPainterPath rectPath;
    rectPath.addRect(QRect(150, 20, 100, 50));
    painter.setPen(QPen(Qt::red, 1, Qt::DashDotLine, Qt::FlatCap,
    Qt::MiterJoin));
    painter.setBrush(Qt::yellow);
    painter.drawPath(rectPath);
```

```
    // Draw Ellipse
    QPainterPath ellipsePath;
    ellipsePath.addEllipse(QPoint(200, 120), 50, 20);
    painter.setPen(QPen(QColor(79, 106, 25), 5, Qt::SolidLine,
    Qt::FlatCap, Qt::MiterJoin));
    painter.setBrush(QColor(122, 163, 39));
    painter.drawPath(ellipsePath);

    painter.end();
}
```

If you build the program now, you should see the following:

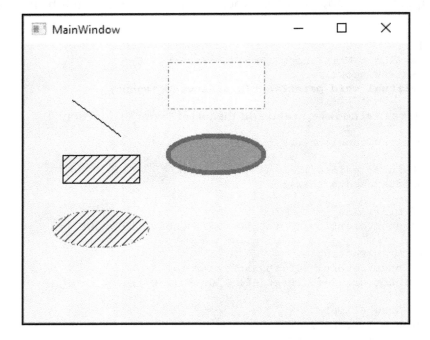

The preceding code is really long. Let's break it down, so it's easier for you to understand. Whenever the paintEvent() is called (usually it will be called once when the window needs to be drawn), we call QPainter::begin() to tell Qt we're about to draw something, and we call QPainter::end() when we're done. Therefore, the code that draws graphics will be contained within QPainter::begin() and QPainter::end().

Let's look at the following steps:

1. The first thing that we drew was a straight line, which is quite simple – just call `QPainter::drawLine()` and insert the start point and end point values to the function. Do note that the coordinate system used by Qt is in pixel format. Its origin starts from the top-left corner of the application window and increases to the right and bottom directions, depending on the *x* and *y* values. The increment of the *x* value moves the position to the right direction, while the increment of the *y* value moves the position to the bottom direction.

2. Next, draw a rectangle that has a hatching pattern within the shape. This time, we called `QPainter::setBrush()` to set the pattern, before calling `drawRect()`.

3. After that, we drew an elliptical shape with a dash-dot outline and hatching pattern within the shape. Since we have already set the pattern in the previous step, we don't have to do it again. Instead, we use the **QPen** class to set the outline style before calling `drawEllipse()`. Just remember that in Qt's terms, a brush is used to define the inner color or pattern of a shape, while a pen is used to define the outline.

4. The next two shapes are basically similar to the previous ones; we only changed different colors and patterns so that you can see the distinctions between them and the previous examples.

Drawing text

Additionally, you can also draw text using the `QPainter` class. All you need to do is to call `QPainter::setFont()` to set the font properties before calling `QPainter::drawText()`, like so:

```
QPainter painter;
painter.begin(this);

// Draw Text
painter.setFont(QFont("Times", 14, QFont::Bold));
painter.drawText(QPoint(20, 30), "Testing");

// Draw Line
painter.drawLine(QPoint(50, 60), QPoint(100, 100))
```

The `setFont()` function is optional as you will get a default font if you don't specify it. Once you're done, build and run the program. You should see the word **Hello World!** displayed in the window:

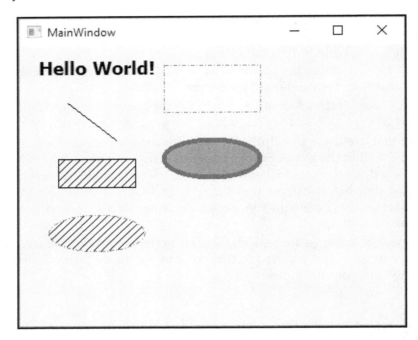

As you can see here, the vector shapes are basically generated by Qt in real time, which looks perfectly fine regardless of how you rescale the window and change its aspect ratio. If you're rendering a bitmap image instead, its visual quality may get degraded when its rescaled along with the window or changed in its aspect ratio.

Saving vector images to an SVG File

Beside drawing vector graphics, Qt allows us to save these graphics into a vector image file, called the **SVG (Scalable Vector Graphics)** file format. The SVG format is an open format used by a lot of software, including web browsers to display vector graphics. In fact, Qt can also read SVG files and render them on screen, but we'll skip that for now. Let's check out how we can save our vector graphics to an SVG file!

This example continues from where we left it in the previous section. Therefore, we don't have to create a new Qt project and can just stick to the previous one.

First, let's add a menu bar to our main window if it doesn't already have one. Then, open `mainwindow.ui`, and in the form editor, right-click on the **MainWindow** object on the hierarchy window and select **Create Menu Bar**:

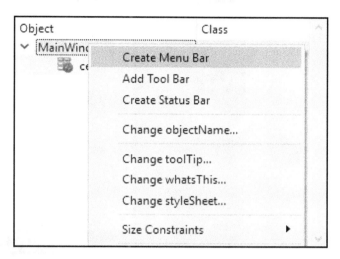

Once you're done, add **File** to the menu bar, followed by **Save as SVG** underneath it:

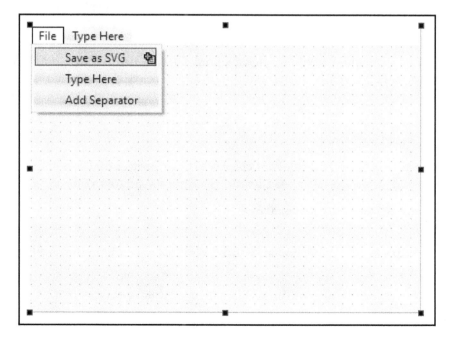

Then, go to the **Action Editor** at the bottom and right-click on the menu option we just added and select **Go to slot...**:

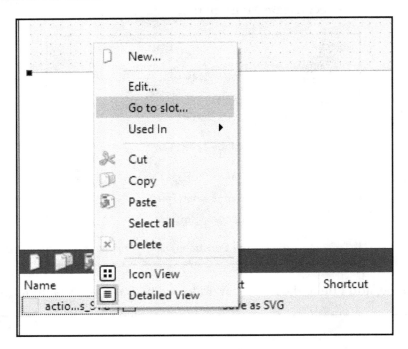

A window will pop up and ask you to pick a signal. Choose **triggered()** and click **OK**. A new slot function will be created for you in `mainwindow.cpp`. Before we open up `mainwindow.cpp`, let's open up our `project file(.pro)` and add the following `svg` module:

```
QT += core gui svg
```

The `svg` keyword tells Qt to add relevant classes to your project that can help you to handle the SVG file format. Then, we also need to add two more headers to our `mainwindow.h`:

```
#include <QtSvg/QSvgGenerator>
#include <QFileDialog>
```

After that, open up `mainwindow.cpp` and add the following code to the slot function we just added in the previous step:

```
void MainWindow::on_actionSave_as_SVG_triggered()
{
    QString filePath = QFileDialog::getSaveFileName(this, "Save SVG",
```

```
"", "SVG files (*.svg)");

    if (filePath == "")
        return;

    QSvgGenerator generator;
    generator.setFileName(filePath);
    generator.setSize(QSize(this->width(), this->height()));
    generator.setViewBox(QRect(0, 0, this->width(), this->height()));
    generator.setTitle("SVG Example");
    generator.setDescription("This SVG file is generated by Qt.");

    paintAll(&generator);
}
```

In the preceding code, we used `QFileDialog` to let the users choose where they want to save their SVG file. Then, we used the `QSvgGenerator` class to export the graphics into an SVG file. Finally, we called the `paintAll()` function, which is a custom function we are going to define in the next step.

Actually, we need to modify the existing `paintAll()` method and put our rendering code into it. Then, pass the `QSvgGenerator` object into the function input as the paint device:

```
void MainWindow::paintAll(QSvgGenerator *generator)
{
    QPainter painter;

    if (generator)
        painter.begin(generator);
    else
        painter.begin(this);

    // Draw Text
    painter.setFont(QFont("Times", 14, QFont::Bold));
    painter.drawText(QPoint(20, 30), "Hello World!");
```

Therefore, our `paintEvent()` now simply looks like this in `mainwindow.cpp`:

```
void MainWindow::paintEvent(QPaintEvent *event)
{
    paintAll();
}
```

The procedure here might seem a little confusing, but what it does is basically call the `paintAll()` function to draw all the graphics once when the window is being created, and then you call `paintAll()` again when you want to save the graphics to an SVG file.

The only difference is the paint device – one is the main window itself, which we use as the drawing canvas, and for the latter one we will pass the `QSvgGenerator` object as the paint device, which will save the graphics into an SVG file instead.

Build and run the program now, click **File | Save SVG File**, you should be able to save the graphics into an SVG file. Try and open up the file with the web browser and see what it looks like:

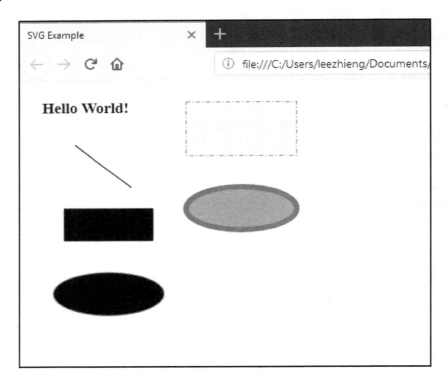

It seems like my web browser (Firefox) does not support the hatching pattern, but other things turn out to be fine. Since vector graphics are generated by the program and the shapes are not stored in the SVG file (only the mathematical formula and its variables are stored), you may need to make sure the features that you use are supported by the user's platform.

In the next section, we will learn how to create our own paint program and draw bitmap images using it!

Creating a paint program

In the following section, we will move over to the realm of pixels and learn how to create a paint program using Qt. Users will be able to express their creativity by using different sizes and colors of the brush to draw pixel images!

Setting up a user interface

Again, for this example, we will create a new Qt Widget Application. After that, open up `mainwindow.ui` and add a menu bar to the main window. Then, add the following options to the menu bar:

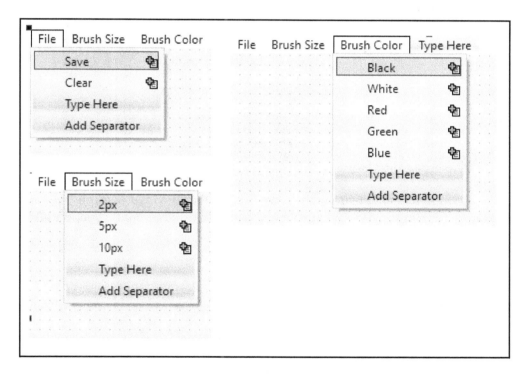

We have three menu items on the menu bar—**File**, **Brush Size**, and **Brush Color**. Under the **File** menu are functions for saving the canvas into a bitmap file, as well as clearing the entire canvas. The **Brush Size** category contains different options for the brush size; last but not least, the **Brush Color** category contains several options for setting the brush color.

You can go for something more *paint-like* or *Photoshop-like* for the GUI design, but we will use this for now for the sake of simplicity.

Once you're done with all that, open up `mainwindow.h` and add the following headers on top:

```
#include <QMainWindow>
#include <QPainter>
#include <QMouseEvent>
#include <QFileDialog>
```

After that, we also declare a few virtual functions, like so:

```
public:
    explicit MainWindow(QWidget *parent = 0);
    ~MainWindow();
    virtual void mousePressEvent(QMouseEvent *event);
    virtual void mouseMoveEvent(QMouseEvent *event);
    virtual void mouseReleaseEvent(QMouseEvent *event);
    virtual void paintEvent(QPaintEvent *event);
    virtual void resizeEvent(QResizeEvent *event);
```

Besides the `paintEvent()` function which we used in the previous example, we can also add a few more for handling mouse events and window resize events. Then, we also add the following variables to our `MainWindow` class:

```
private:
    Ui::MainWindow *ui;
    QImage image;
    bool drawing;
    QPoint lastPoint;
    int brushSize;
    QColor brushColor;
```

After that, let's open up `mainwindow.cpp` and start with the class constructor:

```
MainWindow::MainWindow(QWidget *parent) :
    QMainWindow(parent),
    ui(new Ui::MainWindow)
{
    ui->setupUi(this);
```

```
image = QImage(this->size(), QImage::Format_RGB32);
image.fill(Qt::white);

drawing = false;
brushColor = Qt::black;
brushSize = 2;
}
```

We need to first create a `QImage` object, which acts as the canvas, and set its size to match our window size. Then, we set the default brush color to black and its default size to 2. After that, we will look at each of the event handlers and how they work.

First, let's take a look at the `paintEvent()` function, which we also used in the vector graphics, example. This time, all it does is call `QPainter::drawImage()` and render the `QImage` object (our image buffer) on top of our main window:

```
void MainWindow::paintEvent(QPaintEvent *event)
{
    QPainter canvasPainter(this);
    canvasPainter.drawImage(this->rect(), image, image.rect());
}
```

Next, we will look at the `resizeEvent()` function, which gets triggered whenever the main window is being resized by the user. To avoid image stretching, we must resize our image buffer to match the new window size. This can be achieved by creating a new `QImage` object and setting its size the same as the resized main window, then copying the previous **QImage**'s pixel information and placing it at the exact same spot on the new image buffer.

This means that your image will be cropped if the window size is smaller than the drawing, but at least the canvas will not be stretched and distort the image when the window is resized. Let's take a look at the code:

```
void MainWindow::resizeEvent(QResizeEvent *event)
{
    QImage newImage(event->size(), QImage::Format_RGB32);
    newImage.fill(qRgb(255, 255, 255));

    QPainter painter(&newImage);
    painter.drawImage(QPoint(0, 0), image);
    image = newImage;
}
```

Next, we will look at the mouse event handlers, which we use to apply colors on the canvas. First, the `mousePressEvent()` function, which will be triggered when we start pressing our mouse button (left mouse button in this case). We are still not drawing anything at this point, but set the **drawing** Boolean to `true` and save our cursor position to the `lastPoint` variable:

```
void MainWindow::mousePressEvent(QMouseEvent *event)
{
    if (event->button() == Qt::LeftButton)
    {
        drawing = true;
        lastPoint = event->pos();
    }
}
```

Then, here is the `mouseMoveEvent()` function, which will be called when the mouse cursor is moved:

```
void MainWindow::mouseMoveEvent(QMouseEvent *event)
{
    if ((event->buttons() & Qt::LeftButton) && drawing)
    {
        QPainter painter(&image);
        painter.setPen(QPen(brushColor, brushSize, Qt::SolidLine,
        Qt::RoundCap, Qt::RoundJoin));
        painter.drawLine(lastPoint, event->pos());

        lastPoint = event->pos();
        this->update();
    }
}
```

In the preceding code, we check if indeed we are moving the mouse while holding the left mouse button. If we are, then we draw a line from the previous cursor position to our current cursor position. Then, we save the current cursor position to the `lastPoint` variable and call `update()` to notify Qt to trigger the `paintEvent()` function.

Finally, when we release the left mouse button, the `mouseReleaseEvent()` will be called. We simply set the drawing variable to `false`, and we're done:

```
void MainWindow::mouseReleaseEvent(QMouseEvent *event)
{
    if (event->button() == Qt::LeftButton)
    {
        drawing = false;
    }
}
```

If we build the program and run it now, we should be able to start drawing something on our little paint program:

Even though we can draw something now, it's all the same brush size and with the same color all the time. That's a little boring! Let's right-click on each of the options on the **Brush Size** category in the main menu and select **Go to slot...**, then pick the **triggered()** option and then press **OK**. Qt will then create the slot functions accordingly for us, and what we need to do within these functions is basically change the **brushSize** variable, like so:

```
void MainWindow::on_action2px_triggered()
{
    brushSize = 2;
```

```
}

void MainWindow::on_action5px_triggered()
{
    brushSize = 5;
}

void MainWindow::on_action10px_triggered()
{
    brushSize = 10;
}
```

The same goes for all the options under the **Brush Color** category. This time, we set the
`brushColor` variable accordingly:

```
void MainWindow::on_actionBlack_triggered()
{
    brushColor = Qt::black;
}

void MainWindow::on_actionWhite_triggered()
{
    brushColor = Qt::white;
}

void MainWindow::on_actionRed_triggered()
{
    brushColor = Qt::red;
}

void MainWindow::on_actionGreen_triggered()
{
    brushColor = Qt::green;
}

void MainWindow::on_actionBlue_triggered()
{
    brushColor = Qt::blue;
}
```

If you build and run the program again, you will be able to draw your images with a
variety of settings for your brush:

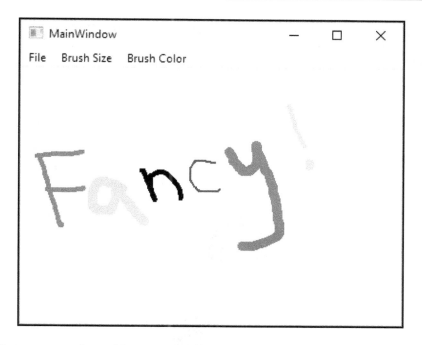

Other than that, we can also add an existing bitmap image to our canvas so that we can draw on top of it. Let's say I have a penguin image in the form of a PNG image (called `tux.png`), we can then add the following code to the class constructor:

```
MainWindow::MainWindow(QWidget *parent) :
    QMainWindow(parent),
    ui(new Ui::MainWindow)
{
    ui->setupUi(this);

    image = QImage(this->size(), QImage::Format_RGB32);
    image.fill(Qt::white);

    QImage tux;
    tux.load(qApp->applicationDirPath() + "/tux.png");
    QPainter painter(&image);
    painter.drawImage(QPoint(100, 100), tux);

    drawing = false;
    brushColor = Qt::black;
    brushSize = 2;
}
```

The preceding code basically opens up the image file and moves it to position 100 x 100 before drawing the image onto our image buffer. Now we can see a penguin on the canvas whenever we start the program:

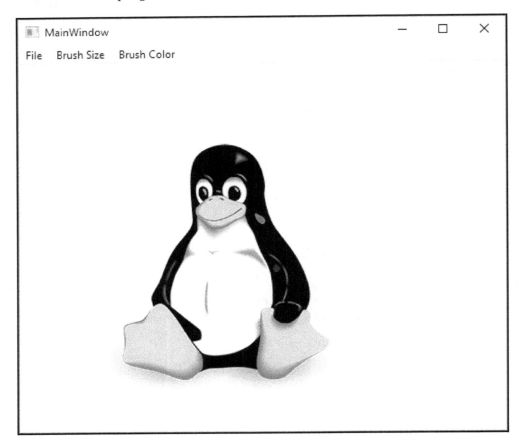

Next, we will look at the **Clear** option under **File**. When the user clicks on this option on the menu bar, we use the following code to clear the entire canvas (including the penguin) and start all over again:

```
void MainWindow::on_actionClear_triggered()
{
    image.fill(Qt::white);
    this->update();
}
```

Finally, when the user clicks on the **Save** option under **File**, we open up a file dialog and let the users save their artwork into a bitmap file. In the following code, we filter out the image formats and only allow the users to save PNG and JPEG formats:

```
void MainWindow::on_actionSave_triggered()
{
    QString filePath = QFileDialog::getSaveFileName(this, "Save Image",
"", "PNG (*.png);;JPEG (*.jpg *.jpeg);;All files (*.*)");

    if (filePath == "")
        return;

    image.save(filePath);
}
```

That's it, we have successfully created a simple paint program from scratch using Qt! You may even combine the knowledge learned from this chapter with the previous chapter to create an online collaborative whiteboard! The only limitation is your creativity. Lastly, I would like to say thank you to all the readers for creating the following masterpiece, using our newly created paint program:

Summary

In this chapter, we have learned how to draw vector and bitmap graphics, and subsequently we created our very own paint program using Qt. In the following chapter, we will look into the aspects of creating a program that transfers and stores our data on to the cloud.

12
Cloud Storage

In the previous chapter, we learned how to draw images on-screen using Qt. In this chapter, however, we are going learn something totally different, which is setting up our own file server and linking it to our Qt application.

In this chapter, we will cover the following topics:

- Setting up the FTP server
- Displaying the file list on the list view
- Uploading files to the FTP server
- Downloading files from the FTP server

Let's get started!

Setting up the FTP server

In the following section, we will learn how to set up an FTP server, which stores all the files uploaded by a user and allows them to download them at any time. This section is not related to Qt, so if you already have a running FTP server, please skip this part and proceed to the next section of this chapter.

Introducing FTP

FTP is an acronym for **File Transfer Protocol**. FTP is used to transfer files from one computer to another on a network, usually over the internet. FTP is just one of the many different forms of cloud storage technology, but it is also a simple one that you can easily set up on your own computer.

There are many different FTP servers that have been developed by different groups of people for a specific operating system. In this section of the chapter, we will learn how to set up a FileZilla server, which runs on the Windows operating system. If you're running other operating systems such as GNU, Linux, or macOS, there are many other FTP server programs that you can use, such as VSFTP and Pure-FTPd.

On Debian, Ubuntu, or other similar variants of Linux, running `sudo apt-get install vsftpd` on the Terminal will install and configure an FTP server. On macOS, open **System Preferences** from the Apple menu and select **Sharing.** Then, click on the **Service** tab and select **FTP access**. Finally, click the **Start** button to start running the FTP server.

If you already have a running FTP server, please skip to the next section, in which we'll start learning about C++ programming.

Downloading FileZilla

FileZilla is really easy to set up and configure. It provides a fully functional and easy-to-use user interface and doesn't require any prior experience to operate it. The first thing we need to do is download FileZilla. We will do it as follows:

1. Open up your browser and hop over to `https://filezilla-project.org`. You will see two download buttons located at the **Home** page.
2. Click on **Download FileZilla Server** and it will bring us to the download page:

3. Once you're at the download page, click on the **Download FileZilla Server** button and start downloading the software. We're not going to use the **FileZilla Client**, so you don't have to download that. Once everything is ready, let's proceed to install the software.

4. Like most Windows software, the installation process is very straightforward. Keep everything as default and click **Next** all the way until the installation process begins. It will take a couple of minutes at most for the installation to complete.

5. Once it's completed, click on the **Close** button and we're done!:

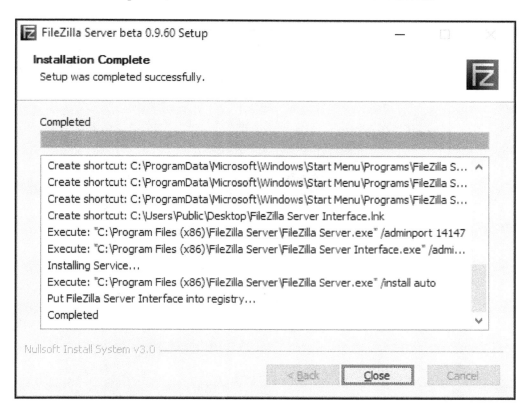

Setting up FileZilla

Once you have installed FileZilla, the control panel will most likely open by itself.

1. Since this is the first time you have launched FileZilla, it will ask you to set up the server. Keep the server IP address as `127.0.0.1` (which means **localhost**) and the admin port to `14147`.

2. Key in your desired password for administrating the server and check on the **Always connect to this server** option. Press **Connect** and the FTP server will now start up! This is shown in the following screenshot:

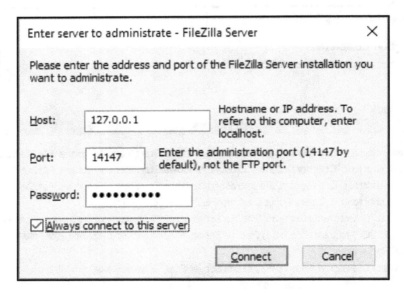

3. After the FTP server has started running, we need to create a user account. Click on the fourth icon from the left to open up the **Users** dialog:

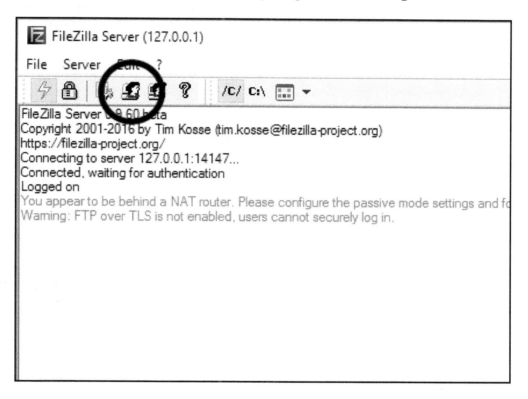

4. Then, under the **General** page, click on the **Add** button located at the right side of the window. Create an account by setting a username and press **OK**.

5. We don't have to set the user to any group for now, as user groups are only useful when you have many users that have the same privilege settings since it is easier to change all users settings at once or move users to different groups. Once you have created the user, check on the **Password** option and key in your desired password. It is always a good practice to put the password on your FTP account:

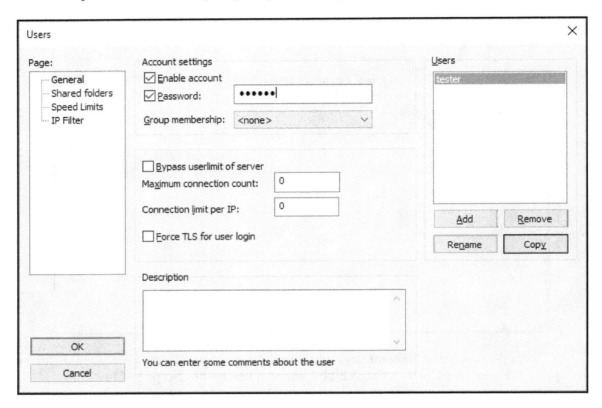

6. After that, we will proceed to the **Shared folders** page and add a shared directory for our newly created user.

7. Make sure the **Delete** and **Append** options are checked so that files that have the same name can be replaced. We will be using that for updating our file list in a moment:

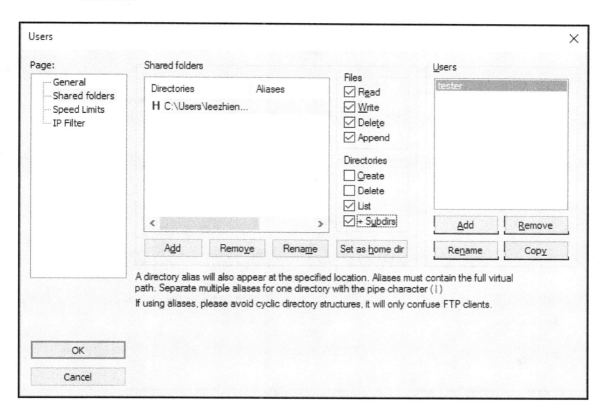

8. If you click on the third icon from the left, the **FileZilla Server options** dialog will appear. You can basically configure everything here to suit your needs. For instance, if you don't want to use the default port number `21`, you can simply change it on the options window, under the **General settings** page:

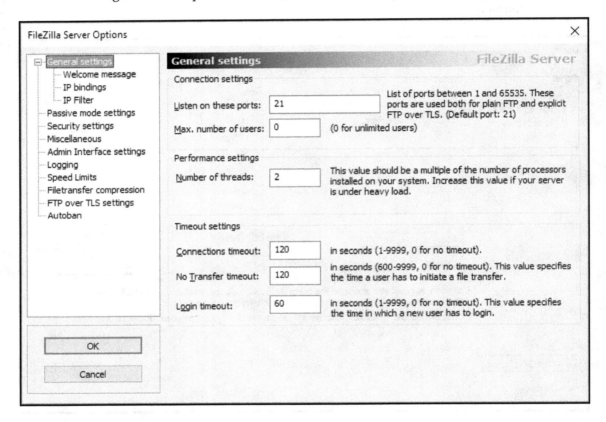

9. You can also set the speed limit for all users or a specific user under the **Speed Limits** page. This can prevent your server from becoming low performance when many users are downloading huge files at the same time:

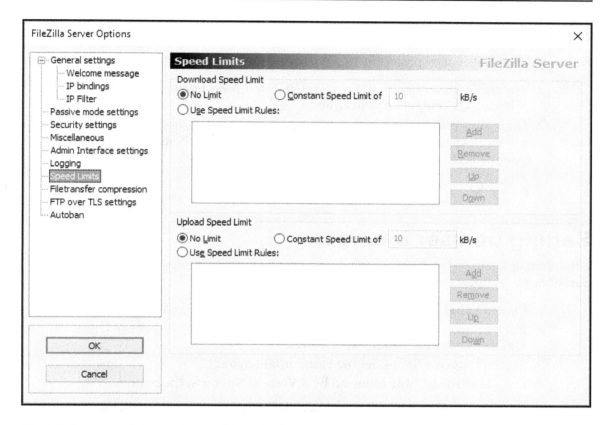

Next, let's proceed to create our Qt project!

Displaying the file list on the list view

In the previous section, we successfully set up a FTP server and kept it running. In the following section, we will learn how to create an FTP client program that displays the file list, uploads files to the FTP server, and finally downloads files from it.

Setting up a project

As usual, let's create a new project using **Qt Creator**. The following steps will help:

1. We can create a new project by going to **File | New File or Project** and selecting **Qt Widgets Application**.
2. Once your project has been created, open your project (.pro) file and add the network keyword so that Qt knows that you need the **Networking module** in your project:

   ```
   QT += core gui network
   ```

Setting up user interface

After that, open up mainwindow.ui and perform the following steps to design the upper part of our user interface for uploading files:

1. Place a **Label** that says **Upload File:** on top of every other widget.
2. Put a horizontal layout and two **Push Buttons** alongside it that say **Open** and **Upload**, under the **Label** respectively.
3. Place a **Progress Bar** under the **Horizontal Layout**.
4. Put a **Horizontal Line** followed by a **Vertical Spacer** at the bottom:

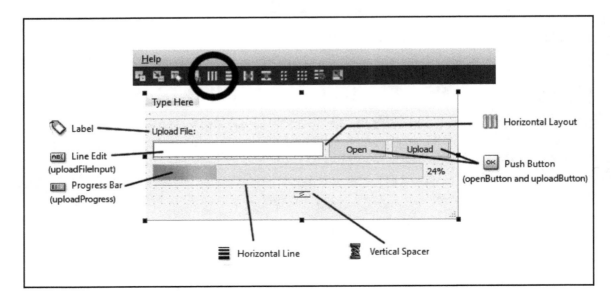

Next, we're going to construct the bottom part of the user interface that is used for downloading files:

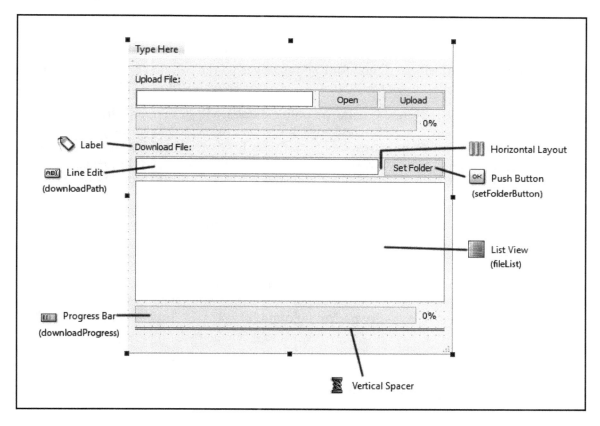

This time, our user interface is very similar to the upper part, except we have added a **List View** before the second **Progress Bar** for displaying the file list. We put everything on the same page for this example program so that it's simpler and less confusing to explain.

Displaying the file list

Next, we will learn how to save and display the file list on the FTP server. Actually, the FTP server does provide the file list by default, and Qt was able to display it using the `qtftp` module back in older versions. However, since Version 5, Qt has completely dropped the `qtftp` module and this feature no longer exists.

If you're still interested in the old `qtftp` module, you can still obtain its source code on GitHub by visiting the following link: `https://github.com/qt/qtftp`

In Qt, we use the `QNetworkAccessManager` class to communicate with our FTP server so features that are specifically designed for FTP no longer work. But, don't worry, we will look into some other alternative methods to achieve the same result.

The best method, in my opinion, is using an online database to store the file list and its information (file size, format, status, and so on). If you're interested in learning how to connect your Qt application to a database, please refer to Chapter 3, *Database Connection*. However, for the sake of simplicity, we will use another method that works just fine but is less secure—by saving the file names directly on a text file and storing it on the FTP server.

 If you're doing a serious project for your client or company, please do not use this method. Check out Chapter 3, *Database Connection*, and learn to use an actual database instead.

Alright, just assume that there is no other way but to use the text file; how are we going to do that? It's very simple: create a text file called `files.txt` and place it into the FTP directory we just created at the very beginning of this chapter.

Writing the code

Next, open up `mainwindow.h` and add the following headers:

```cpp
#include <QMainWindow>
#include <QDebug>
#include <QNetworkAccessManager>
#include <QNetworkRequest>
#include <QNetworkReply>
#include <QFile>
#include <QFileInfo>
#include <QFileDialog>
#include <QListWidgetItem>
#include <QMessageBox>
```

After that, add in the following variables and functions:

```
private:
    Ui::MainWindow *ui;
    QNetworkAccessManager* manager;

    QString ftpAddress;
    int ftpPort;
    QString username;
    QString password;

    QNetworkReply* downloadFileListReply;
    QNetworkReply* uploadFileListReply;

    QNetworkReply* uploadFileReply;
    QNetworkReply* downloadFileReply;

    QStringList fileList;
    QString uploadFileName;
    QString downloadFileName;

public:
    void getFileList();
```

Once you are done with the previous step, open up `mainwindow.cpp` and add the following code to the class constructor:

```
MainWindow::MainWindow(QWidget *parent) :
    QMainWindow(parent),
    ui(new Ui::MainWindow)
{
    ui->setupUi(this);

    manager = new QNetworkAccessManager(this);

    ftpAddress = "ftp://127.0.0.1/";
    ftpPort = 21;
    username = "tester"; // Put your FTP user name here
    password = "123456"; // Put your FTP user password here

    getFileList();
}
```

What we did was basically initialize the `QNetworkAccessManager` object and set up the variables that store our FTP server's information, since we will be repeated using it many times in later steps. After that, we will call the `getFileList()` function to start downloading `files.txt` from our FTP server. The `getFileList()` function looks like the following:

```cpp
void MainWindow::getFileList()
{
    QUrl ftpPath;
    ftpPath.setUrl(ftpAddress + "files.txt");
    ftpPath.setUserName(username);
    ftpPath.setPassword(password);
    ftpPath.setPort(ftpPort);

    QNetworkRequest request;
    request.setUrl(ftpPath);

    downloadFileListReply = manager->get(request);
    connect(downloadFileListReply, &QNetworkReply::finished, this,
    &MainWindow::downloadFileListFinished);
}
```

We used a `QUrl` object to store the information about our server and the location of the file we're trying to download, and then fed it to a `QNetworkRequest` object before sending it off by calling `QNetworkAccessManager::get()`. Since we have no idea when all the files will get downloaded completely, we make use of Qt's SIGNAL and SLOT mechanisms.

We connected the `finished()` signal that comes from our `downloadFileListReply` pointer (which points to a `QNetworkReply` object in `mainwindow.h`) and linked it to the slot function `downloadFileListFinished()`, which we defined as follows:

```cpp
void MainWindow::downloadFileListFinished()
{
    if(downloadFileListReply->error() != QNetworkReply::NoError)
    {
        QMessageBox::warning(this, "Failed", "Failed to load file
        list: " + downloadFileListReply->errorString());
    }
    else
    {
        QByteArray responseData;
        if (downloadFileListReply->isReadable())
        {
            responseData = downloadFileListReply->readAll();
```

```
        }

        // Display file list
        ui->fileList->clear();
        fileList = QString(responseData).split(",");

        if (fileList.size() > 0)
        {
                for (int i = 0; i < fileList.size(); i++)
                {
                        if (fileList.at(i) != "")
                        {
                                ui->fileList->addItem(fileList.at(i));
                        }
                }
        }
    }
}
```

The code is a bit long, so I have broken down the function into the following steps:

1. If any problems occur during the download, display a message box that tells us the nature of the problem.
2. If everything went nicely and the download has completed, we will try and read the data by calling `downloadFileListReply` | `readAll()`.
3. Then, clear the **List Widget** and start parsing the content of the text file. The format we used here is very simple; we only used a comma symbol to separate each file name: `filename1, filename2, filename, . . .` It is important that we do not do this in the actual project.
4. Once we have called `split(",")` to split the string into a string list, do a `for` loop and display each file name on the **List Widget**.

To test whether the preceding code works or not, create a text file called `files.txt` and add the following text to the file:

```
filename1,filename2,filename3
```

Then, place the text file to your FTP directory and run your project. You should be able to see it appear like this on the application:

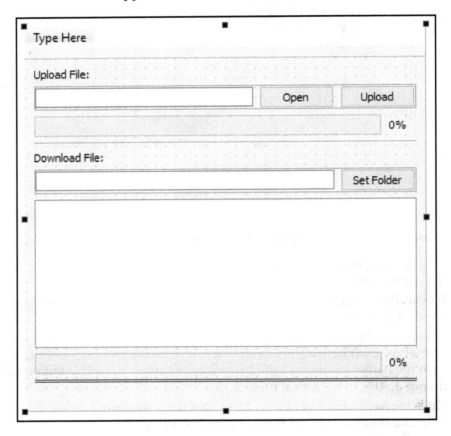

Once it is working, we can clear away the content of the text file and proceed to our next section.

Uploading files to the FTP server

Since we don't have any files in our FTP directory yet (except the file list), let's write the code to allow us to upload our first file.

1. First, open `mainwindow.ui` and right click on the **Open** button. Then, select **Go to slot** and select the **clicked()** option:

2. A `slot` function will be automatically created for you. Then, add the following code to the function to open up the file selector window for our users to select their desired file for upload:

```
void MainWindow::on_openButton_clicked()
{
    QString fileName = QFileDialog::getOpenFileName(this, "Select
    File", qApp->applicationDirPath());
    ui->uploadFileInput->setText(fileName);
}
```

3. After that, repeat this step and do the same for the **Upload** button. This time, the code for its `slot` function looks something like the following:

```
void MainWindow::on_uploadButton_clicked()
{
    QFile* file = new QFile(ui->uploadFileInput->text());
    QFileInfo fileInfo(*file);
    uploadFileName = fileInfo.fileName();

    QUrl ftpPath;
    ftpPath.setUrl(ftpAddress + uploadFileName);
    ftpPath.setUserName(username);
    ftpPath.setPassword(password);
    ftpPath.setPort(ftpPort);

    if (file->open(QIODevice::ReadOnly))
    {
            ui->uploadProgress->setEnabled(true);
            ui->uploadProgress->setValue(0);

            QNetworkRequest request;
            request.setUrl(ftpPath);

            uploadFileReply = manager->put(request, file);
            connect(uploadFileReply,
            SIGNAL(uploadProgress(qint64,qint64)), this,
            SLOT(uploadFileProgress(qint64,qint64)));
            connect(uploadFileReply, SIGNAL(finished()), this,
            SLOT(uploadFileFinished()));
    }
    else
    {
            QMessageBox::warning(this, "Invalid File", "Failed to open
            file for upload.");
    }
}
```

The code looks a bit long, so let's break it down:

1. We used the `QFile` class for opening the file that we want to upload (the file path is taken from `ui->uploadFileInput->text()`). If the file doesn't exist, display a message box to inform the user.
2. Then, we fill in the information of our FTP server and the upload destination into a `QUrl` object before feeding it to a `QNetworkRequest` object.
3. After that, we start reading the content of our file and provide it to the `QNetworkAccessManager::put()` function.

4. Since we have no idea when the file will get uploaded completely, we used the SIGNAL and SLOT mechanisms provided by Qt. We linked the uploadProgress() and finished() signals to our two custom slot function called uploadFileProgress() and uploadFileFinised(), respectively.

The slot function uploadFileProgress() will tell us the current progress of our upload, and therefore we can use it to set the progress bar:

```
void MainWindow::uploadFileProgress(qint64 bytesSent, qint64 bytesTotal)
{
    qint64 percentage = 100 * bytesSent / bytesTotal;
    ui->uploadProgress->setValue((int) percentage);
}
```

Meanwhile, the uploadFileFinished() function will be triggered when the file has been completely uploaded:

```
void MainWindow::uploadFileFinished()
{
    if(uploadFileReply->error() != QNetworkReply::NoError)
    {
        QMessageBox::warning(this, "Failed", "Failed to upload file: "
        + uploadFileReply->errorString());
    }
    else
    {
        QMessageBox::information(this, "Success", "File successfully
        uploaded.");
    }
}
```

We are not done with the preceding function yet. Since a new file has been added to the FTP server, we must update the existing file list and replace the files.txt file stored within the FTP directory. Since the code is slightly longer, we will break the code into several parts, which all are occurring before showing the **File successfully uploaded** message box.

1. First, let's check whether the newly uploaded file has already existed within our file list (replacing an old file on the FTP server). If it does, then we can skip the entire thing; otherwise, append the filename to our fileList string list, as shown in the following code:

```
// Add new file to file list array if not exist yet
bool exists = false;
if (fileList.size() > 0)
{
```

```
        for (int i = 0; i < fileList.size(); i++)
        {
                if (fileList.at(i) == uploadFileName)
                {
                        exists = true;
                }
        }
}

if (!exists)
{
    fileList.append(uploadFileName);
}
```

2. After that, create a temporary text file (`files.txt`) in our application's directory and save the new file list in the text file:

```
// Create new files.txt
QString fileName = "files.txt";
QFile* file = new QFile(qApp->applicationDirPath() + "/" +
fileName);
file->open(QIODevice::ReadWrite);
if (fileList.size() > 0)
{
    for (int j = 0; j < fileList.size(); j++)
    {
            if (fileList.at(j) != "")
            {
                    file->write(QString(fileList.at(j) + ",").toUtf8());
            }
    }
}
file->close();
```

3. Finally, we use the `QFile` class to open the text file we just created, and we upload it again to the FTP server to replace the old file list:

```
// Re-open the file
QFile* newFile = new QFile(qApp->applicationDirPath() + "/" +
fileName);
if (newFile->open(QIODevice::ReadOnly))
{
    // Update file list to server
    QUrl ftpPath;
    ftpPath.setUrl(ftpAddress + fileName);
    ftpPath.setUserName(username);
    ftpPath.setPassword(password);
```

```
    ftpPath.setPort(ftpPort);

    QNetworkRequest request;
    request.setUrl(ftpPath);
    uploadFileListReply = manager->put(request, newFile);
    connect(uploadFileListReply, SIGNAL(finished()), this,
SLOT(uploadFileListFinished()));
    file->close();
}
```

4. Again, we use the `SIGNAL` and `SLOT` mechanisms so that we are notified when the file list has been uploaded. The `slot` function `uploadFileListFinished()` looks something like the following:

```
void MainWindow::uploadFileListFinished()
{
    if(uploadFileListReply->error() != QNetworkReply::NoError)
    {
        QMessageBox::warning(this, "Failed", "Failed to update
file list: " + uploadFileListReply->errorString());
    }
    else
    {
        getFileList();
    }
}
```

5. We basically just call `getFileList()` again after we have updated the file list into the FTP server. If you build and run the project now, you should be able to upload your first file to your local FTP server, hooray!

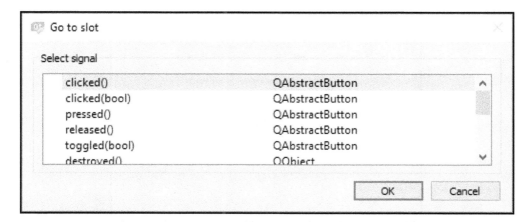

Downloading files from the FTP server

Now that we have successfully uploaded our first file to the FTP server, let's create the feature for downloading the file back onto our computer!

1. First, open `mainwindow.ui` again and right-click on the **Set Folder** button. Select **Go to slot...** and pick the **clicked()** signal to create a `slot` function. The `slot` function is very simple; it will just open up a file selection dialog, but this time it will only let the user select a folder instead since we provided it with a `QFileDialog::ShowDirsOnly` flag:

```
void MainWindow::on_setFolderButton_clicked()
{
    QString folder = QFileDialog::getExistingDirectory(this,
tr("Open Directory"), qApp->applicationDirPath(),
QFileDialog::ShowDirsOnly);
    ui->downloadPath->setText(folder);
}
```

2. Then, right click on the **List Widget** and select **Go to slot...** This time around, we will pick the `itemDoubleClicked(QListWidgetItem*)` option instead:

3. When the user double-clicks on an item in the **List Widget**, the following function will be triggered, which kick-starts the download. The file name can be obtained from the `QListWidgetItem` object by calling `item->text()`:

```cpp
void MainWindow::on_fileList_itemDoubleClicked(QListWidgetItem
*item)
{
    downloadFileName = item->text();

    // Check folder
    QString folder = ui->downloadPath->text();
    if (folder != "" && QDir(folder).exists())
    {
        QUrl ftpPath;
        ftpPath.setUrl(ftpAddress + downloadFileName);
        ftpPath.setUserName(username);
        ftpPath.setPassword(password);
        ftpPath.setPort(ftpPort);

        QNetworkRequest request;
        request.setUrl(ftpPath);

        downloadFileReply = manager->get(request);
        connect(downloadFileReply,
        SIGNAL(downloadProgress(qint64,qint64)), this,
        SLOT(downloadFileProgress(qint64,qint64)));
        connect(downloadFileReply, SIGNAL(finished()), this,
        SLOT(downloadFileFinished()));
    }
    else
    {
        QMessageBox::warning(this, "Invalid Path", "Please set the
        download path before download.");
    }
}
```

4. Just like what we did in the `upload` function, we also used the `SIGNAL` and `SLOT` mechanisms here to obtain the progression of the download process as well as the completed signal. The `slot` function `downloadFileProgress()` will be called during the download process, and we used that to set the value of our second progress bar:

```cpp
void MainWindow::downloadFileProgress(qint64 byteReceived,qint64
bytesTotal)
{
    qint64 percentage = 100 * byteReceived / bytesTotal;
```

```
        ui->downloadProgress->setValue((int) percentage);
    }
```

5. Then, the `slot` function `downloadFileFinished()` will be called when the file has been completely downloaded. What we're going to do after that is read all the data of the file and save it to our desired directory:

```
void MainWindow::downloadFileFinished()
{
    if(downloadFileReply->error() != QNetworkReply::NoError)
    {
        QMessageBox::warning(this, "Failed", "Failed to download
        file: " + downloadFileReply->errorString());
    }
    else
    {
        QByteArray responseData;
        if (downloadFileReply->isReadable())
        {
            responseData = downloadFileReply->readAll();
        }

        if (!responseData.isEmpty())
        {
            // Download finished
            QString folder = ui->downloadPath->text();
            QFile file(folder + "/" + downloadFileName);
            file.open(QIODevice::WriteOnly);
            file.write((responseData));
            file.close();

            QMessageBox::information(this, "Success", "File
            successfully downloaded.");
        }
    }
}
```

6. Build the program now and you should be able to download any files listed on the file list!:

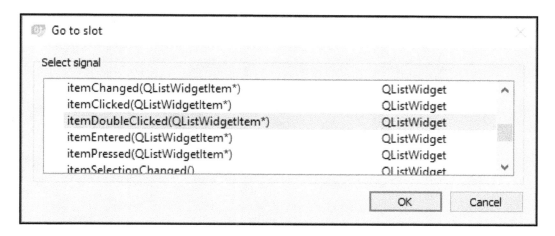

Summary

In this chapter, we learned how to create our own cloud storage client using Qt's Networking module. In the following chapter, we will learn more about the multimedia module and create our own multimedia player from scratch using Qt.

13
Multimedia Viewers

In the previous chapter, we learned how to upload and download files through cloud storage. Now, in this chapter, we are going to learn how to open these files, specifically media files such as images, music, and videos, using Qt's multimedia module.

In this chapter, we will cover the following topics:

- Revisiting the multimedia module
- The image viewer
- The music player
- The video player

Let's get started!

Revisiting the multimedia module

In this chapter, we will be using the multimedia module again, which we covered previously in Chapter 9, *The Camera Module*. However, this time we will be using some other parts of the module, so I thought it would be a good idea to dissect the module and see what's inside it.

Dissecting the module

The multimedia module is a really large module that consists of many different parts, that provide very different features and functionality. The main categories are as follows:

- Audio
- Video
- Camera
- Radio

Do note that classes that handle image formats, such as `QImage`, `QPixmap`, and so on, are not a part of the multimedia module but rather the GUI module. This is because they are an important part of the GUI that cannot be separated. Despite this, we will still cover the `QImage` class within this chapter.

Under each category are subcategories that look something like the following:

- Audio:
    - Audio output
    - Audio recorder
- Video:
    - Video recorder
    - Video player
    - Video playlist
- Camera:
    - Camera viewfinder
    - Camera image capture
    - Camera video recorder
- Radio:
    - Radio tuner (for devices that support analog radio)

Each of the classes is designed to fulfill a different purpose. For example, the `QSoundEffect` is used for playing low latency audio files (such as WAV files). `QAudioOutput`, on the other hand, outputs raw audio data to a specific audio device, which gives you low-level control over your audio output. Finally, the `QMediaPlayer` is a high-level audio (and video) player that supports many different high-latency audio formats. You must understand the differences between all the classes before choosing the right one for your project.

The multimedia module in Qt is such a huge beast that often confuses newcomers, but can be advantageous if you know which to choose from. Another issue with the multimedia module is that it may or may not work on your target platform. This is because underneath all these classes are native implementations for specific platforms. If a particular platform does not support a feature, or there is not yet an implementation for it, then you won't be able to use those functionalities.

For more information regarding the different classes provided by Qt's multimedia module, please visit the following link:
https://doc.qt.io/qt-5.10/qtmultimedia-index.html

The image viewer

Digital images have become an important aspect of our daily life. Whether it's a selfie, prom night photo, or a funny meme, we spend a lot of our time looking at digital images. In the following section, we will learn how to create our own image viewer using Qt and C++.

Designing a user interface for the image viewer

Let's get started with creating our first multimedia program. In this section, we will create an image viewer, which, as its name implies, opens up an image file and displays it on the window:

1. Let's open up **Qt Creator** and create a new **Qt Widgets Application project**.
2. After that, open up `mainwindow.ui` and add a `Label` (name it as `imageDisplay`) to the central widget, which will serve as the canvas for rendering our image. Then, add a layout to the **centralWidget** by selecting it and pressing **Layout Vertically**, located on top of the canvas:

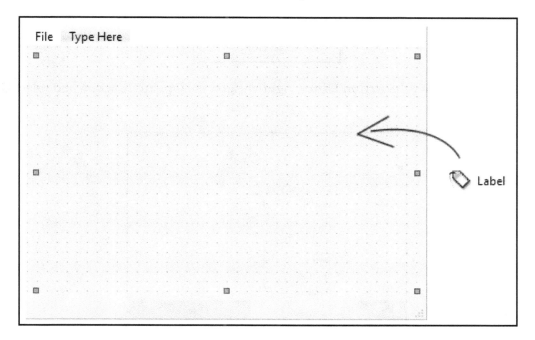

3. You can remove the tool bar and status bar to give space to the `Label`. Also, set the layout margins of the central widget to `0`:

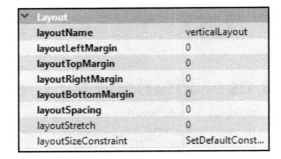

4. After that, double-click on the menu bar and add a **File** action, followed by **Open File** underneath it:

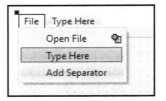

5. Then, under the **Action Editor**, right-click on the **Open File** action and select **Go to slot...**:

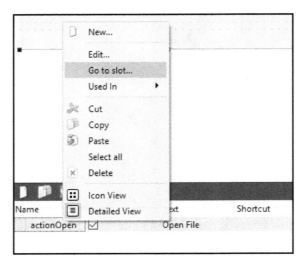

6. A window will pop out and ask you to pick a signal, so choose **triggered()** and click **OK**:

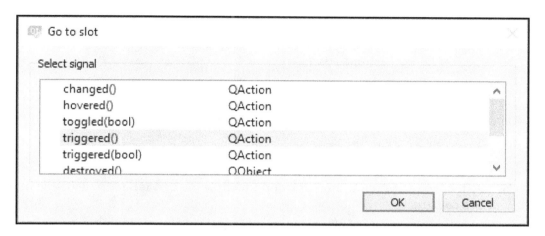

A `slot` function will be created for you automatically, but we will keep that for the next section. We are done with the user interface, and it is really that simple. Next, let's move on and start writing our code!

Writing C++ code for image viewers

Let's get started by using the following steps:

1. First, open up `mainwindow.h` and add the following headers:

```
#include <QMainWindow>
#include <QFileDialog>
#include <QPixmap>
#include <QPainter>
```

2. Then, add the following variable, called `imageBuffer`, which will serve as the pointer that points to the actual image data before rescaling. Then, add the functions as well:

```
private:
    Ui::MainWindow *ui;
    QPixmap* imageBuffer;

public:
    void resizeImage();
    void paintEvent(QPaintEvent *event);

public slots:
    void on_actionOpen_triggered();
```

3. Next, open up `mainwindow.cpp` and initialize the `imageBuffer` variable in the class constructor:

```
MainWindow::MainWindow(QWidget *parent) :
    QMainWindow(parent),
    ui(new Ui::MainWindow)
{
    ui->setupUi(this);
    imageBuffer = nullptr;
}
```

4. After that, add the following code to the `slot` function Qt created for us in the previous section:

```
void MainWindow::on_actionOpen_triggered()
{
    QString fileName = QFileDialog::getOpenFileName(this, "Open
Image File", qApp->applicationDirPath(), "JPG (*.jpg *.jpeg);;PNG
(*.png)");

    if (!fileName.isEmpty())
    {
        imageBuffer = new QPixmap(fileName);
        resizeImage();
    }
}
```

5. The preceding code basically opens up the file-selection dialog, and it creates a QPixmap object with the selected image file. After all that is done, it will call the resizeImage() function, which looks like the following code:

```cpp
void MainWindow::resizeImage()
{
    if (imageBuffer != nullptr)
    {
        QSize size = ui->imageDisplay->size();
        QPixmap pixmap = imageBuffer->scaled(size,
            Qt::KeepAspectRatio);

        // Adjust the position of the image to the center
        QRect rect = ui->imageDisplay->rect();
        rect.setX((this->size().width() - pixmap.width()) / 2);
        rect.setY((this->size().height() - pixmap.height()) / 2);

        QPainter painter;
        painter.begin(this);
        painter.drawPixmap(rect, pixmap,
ui->imageDisplay->rect());
        painter.end();
    }
}
```

What the resizeImage() function does is simply copy the image data from the imageBuffer variable and resize the image to fit the window size before displaying it on the window's canvas. You could be opening an image that is way larger than your screen resolution, and we don't want the image to get cropped when opening such a large image file.

The reason why we use the imageBuffer variable is so that we can keep a copy of the original data and not affect the image quality by resizing it many times.

Lastly, we also call this resizeImage() function within the paintEvent() function. Whenever the main window is being resized or restored from a minimized state, paintEvent() will automatically get called, and so will the resizeImage() function, shown as follows:

```cpp
void MainWindow::paintEvent(QPaintEvent *event)
{
    resizeImage();
}
```

That's it. If you build and run the project now, you should get a pretty neat image viewer that looks like the following:

The music player

In the following section, we will learn how to build our own custom music player using Qt and C++.

Designing a user interface for music players

Let's move on to the next project. In this project, we will be building an audio player using Qt. Perform the following steps:

1. As with the previous project, we will be creating a `Qt Widgets Application` project.
2. Open up the `project file (.pro)`, and add in the `multimedia` module:

   ```
   QT += core gui multimedia
   ```

3. We added the `multimedia` text so that Qt includes classes related to the multimedia module in our project. Next, open up `mainwindow.ui`, and refer to the following screenshot to construct the user interface:

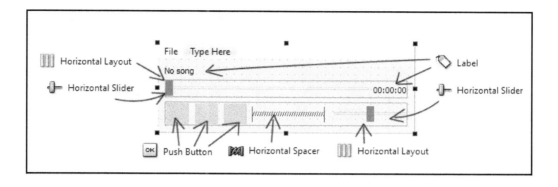

We basically added a **Label** at the top, followed by a **Horizontal Slider** and another **Label** to show the current time of the audio. After that, we added three **Push Buttons** at the bottom for the **Play** button, **Pause** button, and **Stop** button. Located at the right-hand side of these buttons is another **Horizontal Layout** that controls the audio volume.

As you can see, all the **Push Buttons** have no icon for now, and it's very confusing which button is for what purpose.

1. To add icons to the buttons, let's go to **File** | **New File or Project** and select **Qt Resource File** under the **Qt** category. Then, create a prefix called `icons`, and add the icon images to the prefix:

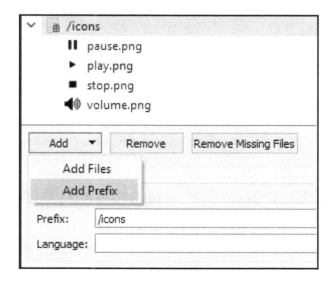

2. After that, add those icons to the **Push Button** by setting its icon property and selecting **Choose Resource...**. Then, set the `pixmap` property of the label, located beside the **volume** slider, as the volume icon:

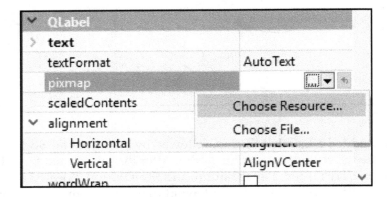

3. After you have added the icons to the **Push Button** and **Label**, the user interface should look a lot better:

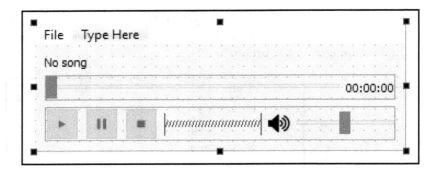

We're done with the user interface; let's move on to the programming part!

Writing C++ code for music players

To write the C++ code for music players, perform the following steps:

1. First and foremost, open up `mainwindow.h` and add the following headers:

```
#include <QMainWindow>
#include <QDebug>
```

```
#include <QFileDialog>
#include <QMediaPlayer>
#include <QMediaMetaData>
#include <QTime>
```

2. After that, add the `player` variable, which is a `QMediaPlayer` pointer. Then, declare the functions that we're going to define later:

```
private:
    Ui::MainWindow *ui;
    QMediaPlayer* player;

public:
    void stateChanged(QMediaPlayer::State state);
    void positionChanged(qint64 position);
```

3. Next, open up `mainwindow.cpp` and initialize the player variable:

```
MainWindow::MainWindow(QWidget *parent) :
    QMainWindow(parent),
    ui(new Ui::MainWindow)
{
    ui->setupUi(this);

    player = new QMediaPlayer(this);
    player->setVolume(ui->volume->value());
    connect(player, &QMediaPlayer::stateChanged, this,
&MainWindow::stateChanged);
    connect(player, &QMediaPlayer::positionChanged, this,
&MainWindow::positionChanged);
}
```

The `QMediaPlayer` class is the main class that is used by our application to play any audio file loaded by it. Thus, we need to know the state of the audio playing and its current position. We can get this information by connecting its `stateChanged()` and `positionChanged()` signals to our custom `slot` functions.

4. The `stateChanged()` signal allows us to obtain information about the current state of the audio playing. Then, we enable and disable the **Push Button** accordingly:

```
void MainWindow::stateChanged(QMediaPlayer::State state)
{
    if (state == QMediaPlayer::PlayingState)
    {
```

```
                    ui->playButton->setEnabled(false);
                    ui->pauseButton->setEnabled(true);
                    ui->stopButton->setEnabled(true);
            }
            else if (state == QMediaPlayer::PausedState)
            {
                    ui->playButton->setEnabled(true);
                    ui->pauseButton->setEnabled(false);
                    ui->stopButton->setEnabled(true);
            }
            else if (state == QMediaPlayer::StoppedState)
            {
                    ui->playButton->setEnabled(true);
                    ui->pauseButton->setEnabled(false);
                    ui->stopButton->setEnabled(false);
            }
    }
```

5. As for the `positionChanged()` and `slot` functions, we use them to set the timeline slider, as well as the timer display:

```
    void MainWindow::positionChanged(qint64 position)
    {
        if (ui->progressbar->maximum() != player->duration())
                ui->progressbar->setMaximum(player->duration());

        ui->progressbar->setValue(position);

        int seconds = (position/1000) % 60;
        int minutes = (position/60000) % 60;
        int hours = (position/3600000) % 24;
        QTime time(hours, minutes,seconds);
        ui->durationDisplay->setText(time.toString());
    }
```

6. Once you're done, open up `mainwindow.ui` and right-click on each of the **Push Buttons**, and select **Go to slot...** followed by selecting the `clicked()` signal. This will generate a `slot` function for each of the **Push Buttons**. The code for these `slot` functions is very simple:

```
    void MainWindow::on_playButton_clicked()
    {
        player->play();
    }

    void MainWindow::on_pauseButton_clicked()
    {
```

```
    player->pause();
}

void MainWindow::on_stopButton_clicked()
{
    player->stop();
}
```

7. After that, right-click on both of the **Horizontal Sliders**, and select **Go to slot...** followed by choosing the `sliderMoved()` signal, and click **OK**:

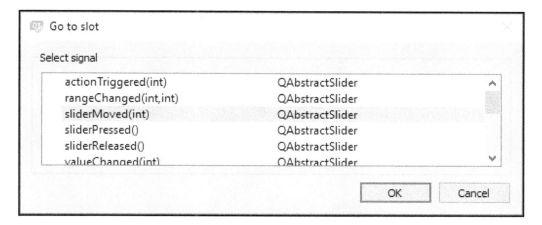

8. The `sliderMoved()` signal will be called whenever the user drags the slider to change its position. We need to send this position to the media player and tell it to adjust the audio volume or change the current audio position. Do be cautious not to set the default position of your volume slider to zero. Consider the following code:

```
void MainWindow::on_volume_sliderMoved(int position)
{
    player->setVolume(position);
}

void MainWindow::on_progressbar_sliderMoved(int position)
{
    player->setPosition(position);
}
```

9. Then, we need to add **File** and **Open File** actions to the menu bar, just like we did in the previous example project.

10. Then, right-click on the **Open File** action in the **Action Editor** and select **Go to slot...** After that, select `triggered()`, and let Qt generate a `slot` function for you. Add the following code to the `slot` function for audio file selection:

```
void MainWindow::on_actionOpen_File_triggered()
{
    QString fileName = QFileDialog::getOpenFileName(this,
        "Select Audio File", qApp->applicationDirPath(),
        "MP3 (*.mp3);;WAV (*.wav)");
    QFileInfo fileInfo(fileName);

    player->setMedia(QUrl::fromLocalFile(fileName));

    if (player->isMetaDataAvailable())
    {
        QString albumTitle = player-
        >metaData(QMediaMetaData::AlbumTitle).toString();
        ui->songNameDisplay->setText("Playing " + albumTitle);
    }
    else
    {
        ui->songNameDisplay->setText("Playing " +
            fileInfo.fileName());
    }

    ui->playButton->setEnabled(true);
    ui->playButton->click();
}
```

The preceding simply opens up a file-selection dialog that only accepts MP3 and WAV files. You can add other formats too if you wish, but the supported formats vary between platforms; therefore, you should test it to make sure the format you want to use is supported.

After that, it will send the selected audio file to the media player for preloading. Then, we try to get the music's title from the metadata and display it on the `Labelwidget`. However, this feature (obtaining metadata) may or may not be supported on your platform, so just in case it won't show up, we replace it with the audio file name. Lastly, we enable the play button and automatically start playing the music.

That's it. If you build and run the project now, you should be able to get a simple but fully functional music player!

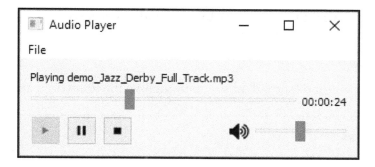

The video player

In the previous section, we have learned how to create an audio player. In this chapter, we will further improvise our program and create a video player using Qt and C++.

Designing a user interface for video players

The next example is that of the video player. Since QMediaPlayer also supports video output, we can use the same user interface and C++ code from the previous audio player example, and just make some minor changes to it.

1. First, open project file (.pro) and add in another keyword, called multimediawidgets:

   ```
   QT += core gui multimedia multimediawidgets
   ```

2. Then, open up mainwindow.ui and add a **Horizontal Layout** (name it as movieLayout) above the timeline slider. After that, right-click on the layout and select **Morph into | QFrame**. We then set its **sizePolicy** property to **Expanding, Expanding**:

⌄ sizePolicy	[Expanding, Exp...
Horizontal Policy	Expanding
Vertical Policy	Expanding

3. After that, we set the QFrame's background to black color by setting its `styleSheet` property, like so:

```
background-color: rgb(0, 0, 0);
```

4. The user interface should look something like the following, and we're done:

Writing C++ code for video players

To write the C++ code for video players, we perform the following steps:

1. For `mainwindow.h`, there aren't many changes to it. All we need to do is to include `QVideoWidget` in the header:

```
#include <QMainWindow>
#include <QDebug>
#include <QFileDialog>
```

```
#include <QMediaPlayer>
#include <QMediaMetaData>
#include <QTime>
#include <QVideoWidget>
```

2. Then, open `mainwindow.cpp`. We must define a `QVideoWidget` object and set it as the video output target, before adding it to the layout of the `QFrame` object we just added in the previous step:

```
MainWindow::MainWindow(QWidget *parent) :
    QMainWindow(parent),
    ui(new Ui::MainWindow)
{
    ui->setupUi(this);

    player = new QMediaPlayer(this);

    QVideoWidget* videoWidget = new QVideoWidget(this);
    player->setVideoOutput(videoWidget);
    ui->movieLayout->addWidget(videoWidget);

    player->setVolume(ui->volume->value());
    connect(player, &QMediaPlayer::stateChanged, this,
&MainWindow::stateChanged);
    connect(player, &QMediaPlayer::positionChanged, this,
&MainWindow::positionChanged);
}
```

3. In the `slot` function thatgets called when the **Open File** action has been triggered, we simply change the file-selection dialog to accept only MP4 and MOV formats. You can add in other video formats too if you wish:

```
QString fileName = QFileDialog::getOpenFileName(this, "Select Movie
File", qApp->applicationDirPath(), "MP4 (*.mp4);;MOV (*.mov)");
```

That's it. The rest of the code is literally the same as the audio player example. The main difference with this example is that we defined the video output widget, and Qt will handle the rest for us.

If we build and run the project now, we should be getting a really slick video player, like what you see here:

On a windows system, there was a case where the video player would throw an error. This problem is similar to the one reported here: `https://stackoverflow.com/questions/32436138/video-play-returns-directshowplayerservicedoseturlsource-unresolved-error-cod`
To resolve this error, simply download and install the K-Lite_Codec_Pack which you can find here: `https://www.codecguide.com/download_k-lite_codec_pack_basic.htm`. After this, the video should play like a charm!

Summary

In this chapter, we have learned how to create our own multimedia players using Qt. What comes next is something quite different from our usual topics. In the following chapter, we will learn how to use QtQuick and QML to create touchscreen-friendly, mobile-friendly, and graphics-oriented applications.

14
Qt Quick and QML

In this chapter, we are going to learn something very different from the rest of the chapters in this book. Qt consists of two different methods for developing an application. The first method is Qt Widgets and C++, which we have covered in all previous chapters. The second method is using Qt Quick controls and the QML scripting language, which we will be covering in this chapter.

In this chapter, we will cover the following topics :

- Introduction to Qt Quick and QML
- Qt Quick Widgets and Controls
- Qt Quick Designer
- Qt Quick Layouts
- Basic QML Scripting

Are you ready? Let's get started!

Introduction to Qt Quick and QML

In the following section, we will learn what Qt Quick and QML are, and how we can make use of them to develop Qt applications without the need for writing C++ code.

Introducing Qt Quick

Qt Quick is a module in Qt that provides a whole set of user-interface engines and language infrastructure for developing touch-oriented and visual-oriented applications. Instead of using the usual Qt Widgets for user-interface design, developers who choose Qt Quick will be using the Qt Quick objects and controls instead.

Furthermore, developers will be writing their code using the QML language, which has similar syntax to **JavaScript**, rather than writing in C++ code. You can, however, use the C++ API provided by Qt to extend the QML application by cross-calling each language's functions (calling C++ functions in QML, and vice versa).

Developers can choose which method they prefer for developing their applications by choosing the right option when creating the project. Instead of choosing the usual **Qt Widgets Application** option, developers can pick **Qt Quick Application**, which tells **Qt Creator** to create different starting files and settings for your project that empowers the **Qt Quick** modules:

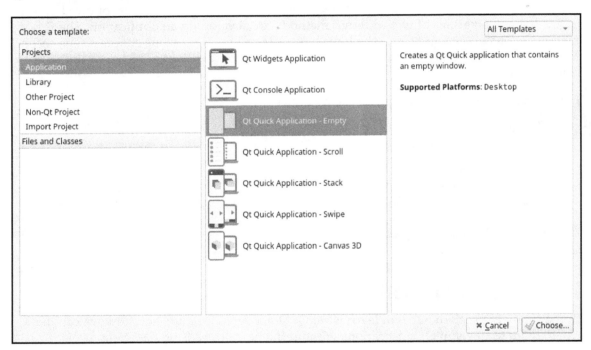

When you're creating a **Qt Quick Application** project, **Qt Creator** will ask you to choose the **Minimal required Qt version** for your project:

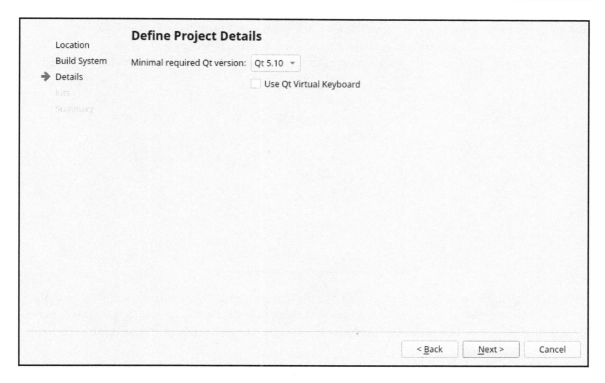

Once you have selected a Qt version, **Qt Quick Designer** will determine which features to enable and which widgets will appear on the **QML Types** window. We will talk more about those in later sections.

Introducing QML

QML (**Qt Modeling Language**) is a user-interface markup language for designing touch-friendly user interfaces, similar to how CSS works on HTML. Unlike **C++** or **JavaScript**, which are both imperative languages, **QML** is a declarative language. In declarative programming, you only express the logic in your script without describing its control flow. It simply tells the computer what to do, instead of how to do it. Imperative programing, however, requires statements to specify actions.

When you open up your newly created Qt Quick project, you will see `main.qml` and `MainForm.ui.qml` in your project, instead of the usual `mainwindow.h` and `mainwindow.cpp` files. You can see this in the project directory in the following screenshot:

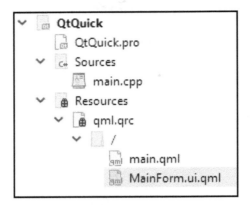

This is because the entire project will be mainly running on QML instead of C++. The only C++ file you will see is `main.cpp`, and all that does is load the `main.qml` file during the application startup. The code that does this in `main.cpp` is shown in the following code:

```
int main(int argc, char *argv[])
{
    QGuiApplication app(argc, argv);

    QQmlApplicationEngine engine;
    engine.load(QUrl(QStringLiteral("qrc:/main.qml")));
    if (engine.rootObjects().isEmpty())
        return -1;

    return app.exec();
}
```

You should have realized that there are two types of QML files, one with the extension `.qml`, and another with extension `.ui.qml`. Even though they are both running on the same syntax and so forth, they serve a very different purpose in your project.

First, the .ui.qml file (with an extra .ui at the beginning) serves as the declarative file for Qt Quick-based user interface design. You can edit a .ui.qml file, using the Qt Quick Designer visual editor, and easily design your application's GUI. You can also add your own code to the file, but there are some limitations on what code they can contain, especially those related to logic code. When you run your Qt Quick application, the Qt Quick engine will read through all the information stored in the .ui.qml file and construct the user interface accordingly, which is very similar to the .ui file used in Qt Widgets applications.

Then, we have another file with only the .qml extension. This file is only used for constructing the logic and functionality in your Qt Quick application, much like the .h and .cpp files used in the Qt Widget application. These two different formats separate the visual definitions of your application from its logic blocks. This allows the developer to apply the same logic code to different user interface templates. You cannot open a .qml file using Qt Quick Designer, since it is not used for GUI declaration. .qml files are written by developers by hand, and they have no restrictions on the QML language features they use.

Let's look at the differences with both of these QML files by first opening up MainForm.ui.qml. By default, **Qt Creator** will open up the user interface designer (Qt Quick Designer); however, let's move over to code-editing mode by pressing the **Edit** button on the left panel:

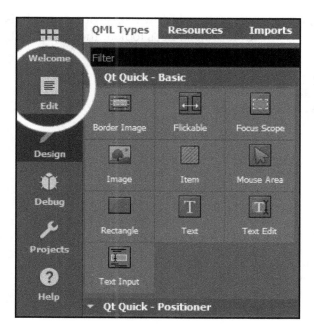

Then, you will be able to see the QML script that forms the user interface you just saw in the design mode. Let's analyze this code to see how QML works compared to C++. The first thing you see in the `MainForm.ui.qml` is this line of code:

```
import QtQuick 2.6
```

This is quite straightforward; we need to import the `Qt Quick` module with the appropriate version number. Different Qt Quick versions may have different functionalities, and support different widget controls. Sometimes, even the syntax could be slightly different. Please make sure you pick the right version for your project, and that it supports the features you need. If you don't know which version to use, do consider the latest version.

Next, we will see different GUI objects (which we call QML types) being declared between two curly braces. The first one that we see is a `Rectangle` type:

```
Rectangle {
    property alias mouseArea: mouseArea
    property alias textEdit: textEdit

    width: 360
    height: 360
    ...
```

The `Rectangle` type, in this case, is the window background, much like the central widget used in the Qt Widget Application project. Let's look at the other QML types that are under the `Rectangle`:

```
MouseArea {
    id: mouseArea
    anchors.fill: parent
}

TextEdit {
    id: textEdit
    text: qsTr("Enter some text...")
    verticalAlignment: Text.AlignVCenter
    anchors.top: parent.top
    anchors.horizontalCenter: parent.horizontalCenter
    anchors.topMargin: 20
    Rectangle {
        anchors.fill: parent
        anchors.margins: -10
        color: "transparent"
        border.width: 1
    }
```

```
    }
```

The `MousArea` type, as its name implies, is an invincible shape that detects mouse clicks and touch events. You can basically turn anything into a button by placing a `MouseArea` on top of it. After that, we also have a `TextEdit` type, which acts exactly like a `Line Edit` widget in a Qt Widget Application.

You may have noticed that there are two properties in the `Rectangle` declaration that carry the `alias` keyword. These two properties expose the `MouseArea` and `TextEdit` types, and allow other QML scripts to interact with them, which we will learn how to do next.

Now, open up `main.qml` and look at its code:

```
import QtQuick 2.6
import QtQuick.Window 2.2

Window {
    visible: true
    width: 640
    height: 480
    title: qsTr("Hello World")

    MainForm {
        anchors.fill: parent
        mouseArea.onClicked: {
            console.log(qsTr('Clicked on background. Text: "' +
            textEdit.text + '"'))
        }
    }
}
```

In the code above, there is a `Window` type that is only available by importing the `QtQuick.Window` module. After setting the properties of the `Window` type, the `MainForm` type is declared. This `MainForm` type is actually the entire user interface we saw previously in `MainForm.ui.qml`. Since the `MouseArea` and `TextEdit` types have been exposed in `MainForm.ui.qml`, we can now access and make use of them in `main.qml`.

QML also uses the signal-and-slot mechanism provided by Qt, but in a slightly different form of writing, since we're no longer writing C++ code. For example, we can see onClicked being used in the code above, which is a built-in signal equivalent to clicked() in a Qt Widgets Application. Since the .qml file is the place where we define the application logic, we can define what happens when onClicked is being called. On the other hand, we cannot do the same in .ui.qml since only visual-related code is allowed in it. You will get warnings from Qt Creator if you try to write logic-related code in a .ui.qml file.

Just like the Qt Widgets Application, you can also build and run the project the same way as before. The default example application looks something like this:

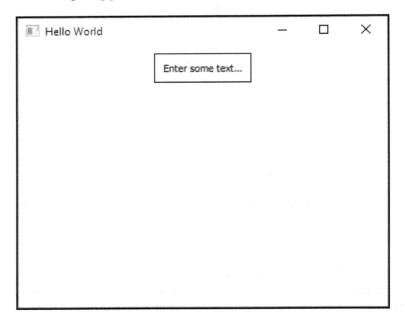

You might realize that the build process is pretty fast. This is because QML code doesn't get compiled into binary by default. QML is an interpreted language, just like JavaScript, and thus it doesn't need to be compiled in order for it to be executed. All the QML files will just get packed into your application's resource system during the build process. Then, the QML files will be loaded and interpreted by the Qt Quick engine once the application is started.

However, you can still choose to compile your QML scripts into binary, using the Qt Quick Compiler program included in Qt, to make the code execution slightly faster than usual. It is an optional step that is not required unless you are trying to run your application on an embedded system that has very limited resources.

Now that we have understood what **Qt Quick** and **QML** language are, let's take a look at all the different QML types provided by Qt.

Qt Quick widgets and controls

In Qt Quick's realm, widgets and controls are known as QML types. By default, **Qt Quick Designer** provides us with a set of basic QML types. You can also import additional QML types that come with different modules. Furthermore, you can even create your own custom QML types if none of the existing ones fit, your needs.

Let's take a look at what QML types come with Qt Quick Designer by default. First off, here are the QML types under the **Basic** category:

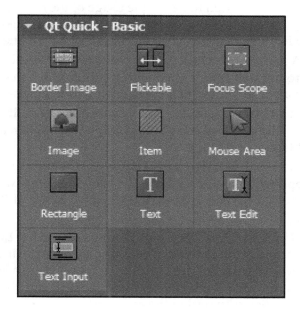

Let's have a look at the different options:

- **Border Image**: Border Image is a QML type that is designed to create scalable rectangular shapes that can maintain their corner shapes and borders.
- **Flickable**: Flickable is a QML type that contains all its children types, and, displays them within its clipping area. Flickable has also been extended and used by the `ListView` and `GridView` types for scrolling long content. It can also be moved by a touchscreen flick gesture.
- **Focus Scope**: Focus Scope is a low-level QML type that is used to facilitate the construction of other QML types that can acquire keyboard focus when being pressed or released. We usually don't directly use this QML type, but rather use other types that are directly inherited from it, such as `GroupBox`, `ScrollView`, `StatusBar`, and so on.
- **Image**: The `Image` type is pretty much self-explanatory. It loads an image either locally or from a network.
- **Item**: The `Item` type is the most basic QML type for all visual items in Qt Quick. All the visual items in Qt Quick inherit from this `Item` type.
- **MouseArea**: We have seen the example usage of the `MouseArea` type in the default Qt Quick Application project. It detects mouse clicks and touch events within a predefined area, and calls the clicked signal whenever it detects one.
- **Rectangle**: A `Rectangle` QML type is pretty similar to the `Item` type, except it has a background that can be filled with solid color or a gradient. Optionally, you can also add a border to it with its own color and thickness.
- **Text**: The `Text` QML type is also pretty self-explanatory. It simply displays a line of text on the window. You can use it to display both plain and rich text with a specific font family and font size.
- **Text Edit**: The Text Edit QML type is equivalent to the `Text Edit` widget in **Qt Widgets Application**. It allows the user to key in the text when being focused. It can display both plain and formatted text, which is very different from the `Text Input` type.
- **Text Input**: The Text Input QML type is equivalent to the **Line Edit** widget in **Qt Widgets Application**, in that it can only display a single line of editable plain text, which is different from the `Text Edit` type. You can also apply an input constraint to it through a validator or input mask. It can also be used for password input fields by setting the `echoMode` to `Password` or `PasswordEchoOnEdit`.

The QML types that we have discussed here are the most basic ones that come with Qt Quick Designer by default. These are also the basic building blocks used for constructing some other more complex QML types. There are many additional modules that come with Qt Quick that we can import into our project, for example, if we add the following line to our `MainForm.ui.qml` file:

```
import QtQuick.Controls 2.2
```

A bunch of additional QML types will then appear on your **Qt Quick Designer** when you switch over to **Design** mode:

We won't go through all these QML types one by one, as there are too many of them. If you are interested in learning more about these QML types, please visit the following link: `https://doc.qt.io/qt-5.10/qtquick-controls-qmlmodule.html`

Qt Quick Designer

Next, we will look at the Qt Quick Designer layout for the Qt Quick Application project. When you open up a `.ui.qml` file, Qt Quick Designer, the designer tool included in the Qt Creator toolset, will be launched automatically for you.

Those of you who have followed all the example projects since the very first chapter of this book may realize the Qt Quick Designer looks a bit different from the one we have been using all this time. This is because the Qt Quick project is very different from the Qt Widgets project, so naturally the designer tool should also look different to suit its needs.

Let's look at how the Qt Quick Designer looks in the Qt Quick project:

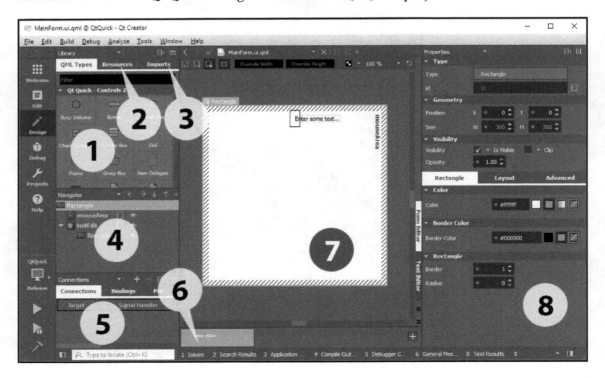

1. Library: The **Library** window displays all the QML types available for the current project. You can click and drag it to the canvas window to add it to your UI. You can also create your own custom QML type and display it here.
2. Resources: The **Resources** window displays all the resources in a list, which can then be used in your UI design.
3. Imports: The **Imports** window allows you to import different **Qt Quick** modules into your current project.
4. Navigator: The **Navigator** window displays the items in the current QML file as a tree structure. It's similar to the object operator window in the **Qt Widgets Application** project.
5. Connections: The **Connections** window consists of several different tabs: **Connections**, **Bindings**, **Properties**, and **Backends**. These tabs allow you to add **Connections** (signal-and-slot), **Bindings**, and **Properties** to your QML file, without switching over to **Edit** mode.
6. State Pane: **State pane** displays the different states in the QML project that typically describe UI configurations, such as the UI controls, their properties and behavior, and available actions.
7. Canvas: **Canvas** is the working area where you design your application UI.
8. Properties Pane: Similar to the property editor we used in **Qt Widgets Application** projects, the **Properties** pane in the QML designer displays the properties of the selected item. You can immediately see the result in the UI after changing the values here.

Qt Quick layouts

Just like the Qt Widget applications, a layout system also exists in Qt Quick applications. The only difference is it's called the **Positioners** in Qt Quick:

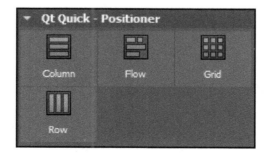

The most noticeable similarity is the **Column** and **Row** positioners. These two are exactly the same as the **Vertical Layout** and **Horizontal Layout** in **Qt Widgets Application**. Besides that, the **Grid** positioner is also the same as the **Grid Layout**.

The only extra thing in Qt Quick is the **Flow** positioner. The items contained within the **Flow** positioner arrange themselves like words on a page, with items arranged in lines along one axis, and lines of items placed next to each other along another axis.

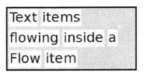

Basic QML scripting

In the following section, we will learn how to create our very first Qt Quick application using Qt Quick Designer and QML!

Setting up the project

Without further ado, let's put our hands on QML and create a **Qt Quick application** ourselves! For this example project, we are going to create a dummy login screen using Qt Quick Designer and a QML script. First, let's open up Qt Creator and create a new project by going to **File** | **New File or Project...**

After that, select **Qt Quick Application** and press **Choose....** After that, press **Next** all the way until the project is created. We are just going to use all the default settings for this example project, including the **Minimal required Qt version**:

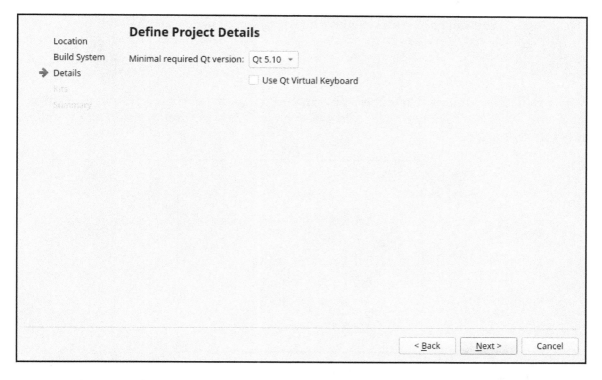

Once the project has been created, we need to add a few image files to our project, so that we can use them later:

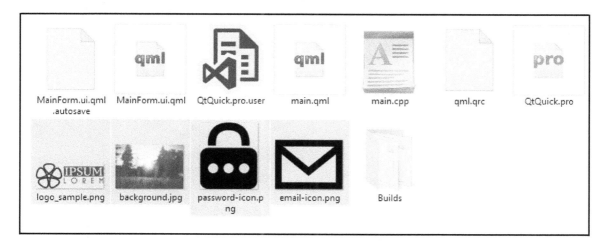

You can get the source files (including these images) at our GitHub page: `http://github.com/PacktPublishing/Hands-On-GUI-Programming-with-C-QT5`

We can add these images to our project by right-clicking on the `qml.qrc` file in the **Project** pane and selecting **Open in Editor**. Add a new prefix called `images`, and add all the image files into that prefix:

After that, open up `MainForm.ui.qml`, and delete everything in the QML file. We start all over by adding an **Item** type to the canvas, set its size to 400 x 400, and call it the `loginForm`. After that, add an `Image` type underneath it, and call it `background`. We then apply the background image to the `Image` type, and the canvas now looks like this:

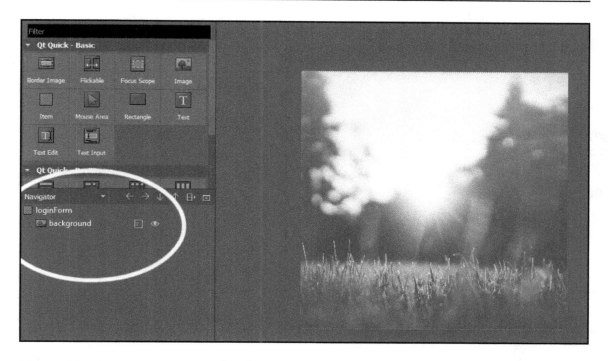

Then, add a `Rectangle` type under the `Image` type (background), and open up the **Layout** tab in the **Properties pane**. Enable both the **vertical** and **horizontal anchor** options. After that, set the `width` to `402`, the `height` to `210`, and the `vertical anchor margin` to `50`:

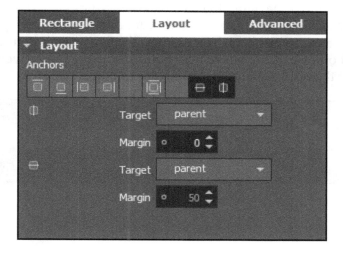

Following that, we set the rectangle's **color** to #fcf9f4 and **border color** to #efedeb, then set the **border** value to 1. The user interface so far looks something like this:

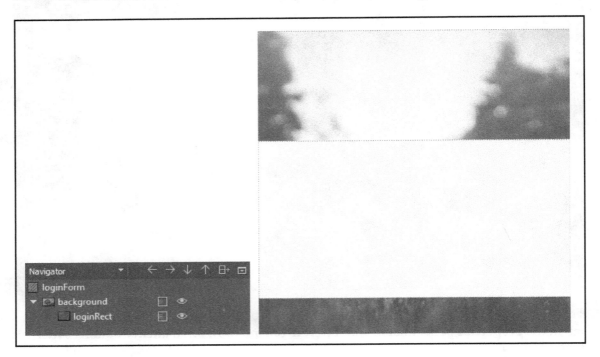

Next, add an **Image** QML type under the rectangle, and set its anchor settings to **top anchor** and **horizontal anchor**. We then set its **top anchor margin** to −110 and apply the logo image to its image source property. You can turn the QML type's **bounding rectangle** and **stripes** on and off by clicking on the little button located on top of your canvas, so that it's easier to look at the result, especially when your canvas is full of stuff:

Then, we add three `Rectangle` types to the canvas under the `loginRect` rectangle, and call them `emailRect`, `passwordRect`, and `loginButton`. The anchor settings for the rectangles are shown as follows:

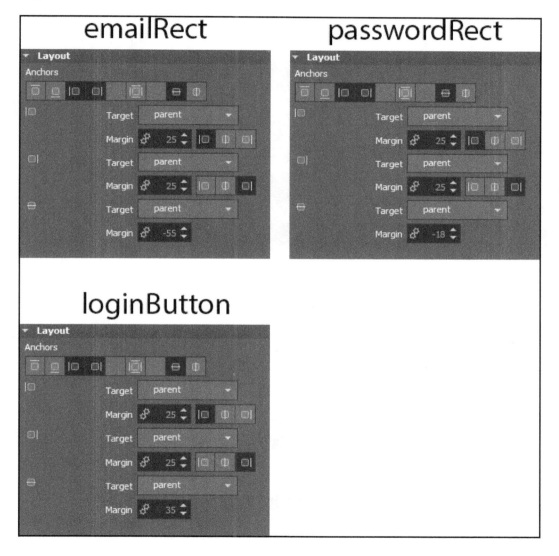

Then, we set the `border` value of both the `emailRect` and `passwordRect` to 1, the `color` to `#ffffff` and the `bordercolor` to `#efedeb`. As for the `loginButton`, we set the `border` to 0, the `radius` to 2 and the `color` to `#27ae61`. The login screen now looks like the following:

Looks good so far. Next, we're going to add a `TextInput`, `Image`, `MouseArea`, and a `Text` QML type to both the `emailRect` and the `passwordRect`. Since there are many QML types here, I will list the properties that need to be set:

- TextInput:
  - **Selection color** set to `#4f0080`
  - Enable **left anchor, right anchor,** and **vertical anchor**
  - **Left anchor margin** `20`, **right anchor margin** `40` and **vertical margin** `3`
  - Set **echoMode** to **Password** for password input only
- Image:
  - Enable **right anchor** and **vertical anchor**
  - **Right anchor margin** set to `10`
  - Set **image source** to **email icon** or **password icon** respectively
  - Set image **fill mode** to **PreserveAspectFit**

- MouseArea:
    - Enable **fill parent item**
- Text:
    - Set the **text** property to `E-Mail` and `Password` respectively
    - Text **color** set to `#cbbdbd`
    - Text **alignment** set to **Left** and **Top**
    - Enable **left anchor**, **right anchor**, and **vertical anchor**
    - **Left anchor margin** 20, **right anchor margin** 40, and **vertical margin** -1

Once you're done, add a `MouseArea` and `Text` to the `loginButton` as well. Enable `fill parent item` for the `MouseArea`, and enable both `vertical` and `horizontal anchors` for the `Text` QML type. Then, set its `text` property to `LOGIN`.

You don't have to follow all my steps by 100%, they are just a guideline for you to achieve a similar result as the screenshot above. However, it's better for you to apply your own design and create something unique!

Phew! After the long process above, our login screen should now look something like this:

One last thing we need to do before moving on to `main.qml` is to expose some of the QML types in our login screen, so that we can link it to our `main.qml` file for logic programming. We can, in fact, do this directly on the designer tool. All you need to do is to click on the small rectangle icon located next to the object name, and make sure the three lines on the icon are penetrating the rectangular box, like this:

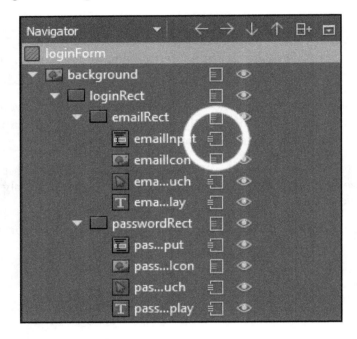

The QML types that we need to expose/export are `emailInput` (TextInput), `emailTouch` (MouseArea), `emailDisplay` (Text), `passwordInput` (TextInput), `passwordTouch` (MouseArea), `passwordDisplay` (Text), and `loginMouseArea` (MouseArea). Once you have done all that, let's open up `main.qml`.

At first, our `main.qml` should look something like this, which will just open an empty window:

```
import QtQuick 2.6
import QtQuick.Window 2.2

Window {
    id: window
    visible: true
    width: 800
    height: 600
```

```
        title: qsTr("My App")
    }
```

After that, add in the `MainForm` object, and set its anchor setting to `anchors.fill:` `parent`. Then, print out a line of text, `Login pressed`, on the console window when the `loginButton` is clicked (or touched, if running on the touch device):

```
Window {
    id: window
    visible: true
    width: 800
    height: 600
    title: qsTr("My App")

    MainForm
    {
        anchors.fill: parent

        loginMouseArea.onClicked:
        {
            console.log("Login pressed");
        }
    }
}
```

After that, we are going to program the behavior when the `MouseArea` on the email input is clicked/touched. Since we are manually creating our own text field, instead of using the `TextField` QML type provided by the `QtQuick.Controls` module, we must manually hide and show the `E-Mail` and `Password` text displays, as well as changing the input focus when the user clicks/touches down on the `MouseArea`.

The reason why I chose not to use the `TextField` type is that I can hardly customize the `TextField`'s visual presentation, so why don't I create my own? The code for doing manual focus for the email input looks like the following:

```
emailTouch.onClicked:
{
    emailDisplay.visible = false;      // Hide emailDisplay
    emailInput.forceActiveFocus();     // Focus emailInput
    Qt.inputMethod.show();          // Activate virtual keyboard
}

emailInput.onFocusChanged:
{
    if (emailInput.focus == false && emailInput.text == "")
    {
```

```
            emailDisplay.visible = true;    // Show emailDisplay if
            emailInput is empty when loses focus
        }
    }
```

After that, do the same for the password field:

```
    passwordTouch.onClicked:
    {
        passwordDisplay.visible = false;    // Hide passwordDisplay
        passwordInput.forceActiveFocus();  // Focus passwordInput
        Qt.inputMethod.show();             // Activate virtual keyboard
    }

    passwordInput.onFocusChanged:
    {
        if (passwordInput.focus == false && passwordInput.text == "")
        {
            passwordDisplay.visible = true;        // Show passwordDisplay if
            passwordInput is empty when loses focus
        }
    }
```

That's it; we're done! You can now compile and run the program. You should get something like this:

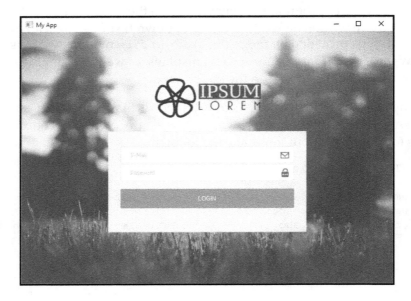

If you're not seeing the images, and are getting error messages that say Qt is unable to open the images, please go back to your `MainForm.ui.qml` and add in the prefix `image/` to the front of the source property. This is because Qt Quick Designer loads the images without the prefix, while your final program needs the prefix. After you have added the prefix, you may realize you no longer see the images getting displayed on Qt Quick Designer, but it will work just fine in your final program.

I'm not sure if this is a bug or if they intended it like that. Hopefully, Qt's developers can get it fixed, and we won't have to do that extra step anymore. That's it; hopefully, you have understood the similarities and differences between **Qt Widgets Application** and **Qt Quick Application**. You can now pick the best option from the two to fit your project's needs!

Summary

In this chapter, we have learned what Qt Quick is and how to create a program using the QML language. In the following chapter, we are going to learn how to export our Qt project to different platforms without much hassle. Let's go!

Cross-Platform Development 15

Qt has been known for its cross-platform capability since its first release. It was also one of the main goals of the founders when they decided to create this framework, long before it was taken over by **Nokia**, and later **The Qt Company**.

In this chapter, we will cover the following topics:

- Compilers
- Build settings
- Deploying to PC platforms
- Deploying to mobile platforms

Let's get started.

Understanding compilers

In this chapter, we will learn about the process of generating an executable file from a Qt project. This process is what we call **compile** or **build**. The tool that is used for this purpose is called a **compiler**. In the following section, we will learn what a compiler is and how to use it to generate an executable file for our Qt project.

What is a compiler?

When we develop an application, either using Qt or any other software development kit, we often have to compile our project into an executable, but what is actually going on when we're compiling our project?

A **compiler** is a piece of software that transforms computer code written in a high-level programming language or computer instructions into a machine code or lower-level form that can be read and executed by a computer. This low-level machine code is very different depending on the operating system and computer processor you're running, but you don't have to worry about it as the compiler will convert it for you.

That means all you need to worry about is writing your logic code in a human-readable programming language, and let the compiler do the job for you. By using different compilers, theoretically, you should be able to compile your code into executable programs that can be run on different operating systems and hardware. I'm using the word *theoretically* here because in practice it's actually much more difficult than just using different compilers, you may also need to implement libraries that support the target platform. However, Qt has already handled all this for you, so you don't have to do the extra work.

In the current version, Qt supports the following compilers:

- **GNU Compiler Collection (GCC)**: GCC is a compiler for Linux and macOS
- **MinGW (Minimalist GNU for Windows)**: MinGW is a native software port of GCC and GNU Binutils (binary utilities) for developing applications on Windows
- **Microsoft Visual C++ (MSVC)**: Qt supports MSVC 2013, 2015, and 2017 for building Windows applications
- **XCode**: XCode is the primary compiler used by developers who develop applications for macOS and iOS
- **Linux ICC (Intel C++ Compiler)**: Linux ICC is a set of compilers of C and C++ compilers developed by Intel for Linux application development
- **Clang**: Clang is a C, C++, Objective C, and Objective C++ frontend for the LLVM compiler for Windows, Linux, and macOS
- **Nim**: Nim is the Nim compiler for Windows, Linux, and macOS
- **QCC**: QCC is the interface for compiling C++ applications for the QNX operating system

Build automation with Make

In software development, **Make** is a build automation tool that automatically builds executable programs and libraries from source code by reading configuration files called **Makefiles** that specify how to derive the target platform. In a nutshell, a Make program generates build configuration files and uses them to tell the compiler what to do before generating the final executable program.

Qt supports two types of Make programs:

- **qmake**: It is the native Make program developed by the Qt team. It works best on Qt Creator, and I strongly recommend using it for all Qt projects.
- **CMake**: On the other hand, although this is a very powerful build system, it doesn't do all the things that qmake does specifically for a Qt project, such as:
  - Running the **Meta Object Compiler (MOC)**
  - Telling the compiler where to look for Qt headers
  - Telling the linker where to look for Qt libraries

You have to do the preceding steps manually on CMake in order to successfully compile a Qt project. You should use CMake only if:

- You're working on a non-Qt project but wish to use Qt Creator for writing the code

- You're dealing with a massive project that requires complex configurations, which qmake simply cannot handle

- You really love to use CMake and you know exactly what you're doing

Qt is really flexible when it comes to choosing the right tools for your project. It doesn't stick to just its own build system and compiler. It gives the developers freedom to choose what suits best for their projects.

Build settings

Before a project is compiled or built, the compiler needs to know several details before proceeding. These details are known as the **build settings**, which are a very important aspect of the compilation process. In the following section, we will learn what the build settings are and how we can configure them in an accurate manner.

Qt Project (.pro) File

I'm sure you already know about the **Qt Project File** since we have mentioned it countless times throughout the book. A `.pro` file is actually the project file used by *qmake* to build your application, library, or plugin. It contains all the information, such as links to the headers and source files, libraries required by the project, custom-build processes for different platforms/environments, and so on. A simple project file could look something like this:

```
QT += core gui widgets

TARGET = MyApp
TEMPLATE = app

SOURCES +=
        main.cpp
        mainwindow.cpp

HEADERS +=
        mainwindow.h

FORMS +=
        mainwindow.ui

RESOURCES +=
    resource.qrc
```

It simply tells qmake which Qt modules should be included in the project, what the name of the executable program is, what's the type of the application, and finally the links to the header files, source files, form declaration files, and resource files that need to be included in the project. All of this information is crucial in order for qmake to generate the configuration files and successfully build the application. For a more complex project, you may want to configure your project differently for different operating systems. This can also be done easily in the Qt Project File.

 To learn more about how you can configure your project differently for different operating systems, please refer to the following link: `http://doc.qt.io/qt-5/qmake-language.html#scopes-and-conditions`.

Comment

You can add your own comments in the project file to remind yourself of the purpose of adding a specific line of configuration, so that you won't forget why you added a line after not touching it for a while. A comment starts with the hash symbol (#) after which you can write anything since the build system will simply ignore the entire line of text. For example:

```
# The following define makes your compiler emit warnings if you use
# any feature of Qt which has been marked as deprecated (the exact warnings
# depend on your compiler). Please consult the documentation of the
# deprecated API in order to know how to port your code away from it.
DEFINES += QT_DEPRECATED_WARNINGS
```

You can also add dash lines or use spaces to make your comment stand out from others:

```
#-------------------------------------------------
#
# Project created by QtCreator 2018-02-18T01:59:44
#
#-------------------------------------------------
```

Modules, configurations, and definitions

You can add different Qt modules, configuration options, and definitions to your project. Let's take a look at how we can achieve these. To add additional modules, you simply add the module keyword behind QT +=, like so:

```
QT += core gui sql printsupport charts multimedia
```

Or you can also add in a condition in front to determine when to add a specific module to your project:

```
greaterThan(QT_MAJOR_VERSION, 4): QT += widgets
```

You can also add configuration settings to your project. For example, we want to specifically ask the compiler to follow the 2011 version of the C++ specifications (known as C++11) when compiling our project, as well as making it a multithreaded application:

```
CONFIG += qt c++11 thread
```

You must use +=, not =, or qmake will not be able to use Qt's configuration to determine the settings needed for your project. Alternatively, you can also use -= to remove a module, configuration, and definition from your project.

As for adding definitions (or variables) to our compiler, we use the DEFINES keyword, like so:

```
DEFINES += QT_DEPRECATED_WARNINGS
```

Qmake adds the values of this variable as a compiler C preprocessor macro (-D option) before compiling your project. The earlier definition tells the Qt compiler to emit warnings if you have used any feature of Qt that has been marked as deprecated.

Platform-specific settings

You can set different configurations or settings for different platforms, since not every setting can fit all use cases. For example, if we want to include different header paths for different operating systems, we can do the following:

```
win32:INCLUDEPATH += "C:/mylibs/extra headers"
unix:INCLUDEPATH += "/home/user/extra headers"
```

Alternatively, you can also put your settings in curly braces which behave like the if statements in a programming language:

```
win32 {
    SOURCES += extra_code.cpp
}
```

You can check out all the settings you can use in your project file by visiting the following link:
http://doc.qt.io/qt-5/qmake-variable-reference.html.

Deploying to PC platforms

Let's move on to learn how to deploy our applications on platforms such as Windows, Linux, and macOS.

Windows

In this section, we will learn how to deploy our application to different operating systems. Even though Qt supports all major platforms out of the box, there might be some configurations which you need to set in order to make your application easily deployable to all platforms.

The first operating system we're going to cover is the most common one, **Microsoft Windows**.

 Starting from Qt 5.6, **Windows XP** is no longer supported by Qt.

There could be certain plugins that may not work properly on the Windows version you're trying to deploy, so do check out the documentation before you decide to work on your project. However, it's safe to say most of the features will work out of the box on Qt.

By default, the **MinGW** 32-bit compiler comes together with Qt when you're installing it to your Windows PC. Unfortunately, it doesn't support 64-bit by default unless you compile Qt from source. If you need to build 64-bit applications, you can consider installing the MSVC version of Qt alongside the **Microsoft Visual Studio**. Microsoft Visual Studio can be obtained for free from the following link: https://www.visualstudio.com/vs.

You can set up your compiler settings in **Qt Creator** by going to **Tools | Options**, then go to the **Build & Run** category and select the **Kits** tab:

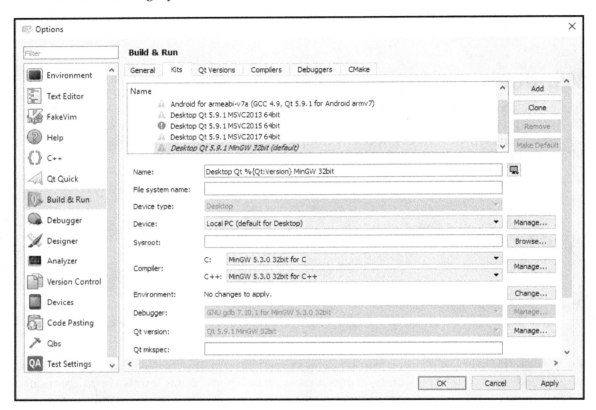

As you can see, there are multiple kits that run on different compilers, in which you can configure. By default, Qt already comes with five kits—one for Android, one for MinGW, and three for MSVC (version 2013, 2015, and 2017). Qt will automatically detect the existence of these compilers and configure these settings for you accordingly.

If you have not installed **Visual Studio** or **Android SDK**, there will be a red icon with an exclamation mark appearing in front of the kit option. After you have installed the compiler you need, try restarting **Qt Creator**. It will now detect the newly installed compilers. You should have no problem compiling for the Windows platform as Qt will handle the rest for you. We will talk more about the Android platform in another section.

Once you have compiled your application, open up the folder in which you installed Qt. Copy the relevant DLL files to your application folder, and pack it together before distributing it to your users. Without these DLL files, your users may not be able to run the Qt application.

 For more information, please visit the following link: http://doc.qt.io/qt-5/windows-deployment.html.

As for setting a custom icon for your application, you must add the following code to your project (.pro) file:

```
win32:RC_ICONS = myappico.ico
```

The preceding code only works on Windows platforms, which is why we have to add the win32 keyword before it.

Linux

Linux (or GNU/Linux) in general is considered a major operating system that dominates the cloud/server market. Since Linux is not a single operating system (Linux is offered by different vendors in the form of different Linux distributions that are not entirely compatible) like Windows or macOS, it is very hard for developers to build their applications and expect them to run flawlessly on different Linux distributions (**distros**). However, if you develop your Linux application on Qt, there is a high chance that it will work on most distributions, if not on all of the major distros out there, as long as the Qt library exists on the target system.

The default kit selection on Linux is much simpler than Windows. Since a 64-bit application has been mainstream and standard on most Linux distros for some time now, we only need to include the **GCC** 64-bit compiler when installing Qt. There is also an option for Android, but we will talk more about it later:

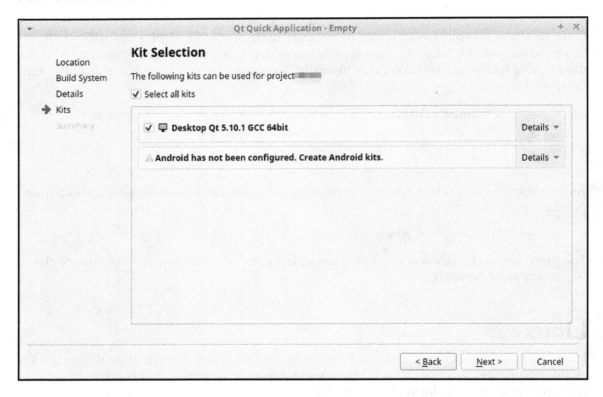

If you are compiling your Linux application on **Qt Creator** for the first time, I'm pretty sure you will get the following error:

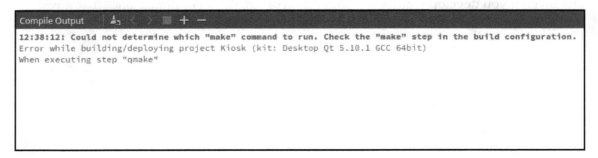

This is because you have not installed the relevant tools required to build Linux applications, such as Make, GCC, and other programs.

Different Linux distros have a slightly different method to install programs, but I won't be explaining every single one of them here. In my case, I'm using an Ubuntu distro, so I did was first opened up the terminal and typed the following command to install the `build-essential` package which includes Make and GCC:

```
sudo apt-get install build-essential
```

The preceding command only works on distros that inherit from **Debian** and **Ubuntu**, and it may not work on other distributions such as **Fedora**, **Gentoo**, **Slackware**, and so on. You should search for the appropriate command used by your Linux distro to install these packages, as shown in the following screenshot:

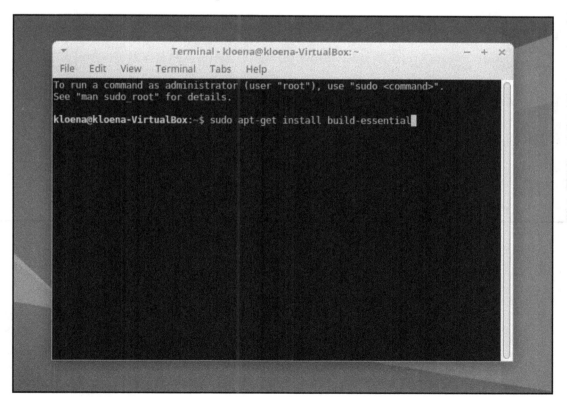

Once you have installed the appropriate packages, restart **Qt Creator** and go to **Tools** | **Options**. Then, go to the **Build & Run** category and open up the **Kits** tab. You should now be able to select the compilers for both C and C++ options for your **Desktop** kit:

However, you might get another error that says **cannot find -lGL** when trying to compile
again:

```
Compile Output
DQT_NETWORK_LIB -DQT_CORE_LIB -I../../Kiosk -I. -I../../../Qt/5.10.1/gcc_64/includ
5.10.1/gcc_64/include/QtGui -I../../../Qt/5.10.1/gcc_64/include/QtQml -I../../../Q
gcc_64/include/QtCore -I. -isystem /usr/include/libdrm -I../../../Qt/5.10.1/gcc_64
g++ -Wl,-O1 -Wl,-rpath,/home/kloena/Qt/5.10.1/gcc_64/lib -o Kiosk main.o qrc_qml.o
lQt5Qml -lQt5Network -lQt5Core -lGL -lpthread
/usr/bin/ld: cannot find -lGL
collect2: error: ld returned 1 exit status
Makefile:246: recipe for target 'Kiosk' failed
make: *** [Kiosk] Error 1
13:06:34: The process "/usr/bin/make" exited with code 2.
Error while building/deploying project Kiosk (kit: Desktop Qt 5.10.1 GCC 64bit)
When executing step "Make"
13:06:34: Elapsed time: 00:06.
```

This is because Qt is trying to look for the OpenGL libraries, and it can't find them on your
system. This can be easily fixed by installing the Mesa development library package with
the following command:

```
sudo apt-get install libgl1-mesa-dev
```

Again, the preceding command only works on Debian and Ubuntu variants. Please look for the appropriate command for your Linux distro if you're not running one of the Debian or Ubuntu forks:

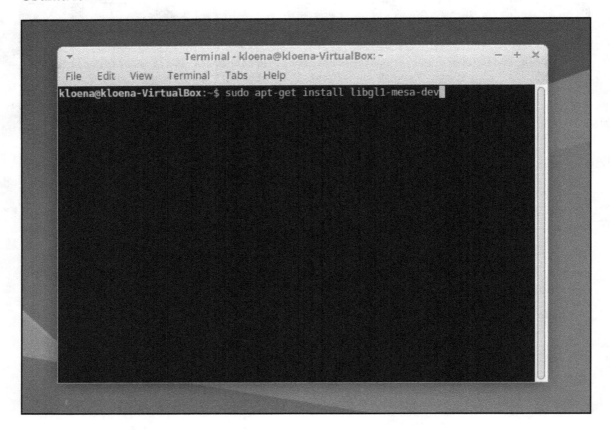

Once the package has been installed, you should be able to compile and run your Qt application without any problem:

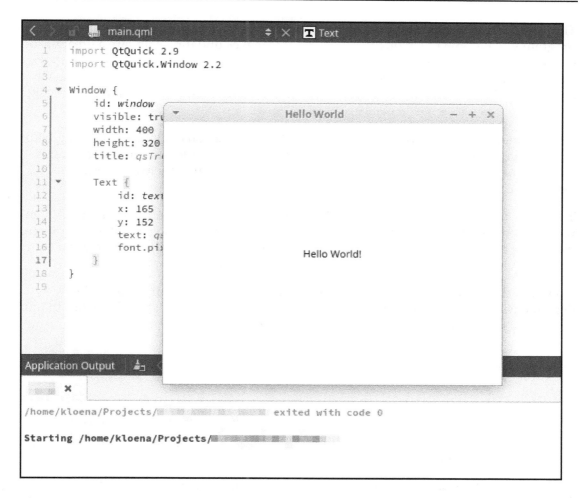

As for using one of the other compilers that are less popular, such as **Linux ICC**, **Nim**, or **QCC**, you must set it manually by clicking on the **Add** button located on the right-hand side of the **Kits** interface, then key in all the appropriate settings to get it to work. Most people do not use these compilers, so we'll just skip them for now.

When it comes to distributing Linux applications, it's a lot more complicated than Windows or macOS. This is owing to the fact that Linux is not a single operating system, but rather a bunch of different distros with their own dependencies and configurations, which makes distributing programs very difficult.

The safest way is to compile your program statically, which has its own pros and cons. Your program will become really huge in size, and that makes updating software a great burden to users who have slow internet connections. Other than that, the Qt license also forbids you from building statically if you're not doing an open source project and do not have a Qt commercial license. To learn more about Qt's licensing options, please visit the following link: https://www1.qt.io/licensing-compariso.n.

Another method is to ask your users to install the right version of Qt before running your application, but that will yield a ton of problems on the user side since not every user is very tech savvy and has the patience to go through all those hassles to avoid the dependency hell.

Therefore, the best way is to distribute the Qt library alongside your application, just like we did on the Windows platform. The library might not work on some of the Linux distros (rarely the case, but there is a slight possibility), but that can be easily overcome by creating a different installer for different distros, and everyone's happy now.

However, due to security reasons, a Linux application doesn't usually look for its dependencies in its local directory by default. You must use the $ORIGIN keyword in the executable's rpath setting in your qmake project (.pro) file:

```
unix:!mac{
QMAKE_LFLAGS += -Wl,--rpath=$$ORIGIN
QMAKE_RPATH=
}
```

Setting the QMAKE_RPATH clears the default rpath setting for the Qt libraries. This allows for bundling the Qt libraries with the application. If you want the rpath to include the path to the Qt libraries, don't set QMAKE_RPATH.

After that, just copy all the library files from the Qt installation folder to your application's folder and remove its minor version numbers from the filename. For example, rename libQtCore.so.5.8.1 to libQtCore.so.5 and now it should be able to get detected by your Linux application.

As for application icons, you can't apply any icon to Linux applications by default as it is not supported. Even though some desktop environments such as KDE and GNOME do support application icons, the icon has to be installed and configured manually, which is not very convenient to the users. It may not even work on some user's PC since every distro works a little bit differently than the others. The best way to set icons for your application is to create a desktop shortcut (symlink) during installation and apply the icon to the shortcut.

macOS

In my opinion, **macOS** is the single most centralized operating system in the software world. Not only is it designed to run only on the Macintosh machines, you are also required to download or buy software only from the Apple App Store.

No doubt this has caused an uneasy feeling for some people who care about freedom of choice, but on the other hand it also means that developers have less problems to deal with when it comes to application building and distribution.

Other than that, macOS applications behave pretty much similar to a ZIP archive, where each and every application has its own directory that carries the appropriate libraries with it. Therefore, there is no need for the users to install the Qt libraries on their operating system beforehand and everything just works out of the box.

As for the **Kit Selection**, Qt for macOS supports kits for Android, clang 64-bit, iOS, and iOS Simulator:

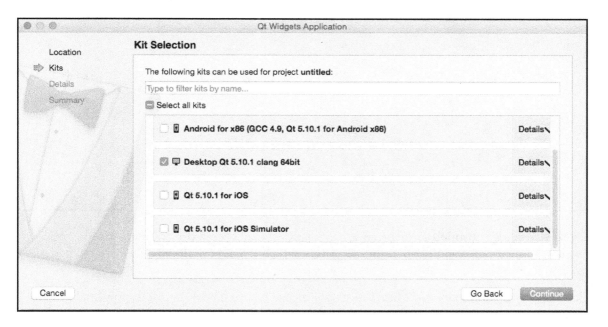

As of Qt 5.10 and above, Qt no longer supports 32-bit builds for macOS. Also, Qt does not support OS X on PowerPC; and since Qt uses Cocoa internally, building for Carbon is also not possible, please be aware of that.

Before compiling your macOS applications, please install **Xcode** from the App Store before proceeding. **Xcode** is an integrated development environment for macOS, containing a suite of software development tools developed by Apple for developing software for macOS and iOS. Once you have installed **Xcode**, Qt Creator will detect its existence and automatically set the compiler settings for you, which is great:

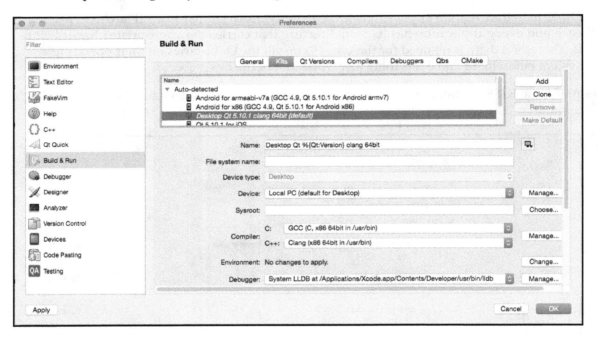

Once you have compiled your project, the resulting executable program is a single app bundle that can be easily distributed to your users. Since all the library files are packed within the application bundle, it should work out of the box on the user's PC.

Setting application icons for Mac is quite a simple task. Just add the following line of code to your project (.pro) file and we're good to go:

```
ICON = myapp.icns
```

Do note that the icon format is .icns, instead of .ico, which we usually use for Windows.

Deploying to mobile platforms

Apart from platforms such as Windows, Linux, and macOS, mobile platforms do hold equal importance. There are many developers who would like to deploy their applications to mobile platforms. Let's see how that's done. We will cover two major platforms, they are, iOS and Android.

iOS

Deploying Qt applications on iOS is really simple and easy. Just like we did previously for macOS, you need to first install **Xcode** on your development PC:

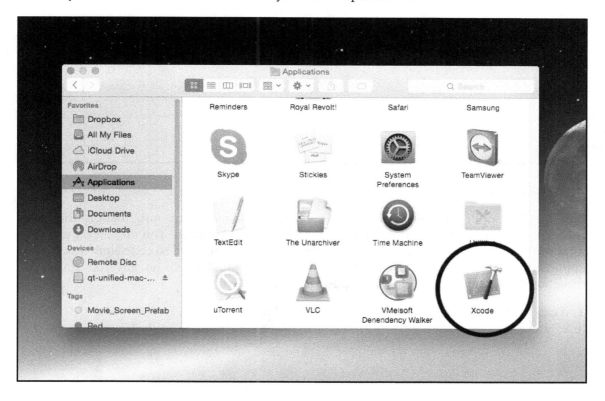

Then, restart Qt Creator. It should now detect the existence of **Xcode**, and it will then automatically set the compiler settings for you:

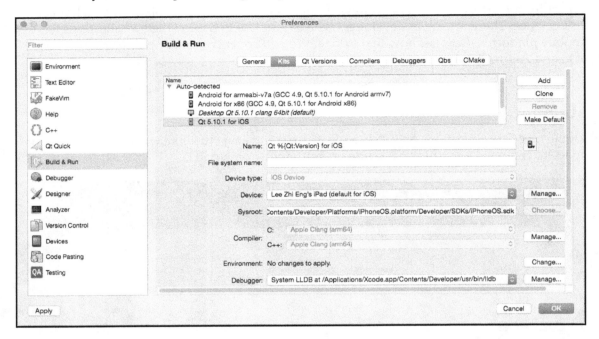

After that, just plug in your iPhone and hit the **Run** button!

Building iOS applications on Qt is really that easy. However, distributing them is not. This is because iOS is a very closed ecosystem, just like a walled garden. You are not only required to register as an app developer with Apple, you also need to code sign your iOS applications before you're able to distribute it to your users. There is no way you can avoid these steps if you want to build your apps for the iOS.

You can learn more about these by visiting the following link: https://developer.apple.com/app-store/submissions.

Android

Even though Android is a Linux-based operating system, it is very different when comparing it to the Linux platforms that you run on your PC. To build Android applications on Qt, you must first install **Android SDK**, **Android NDK**, and **Apache ANT** to your development PC, regardless of whether you're running Windows, Linux, or macOS:

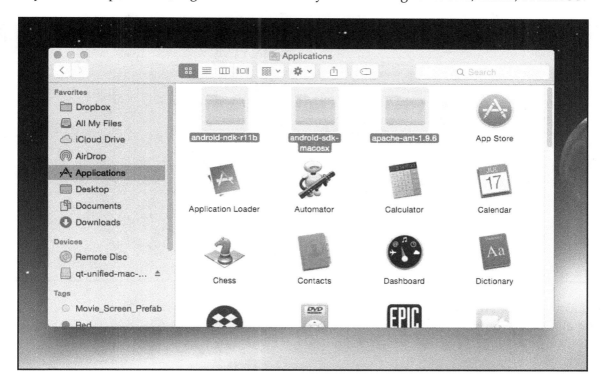

These three packages are essential when it comes to building Android applications on Qt. Once all of them have been installed, restart **Qt Creator**, and voilà, it should have now detected their existence and the build settings will now have been set automatically:

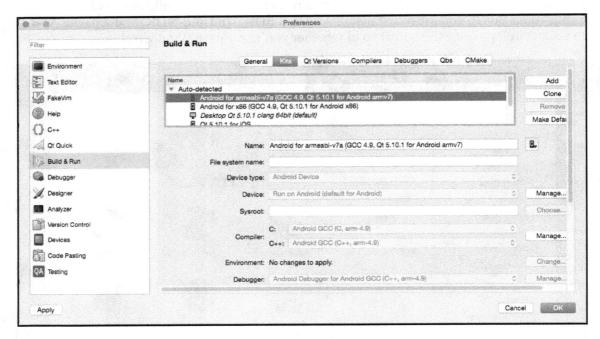

Lastly, you can configure your Android app by opening the `AndroidManifect.xml` file with Qt Creator:

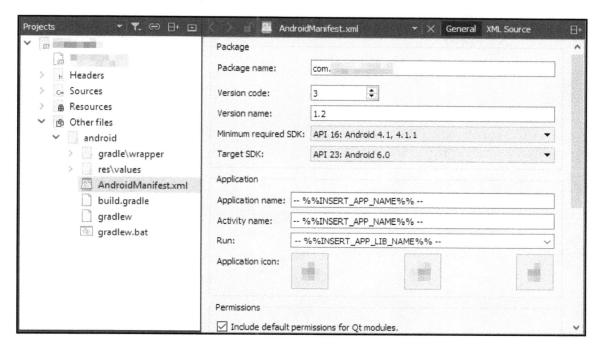

You can set everything here, such as the package name, version code, SDK version, application icon, permissions, and so on.

Android is an open system compared to iOS, so there is no need for you to do anything before you're able to distribute your applications to your users. You can, however, choose to register as a Google Play developer if you want to distribute your apps on the Google Play Store.

Summary

In this chapter, we have learned how to compile and distribute our Qt applications for different platforms, such as Windows, Linux, macOS, Android, and iOS. In the next chapter, we will learn different debugging methods that could save development time. Let's check it out!

16
Testing and Debugging

We often see the word *debug* when reading tutorials or articles related to programming. But do you know what debugging means? A *bug* in programming terms means an error or defect within a computer program that prevents the software from operating correctly, which often leads to incorrect output or even a crash.

In this chapter, we will cover the following topics and learn how to debug our Qt project:

- Debugging techniques
- Debuggers supported by Qt
- Unit testing

Let's get started.

Debugging techniques

Technical issues occur all the time during the development process. To tackle these problems, we need to find out all these issues and solve them before releasing our application to the users, so as not to affect the company/team's reputation. The method used to look for technical issues is called debugging. In this section, we will look at the common debugging techniques used by professionals to ensure their program is reliable and of a high quality.

Identifying the problem

The most important thing when it comes to debugging your program, regardless of programming language or platform, is to know which part of your code is causing the problem. There are several ways you can identify your problematic code:

- Ask the user at which point the bug happened; for example, which button was pressed, what were the steps leading to the crash, and so on.
- Comment away part of your code, then build and run the program again to check whether the problem still occurs or not. If it still does, continue to comment out more code until you find the problematic line of code.
- Use the built-in debugger to check for the variable changes within your targeted function by setting a data breakpoint. You can easily spot if one of your variables has changed to an unexpected value or an object pointer has become an undefined pointer.
- Make sure all the libraries that you included in the installer for your users have matching version numbers with the ones used in your project.

Print variables using QDebug

You can also print out the value of a variable to the application output window, using the QDebug class. QDebug is quite similar to `std::cout` in the standard library, but the advantage of using QDebug is that since it is part of Qt, it supports Qt classes out of the box, and it is able to output its value without the need for any conversion.

To enable QDebug, we must first include its header:

```
#include <QDebug>
```

After that, we can call `qDebug()` to print out variables to the application output window:

```
int amount = 100;
qDebug() << "You have obtained" << amount << "apples!";
```

The result will look like this:

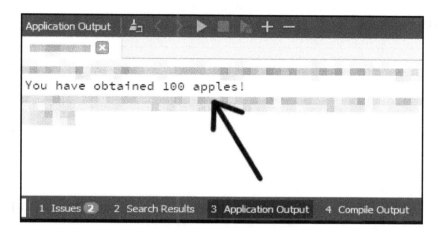

By using QDebug, we will be able to check if our function is running correctly. You can just comment out the particular line of code that contains qDebug() after you have finished checking for the problem.

Setting breakpoints

Setting a breakpoint is another good way to debug your program. When you right-click on the line number of your script in Qt Creator, you will get a pop-up menu with three options, which you can see in the following screenshot:

```
1    #include "mainwindow.h"
2    #include <QApplication>
3
4  ⌄ int main(int argc, char *argv[])
5    {
6        QApplication a(argc, argv);
7        MainWindow w;
8    │  Set Breakpoint at Line 7
9    │
10   │  Set Message Tracepoint at Line 7...
11   │
     │  Toggle Bookmark
12
```

The first option is called **Set Breakpoint at Line...**, which lets you set a breakpoint at a specific line on your script. A red dot icon will appear beside the line number once you have created a breakpoint:

```
1    #include "mainwindow.h"
2    #include "ui_mainwindow.h"
3
4    MainWindow::MainWindow(QWidget *parent) :
5        QMainWindow(parent),
6 ✓      ui(new Ui::MainWindow)
7    {
8        ui->setupUi(this);
9    }
10
11   MainWindow::~MainWindow()
12   {
13       delete ui;
14   }
15
```

The second option is called **Set Message Tracepoint at Line...**, which prints a message when the program reaches this particular line of code. An eye icon will appear beside the line number once you have created a breakpoint:

```
1    #include "mainwindow.h"
2    #include "ui_mainwindow.h"
3
4    MainWindow::MainWindow(QWidget *parent) :
5        QMainWindow(parent),
6 ✓      ui(new Ui::MainWindow)
7    {
8        ui->setupUi(this);
9    }
10
11   MainWindow::~MainWindow()
12   {
13       delete ui;
14   }
15
```

The third option is **Toggle Bookmark,** which lets you set a bookmark for your own reference. Let's create a function called `test()` to try out the breakpoint:

```
void MainWindow::test()
{
    int amount = 100;
    amount -= 10;
    qDebug() << "You have obtained" << amount << "apples!";
}
```

After that, we call the `test()` function at the `MainWindow` constructor:

```
MainWindow::MainWindow(QWidget *parent) :
    QMainWindow(parent),
    ui(new Ui::MainWindow)
{
    ui->setupUi(this);
    test();
}
```

Then, press the **start debug** button located at the bottom left of your Qt Creator window:

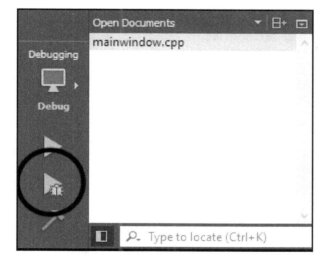

You may get an error message that looks like this:

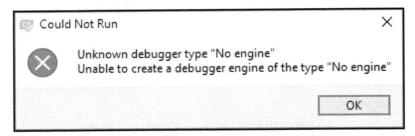

In this case, make sure your project kit has a debugger linked to it. If this error still occurs, close your Qt Creator, go to your project folder and delete the .pro.user file. After that, open up your project with Qt Creator. Qt Creator will reconfigure your project again, and the debug mode should work by now.

Let's add two breakpoints to our code and run it. Once our program has been started, we will see a yellow arrow appearing on top of the first red dot:

```
17  ✔  void MainWindow::test()
18     {
19         int amount = 100;
20 ⬦    |  amount -= 10;
21 ●       qDebug() << "You have obtained" << amount << "apples!";
22     }
23
```

This means that the debugger has stopped at the first breakpoint. The **Locals and Expression** window, which is located on the right-hand side of your Qt Creator, will now display the variable along with its **value** and **type** here:

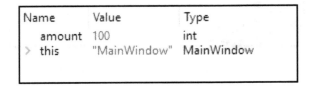

Name	Value	Type
amount	100	int
> this	"MainWindow"	MainWindow

In the preceding image, you can see the value is still at **100** because at this point the minus operation has not yet been run. The next thing we need to do is to click on the **Step Into** button on top of the **Stack** window located at the bottom of your Qt Creator:

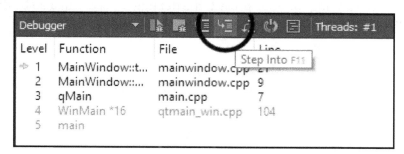

After that, the debugger will move on to the next breakpoint, and here we can see the value has decreased to **90** as expected:

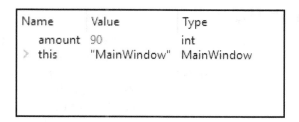

You can use this method to easily examine your application. To delete a breakpoint, you just have to click on the red dot icon again.

Do note that you must run this in the debug mode. This is because when compiling in debug mode, additional debugging symbols will be embedded into your application or library that allow your debugger to gain access to information from the source code of the binary, such as the name of identifiers, variables, and routines. This is also the reason why your application or library will be much bigger in file size if compiled in debug mode.

Debuggers supported by Qt

There are different types of debuggers that are supported by Qt. Depending on the platform and compiler you're running for your project, the debugger used will also be different. The following is the list of debuggers commonly supported by Qt:

- **Windows (MinGW):** GDB (GNU Debugger)
- **Windows (MSVC):** CDB (Debugging Tools for Windows)
- **macOS**: LLDB (LLVM Debugger), FSF GDB (Experimental)
- **Linux**: GDB, LLDB (Experimental)
- **Unix** (FreeBSD, OpenBSD, etc.): GDB
- **Android**: GDB
- **iOS**: LLDB

Debugging for PC

With **GDB (GNU Debugger),** there is no need for any manual setup if you're using MinGW compiler on Windows, as it usually comes together with your Qt installation. If you're running other operating systems such as Linux, you may need to install it manually before linking it up with your Qt Creator. Qt Creator detects the existence of GDB and links it with your project automatically. If it doesn't, you can easily find the GDB executable located in your Qt directory and link it by yourself.

CDB (Debugging Tools for Windows) on the other hand, needs to be installed manually on your Windows machine. Do note that Qt doesn't support the built-in debugger of Visual Studio. Therefore, you need to install the CDB debugger separately by selecting an optional component called **debugging tools for windows** while installing the Windows SDK. Qt Creator also normally would recognize the existence of CDB and put it on the debugger list under the Debuggers **Options** page. You can go to **Tools** | **Options** | **Build and Run** | **Debuggers** to look for the settings as seen in the following screenshot:

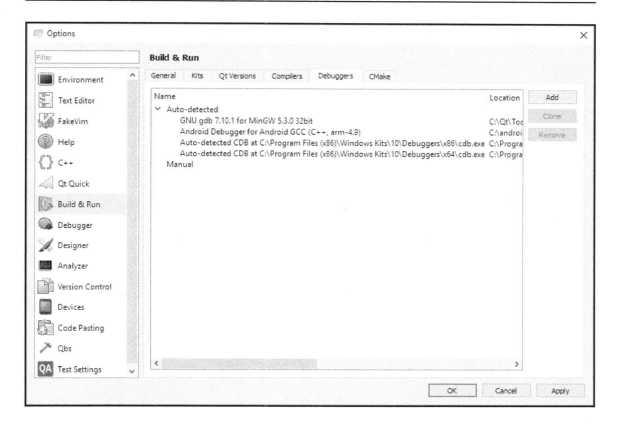

Debugging for Android devices

Debugging for Android devices is slightly more complicated than for a PC. You must install all the necessary packages for Android development, such as JDK (version 6 or later), Android SDK, and Android NDK. Then you also need the Android Debug Bridge (ADB) driver on the Windows platform to enable USB debugging, since the default USB driver on Windows does not allow for debugging.

Debugging for macOS and iOS

As for macOS and iOS, the debugger used is **LLDB (LLVM Debugger)**, which comes with Xcode by default. Qt Creator will also recognize its existence and link it with your project automatically.

Every debugger is a little different from another and may behave differently on Qt Creator. You can also run the non-GDB debuggers on their respective IDE (Visual Studio, XCode, and so on), if you are familiar with those tools and know what you're doing.

If you need to add other debuggers to your project, you can go over to **Tools** | **Options** | **Build and Run** | **Kits** and click **Clone** to copy an existing kit. Then, under the **Debuggers** tab, click on the **Add** button to add a new debugger selection:

In the **Name** field, type in the descriptive name for the debugger so you can easily remember its purpose. Then, specify the path to the debugger binary in the **Path** field so that Qt Creator knows which executable to run when you start the debugging process. Other than that, the **Type** and **Version** fields are used by Qt Creator to identify the types of version of the debugger. In addition, Qt Creator shows the ABI version that will be used on embedded devices in the **ABIs** field.

To learn more about the in-depth information on how to set up different debuggers in Qt, please visit the following link:
`http://doc.qt.io/qtcreator/creator-debugger-engines.html`.

Unit testing

Unit testing is an automated process for testing an individual module, class, or method in your application. Unit testing finds problems early in the development cycle. This includes both bugs in the programmer's implementation and flaws or missing parts of the specification for the unit.

Unit testing in Qt

Qt comes with a built-in unit testing module, which we can use by adding the `testlib` keyword to our project file (`.pro`):

```
QT += core gui testlib
```

After that, add the following header to our source code:

```
#include <QtTest/QtTest>
```

Then, we can start testing our code. We must declare our test functions as private slots. Other than that, the class must also inherit from the `QObject` class. For example, I created two text functions called `testString()` and `testGui()`, like so:

```
private slots:
    void testString();
    void testGui();
```

The function definitions look something like this:

```
void MainWindow::testString()
{
    QString text = "Testing";
    QVERIFY(text.toUpper() == "TESTING");
}

void MainWindow::testGui()
{
    QTest::keyClicks(ui->lineEdit, "testing gui");
```

```
        QCOMPARE(ui->lineEdit->text(), QString("testing gui"));
}
```

We used some of the macros provided by the QTest class, such as QVERIFY, QCOMPARE, and so on, to evaluate the expression passed as its argument. If the expression evaluates to true, the execution of the test function continues. Otherwise, a message describing the failure is appended to the test log, and the test function stops executing.

We also used QTest::keyClicks() to simulate mouse clicking in our application. In the earlier example, we simulate clicking on the line edit widget on our main window widget. Then, we input a line of text to the line edit and use QCOMPARE macro to test if the text has been correctly inserting into the line edit widget. If anything wrong happened, Qt will show us the problem in the application output window.

After that, comment out our main() function and use the QTEST_MAIN() function instead to start testing our MainWindow class:

```
/*int main(int argc, char *argv[])
{
    QApplication a(argc, argv);
    MainWindow w;
    w.show();

    return a.exec();
}*/
QTEST_MAIN(MainWindow)
```

If we build and run our project now, we should be getting similar results as follows:

```
********* Start testing of MainWindow *********
Config: Using QtTest library 5.9.1, Qt 5.9.1 (i386-little_endian-ilp32
shared (dynamic) debug build; by GCC 5.3.0)
PASS   : MainWindow::initTestCase()
PASS   : MainWindow::_q_showIfNotHidden()
PASS   : MainWindow::testString()
PASS   : MainWindow::testGui()
PASS   : MainWindow::cleanupTestCase()
Totals: 5 passed, 0 failed, 0 skipped, 0 blacklisted, 880ms
********* Finished testing of MainWindow *********
```

There are many more macros that you can use to test your application.

For more information, please visit the following link:
http://doc.qt.io/qt-5/qtest.html#macros

Summary

In this chapter, we have learned how to identify technical issues in our Qt project by using multiple debugging techniques. Other than that, we have also learned about different debuggers that are supported by Qt on different operating systems. Finally, we also learned how to automate some of the debugging steps through unit testing.

That's it! We have reached the end of this book. Hopefully, you have found this book useful on learning how to build your own applications from scratch using Qt. You can look for all the source code on GitHub. I wish you all the best!

Other Books You May Enjoy

If you enjoyed this book, you may be interested in these other books by Packt:

Mastering the C++17 STL
Arthur O'Dwyer

ISBN: 978-1-78712-682-4

- Make your own iterator types, allocators, and thread pools.
- Master every standard container and every standard algorithm.
- Improve your code by replacing new/delete with smart pointers.
- Understand the difference between monomorphic algorithms, polymorphic algorithms, and generic algorithms.
- Learn the meaning and applications of vocabulary type, product type and sum type.

C++17 By Example
Stefan Björnander

ISBN: 978-1-78839-181-8

- Acquire the key skills of ethical hacking to perform penetration testing
- Learn how to perform network reconnaissance
- Discover vulnerabilities in hosts
- Attack vulnerabilities to take control of workstations and servers
- Understand password cracking to bypass security
- Learn how to hack into wireless networks
- Attack web and database servers to exfiltrate data
- Obfuscate your command and control connections to avoid firewall and IPS detection

Leave a review - let other readers know what you think

Please share your thoughts on this book with others by leaving a review on the site that you bought it from. If you purchased the book from Amazon, please leave us an honest review on this book's Amazon page. This is vital so that other potential readers can see and use your unbiased opinion to make purchasing decisions, we can understand what our customers think about our products, and our authors can see your feedback on the title that they have worked with Packt to create. It will only take a few minutes of your time, but is valuable to other potential customers, our authors, and Packt. Thank you!

Index

A

American National Standards Institute (ANSI) 66
AMPPS 56
Android 363, 364
Android NDK 363
Android SDK 351, 363
Apache 56
Apache ANT 363
Apache Friends 56
AppServ 56
area chart 96

B

bar chart 93
box-and-whiskers chart 98
build 343
build settings
  about 345
  comment 347
  configurations 347, 348
  definitions 347, 348
  modules 347, 348
  platform-specific settings 348
  Qt Project (.pro) File 346

C

C++ code
  writing, for image viewers 303, 305
  writing, for music players 308, 311, 312
  writing, for video players 314, 316
C++
  functions, calling from JavaScript 168, 170, 172
  integrating 164
cache
  about 162
  managing 163
camera image
  capturing, to file using Qt multimedia module 231, 232
camera video
  recording, to file using Qt multimedia module 232, 234
camera
  connecting, Qt multimedia module used 226, 230
candlestick charts 98
Cascading Style Sheet (CSS) 45, 145
chart
  implementing 99, 101, 102
  types, in Qt 92
Chromium 146
compile 343
compiler
  about 343, 344
  automation, building with Make tool 344, 345
  Clang 344
  GNU Compiler Collection (GCC) 344
  Linux ICC (Intel C++ Compiler) 344
  Microsoft Visual C++ (MSVC) 344
  Minimalist GNU for Windows (MinGW) 344
  Nim 344
  QCC 344
  XCode 344
cookie
  about 162
  managing 162
cryptographic hash function 66

D

dashboard page
  creating 106, 107, 108, 111, 113, 115

database connection
  in Qt 75, 76, 78, 80, 81, 82, 83
Debian 353
debugging techniques
  about 367
  breakpoints, setting 369, 371, 372, 373
  for Android devices 375
  for PC 374
  macOS and iOS 375
  problem, identifying 368
  variables, printing with QDebug 368
DELETE statement
  reference link 69
dialog boxes
  working 128, 130, 132, 133
Digital Rights Management (DRM) 13

F

Fedora 353
file list
  code, writing 284, 285, 286, 288
  displaying 283, 284
  displaying, list view 281
  project, setting up 282
  user interface, setting up 282, 283
file selection dialogs
  creating 134
  reference link 136
File Transfer Protocol (FTP) 273, 274
files
  downloading, from FTP server 294, 295
  downloading, to FTP server 297
  uploading, to FTP server 288, 290, 291
FileZilla
  downloading 274, 275
  setting up 276, 277, 278, 279, 280
  URL 274
FTP server
  setting up 273
functional login page
  creating 83, 84, 86, 87, 88, 89

G

GCC 64-bit compiler 352

Gentoo 353
Geo Routing Request 193, 194, 195, 196
GNU licenses
  reference link 91
graphical user interface (GUI) 27
Graphics View framework
  about 197
  movable graphics items 201, 202, 204
  organization chart, creating 204, 205, 206, 207,
    208, 210, 211, 212, 213, 214, 215, 216, 217,
    218, 219, 220
  Qt Widgets Application project, setting up 198,
    200, 201
graphs
  implementing 99, 101, 102
  types, in Qt 92

H

Hello World Qt program
  executing 19, 22, 23, 25
Homebrew 80
Hypertext Markup Language (HTML) 145

I

image viewer
  about 301
  C++ code, writing 303
  C++, writing 305
  user interface, designing 301, 303
image
  cropping 136, 138, 140, 142
  scaling 136, 138, 140, 142
INNER JOIN 83
INSERT statement
  reference link 68
instant messaging client
  chat features, implementing 247, 248, 249, 250
  creating 243
  user interface, creating 247
  user interface, designing 244, 246
instant messaging server
  clients, listening 240
  creating 238
  TCP Server, creating 238

International Organization for Standardization
(ISO) 66
iOS 361, 362
item view widgets
working 117

J

JavaScript
about 318
functions, calling from C++ 164, 166, 167
integrating 164
JOIN statement
reference link 72

L

LAMP 56
layouts
about 35
form layout 36
grid layout 36
horizontal layout 35
vertical layout 35
license, Qt
Commercial License 8
Open Source License 8
line and spline chart 92
Linux 351, 352, 353, 354, 355, 356, 358
List Widget
about 119
functional, creating 124, 126
LLDB (LLVM Debugger) 375

M

macOS 359, 360
Make tool
about 344
CMake 345
qmake 345
Makefiles 344
map display
about 173
creating 174, 176, 178
Qt location module, setting up 174
MariaDB 54, 56, 66

MariaDB binary tarballs, on Linux
URL, for installing 80
MariaDB Connector
URL, for downloading 78
marker 178
Meta Object Compiler (MOC) 345
Microsoft SQL 66
Microsoft Visual Studio 146, 349
URL 349
MinGW 32-bit compiler 349
mobile platforms
Android 363, 364
deploying 361
iOS 361, 362
model-view architecture 118
modules, Qt
reference link 11
MSVC 146
multimedia module
about 299
dissecting 299, 300
reference link 300
music player
about 306
C++ code ,writing 308, 310, 312
user interface, designing 306, 308
MySQL AB 54
MySQL Connector
reference link 78
MySQL database system 54
MySQL database
setting up 56, 57, 58, 60, 62, 63, 64, 66
MySQL
about 54, 66
URL 55

O

Open Street Map (OSM) 177, 193
Oracle SQL 66

P

paint program
creating 263
user interface, setting up 263, 264, 266, 267,

270, 271
PC platforms
 deploying 349
 Linux 351, 352, 353, 354, 355, 356, 358
 macOS 359, 360
 Windows 349, 350, 351
Percona Server 54
PHP 56
phpMyAdmin 60
pie charts 94
polar charts 95
position markers
 displaying, on map 179, 180, 182, 183, 184,
 185, 187

Q

QGraphicsItem class
 reference link 201
QStackedWidget 107
Qt Charts
 reference link 99
Qt Console Application project
 setting up 237
Qt Creator 282
Qt Designer 28, 30, 32
 about 10
 action editor 34
 build shortcuts 34
 form editor 34
 form toolbar 34
 menu bar 33
 mode selector 34
 object inspector 34
 output panes 34
 property editor 34
 signals 34
 slots editor 34
 widget box 33
Qt Media Encoding Library (QtMEL) 234
Qt Modeling Language (QML)
 about 174, 317, 319, 320, 321, 322, 324, 325
 project, scripting 337
 project, setting up 330, 332, 334, 335, 336,
 339, 341
 scripting 330

Qt multimedia module
 about 221
 used, for capturing camera image to file 231,
 232
 used, for connecting camera 226, 230
 used, for recording camera video to file 232, 234
Qt networking module
 about 235
 connection protocols 235, 236, 237
Qt Project (.pro) File
 about 346
 reference link 346
Qt Quick Designer 11, 325
Qt Quick
 about 317, 318, 325
 controls 327
 designer 328, 329
 layouts 329, 330
 widgets 327
 widgets and controls 325
Qt Style Sheets 45, 48, 49, 52
Qt Style Sheets, syntax and properties
 reference link 45
Qt WebEngine
 reference link 161
Qt Widgets Application project
 setting up 221, 222, 223, 224, 226
QT Widgets application
 creating 120, 122
Qt widgets
 about 35, 38, 40, 42, 44
 layouts 35
 spacers 35
Qt's licensing options
 reference link 358
Qt's licensing
 reference link 8
Qt, for Windows deployment
 reference link 351
Qt
 about 8
 charts, types 92
 database connection in 75, 76, 78, 80, 81, 82,
 83
 downloading 12, 14

graphs, types 92
installing 12, 14
tools, discovering 9
unit testing 377
using 9
working environment, setting up 15, 16, 18

S

Scalable Vector Graphics (SVG) 258
scatter charts 96
SELECT statement
  reference link 67
session
  about 162
  managing 162
shape display 178
shapes
  displaying, on map 188
signal-slot architecture 118
Slackware 353
spacers
  about 35
  horizontal spacer 36
  vertical spacer 36
SQL commands
  about 66
  DELETE statement 69
  INSERT statement 68
  JOIN statement 69, 70, 71, 72, 74, 75
  SELECT statement 67
  UPDATE statement 68
StackOverflow 55
Structured Query Language (SQL) 54, 66
supported debuggers, Qt
  about 374
  CDB (Debugging Tools for Windows) 374
  dGDB (GNU Debugger) 374
  reference link 376
SVG file
  vector images, saving 258, 259, 260, 262

T

table view 117
Table Widget 119, 127

Transmission Control Protocol (TCP)
  about 235
  versus User Datagram Protocol (UDP) 236
Tree Widget
  about 119
  functionality, adding 127

U

Ubuntu 353
unit testing
  about 377
  in Qt 377, 378
  reference link 378
UPDATE statement
  about 68
  reference link 68
User Datagram Protocol (UDP)
  about 235
  versus Transmission Control Protocol (TCP) 236
user interface
  designing, for image viewer 301, 303
  designing, for music players 306, 308
  designing, for video players 313
user's location
  obtaining 191, 192

V

vector images
  saving, to an SVG file 258, 259, 260, 262
vector shapes
  drawing 253
  drawing, QPainter used 255, 257
  text, drawing 257, 258
  vector, versus bitmap 253, 254
video player
  ++ code, writing 316
  about 313
  C++ code, writing 314
  reference link 316
  user interface, designing 313
Visual C++ 146
Visual Studio 351

W

WAMP 56
web browser
    creating 145
    history, managing 161
    UI, creating 150, 152, 154, 156, 158, 160
    view widget, adding 147
web view, printing
    reference link 161
WebEngine 145
WebKit 145
What-You-See-Is-What-You-Get (WYSIWYG)
    approach 35
widgets and controls, Qt Quick
    Border Image 326
    Flickable 326

Focus Scope 326
Image 326
Item 326
MouseArea 326
Rectangle 326
Text 326
Text Edit 326
Text Input 326
Windows 349, 350, 351
Windows XP 349

X

XAMPP 56

Z

ZendServer 56

www.ingramcontent.com/pod-product-compliance
Lightning Source LLC
Chambersburg PA
CBHW080606060326
40690CB00021B/4608